THE ENGLISH INN

THE ENGLISH INN

JOHN BURKE

HM

Holmes & Meier Publishers, Inc.   New York

In memory of
George Carruthers
and
Peter Leggett
whose like I keep seeking
but with diminishing hope

This life at best is but an inn,
And we the passengers.
James Howell

First published in the
United States of America 1981 by
HOLMES & MEIER PUBLISHERS, INC.
30 Irving Place, New York, N.Y. 10003

Printed in Great Britain

Library of Congress Cataloging in Publication Data

Burke, John Frederick, 1922–
    The English inn.

    Bibliography: p. 189
    Includes index.
    1. Hotels, taverns, etc.—England.   I. Title.
TX910.G7B79   1981   647′.944201   81–4292
                                            AACR2

            ISBN 0–8419–0706–4

CONTENTS

ACKNOWLEDGEMENTS

Many anonymous donors have contributed to this book. A chat in an inn, a casually bestowed story, a host of remembered snippets: these have been as rewarding as books, brochures and documents, and I am sorry that I cannot put a name to each friendly informant and each generous landlord.

Some names must however be recorded with special gratitude. The Editor of the *Eastern Daily Press* has been kind enough to let me quote from one of his issues (page 86), and I am indebted for encouragement and advice (not to mention transport and running commentary) to Bert and Biddy Bales, Dick and Connie Bearden, Barry Davies, Peter Davies, Maurice and Sheila Eves, Mike and Irna Mortlock, Stephen Pennington, Ian Parrott, Humphrey and Pauline Phelps, Chick Webb, Eric Woods and, as so many times before, to John Tustin for the use of his unlicensed but always welcoming premises.

Most of the photographs were taken by Ian Pleeth, who not only sought out every subject I wished to feature, no matter what the weather or distance, but so often drew my attention to things I would otherwise have missed. Publisher and author wish also to thank the following for permission to reproduce supplementary illustrations: Arthur Ackermann & Son Ltd (colour plate 3); Adnams & Co Ltd of Southwold, and Stephen Wolfenden (colour plates 6 and 7); A. F. Kersting (35); Mary Evans Picture Library (colour plates 1 and 2; 20, 21, 23, 29).

LIST OF ILLUSTRATIONS

1

Opening Time

No, Sir, there is nothing which has yet been
contrived by man, by which so much happiness
is produced, as by a good tavern or inn.

Samuel Johnson

Tavern or inn: how do we distinguish the one from the other? At times in our history the words have been virtually synonymous. At others, royal decrees of one kind and another separated them; and in our own time successive legal definitions and restrictions have been laid down. But often we find that what is classified by modern licensing laws as a public house was once a wayside inn, and still carries the description in its sign. Since 1956, most regulations for inns and hotels have been lumped together under the Hotel Proprietors Act, and the Catering Wages Act makes an even broader classification, including hotels, inns, boarding-houses and pretty well any establishment with four or more guest-rooms. Does this mean, then, that we can reasonably refer to the London Hilton or the Grand Hotel, Eastbourne, as an inn? Somehow the picture doesn't seem quite right.

Most of us have an idealized picture of an archetypal inn: thatched roof, leaded windows, a log fire with an ancient ingle-nook, and a jovial host whose buxom wife scurries cheerfully to and fro with loaded plates of traditional English fare. Often enough this vision turns out to be misleading from a purely legalistic point of view. What was once a country inn has lost trade since the decline of the stage coach, no longer offers food other than unadventurous bar snacks, and certainly doesn't offer accommodation. So technically it is not an inn any longer but merely a tavern or public house, whose licensee does not 'hold out' that he supplies food or shelter for the traveller. Yet still it calls itself the White Hart Inn, as it has done for centuries.

Lawyers, magistrates and health inspectors find professional gratification in quibbling over these niceties. Perhaps we may allow ourselves more latitude and blur distinctions when there are historic grounds for so doing. I intend to risk it. I will even risk repeating a friend's remark when we were discussing the approach to this problem in this book: 'The author's opinion is inn-decisive.'

Perhaps, also, we can resolve some of the conflicts by studying the broad picture throughout the centuries: growing, fading, being restored and then damaged and then repainted in a different form. One could almost build a novel in the fashionable 'saga' genre around a single hostelry and its site, its changing fortunes, its tenants and guests and despoilers.

Of course it is unlikely that any one establishment has survived in any one place for the full term of our saga, though some do claim great longevity. According to the *Guinness Book of Records*, foremost contenders for the title of England's oldest inn are led by the Angel (now the Angel and Royal) at

1 Ye Olde Trip to Jerusalem, built into the rock below Nottingham Castle

Grantham, and the George at Norton St Philip. These are challenged by Ye Olde Trip to Jerusalem in Nottingham, where a number of Crusaders are said to have met for refreshment in A.D. 1189 before setting out for the Holy Land. There is little reliable evidence for this, however, and nothing in the building itself dates from earlier than the eighteenth century. The less well known Olde Salutation Inn in Nottingham is verifiably older, with cellars and an old well which could actually have existed since the twelfth century, though the rest of the fabric is of later date.

The Fighting Cocks at St Albans makes the bolder claim of having been licensed since 'Before the Flood'. The inundation referred to is not, however, the Old Testament one, but a flooding of neighbouring water meadows centuries ago. The oddly shaped structure was originally set over the water-gate of St Albans abbey, served as a dovecot in the fourteenth century, and after reconstruction in Elizabeth's reign acquired its present name from its popularity as a cock-fighting venue.

But whichever of these may pretend with the greatest flourish to be the oldest surviving licensed premises, there had been a wide range of houses of rest and refreshment long before that.

Grapevine and ale-stake

Neither the Roman merchant nor the medieval wayfarer would have faced quite our problems of parking space, VAT, service charges, or AA and RAC ratings of inns along his route. He would not have been tempted—or deterred—by the insignia of well-known hotel and catering chains and combines on the façade, the name of the brewer, or the colourful signboards with the arms of some local magnate or a favoured animal, wild or domestic. The Roman was offered an indication of where to seek sustenance by means of a long pole from the end of which hung a grapevine or a cluster of ivy leaves. When Romano-British wine had given way to Saxon ale, the bushy sign became that of an ale-stake—a pole with a broomhead tied to its end.

Let's start with a site beside one of the military roads built to supply Roman legionary garrisons along the northern borders of the province. Messengers, army contractors and merchants have to make long journeys from ports and supply bases in the south to those distant bastions. Farmers have to deliver to appointed collection points over a wide area. Horses and travellers, military or civilian, need posting houses at which to rest and feed; and the men need drink and entertainment while breaking their journey. As well as the vine-leaf garland, some Roman establishments advertise facilities for the favourite game of chess by painting a chequer-board on their doorpost—which can also, confusingly, be the sign of a money-lender. This may be the oldest true inn sign as we know it, surviving on through the centuries as the Chequers and acquiring added significance in the reign of Henry IV with the granting to the Warenne family, whose escutcheon was a blue and gold chequer-board, of the monopoly of ale-house licensing.

Excessive drinking and violence have also been sadly associated since time immemorial. Under the floor of the tavern at Housesteads (*Vercovicium*) on Hadrian's Wall has been found a skeleton with a knife blade driven into the ribs—all too probably the loser in a drunken brawl. There will be many others in the years to come: Christopher Marlowe, killed on Deptford Green in a scuffle following an argument about a tavern bill; Richard Everard, murdered by Roger Greene in the entrance hall of the Bull at Long Melford, Suffolk, in 1648, and thereafter haunting the place and repeatedly opening the dining room door; the landlord of the Lamb in Norwich, killed when he caught his brother-in-law lashing out free beer to friends in the cellar in 1787.

If the Romans could afford to import and drink wine, and even grow small quantities in their Britannic outposts, the natives had already discovered the pleasures of ale. They brewed it for home consumption and met in taverns where it was served—unless, growing prosperous by collaboration with their masters, they preferred to ape Roman ways and spend their earnings on wine.

The next invaders preferred ale anyway, and preferred a way of life quite different from that of the Romans.

Saxon homes were built largely of wood. Sumptuous feasting and great drinking bouts of mead and ale were a regular feature in the timbered halls of the chieftains. Roman wine was forgotten. Roman buildings were neglected. Even the Roman roads were allowed to decay. Only gradually did the Saxon tribes come together in some sort of national community, and then more sophisticated communications again became necessary. Key sites in any part of the country were much the same for successive conquerors and developers: settlements at river crossings controlled important roads, fords and ferries; and where old trackways intersected just as they had done in pre-Roman times, in Roman times, and now under Saxon rule, urban communities and sociable inns inevitably grew up.

Our Roman inn, long neglected but now profiting from the revived importance of the road junction at which it stands, is refurbished with new timbers or completely recreated in wattle and daub . . . only to find itself in competition with a much more powerful rival a few miles away in a fertile valley, offering food, drink and lodging not merely at cut rates but even, all too often, free.

When Christian missionaries came over in the wake of St Augustine, England was drawn under a different kind of Roman domination: that of the Church. Monasteries were built throughout the land. Travellers, whether on religious errands or on trading trips, could rely on obtaining food and accommodation at such places. Separate quarters for visiting wayfarers soon developed into virtual inns. In fact the word 'inn' derives from a Saxon word meaning simply a room, extended in due course to imply a suite of rooms, permanent or, more usually, the temporary residence of students: hence the original University Inns, the Inns of Court and Inns of Chancery, Lincoln's Inn, Gray's Inn, and so on.

Many traces of monastic hospices, sturdily built of stone, remain. Few of the Saxon wooden taverns could have survived long, but their existence is attested by many an episcopal stricture. According to St Boniface, drunkenness was a particularly English trait:

Neither the Franks nor the Gauls nor the Lombards nor the Romans nor the Greeks commit it. Let us then repress this iniquity by deeds of synods and the prohibition of the scriptures, if we are able.

If they were able . . .!

King Edgar ruled in the middle of the tenth century that the excessive number of ale-houses should be cut down, and that there should be not more than one in each village. He also, for the first time, laid down a standard measure for drinking horns.

When the Saxons succumbed to William the Conqueror, this fierce Norman Christian not merely encouraged but commanded a spread of monastic building and endowments. Many great religious houses grew rich on lands and gifts presented to them. Still they had charitably to furnish food and shelter for the traveller. Throughout the Middle Ages their power grew; and their responsibilities grew. Pilgrimages to the shrines of such saints as Edmund,

Thomas Becket and Cuthbert were recommended as a means of acquiring virtue, and roads were soon busy with not merely a local and national traffic but devout seekers from the Continent. Hospitable religious houses were too far apart to supply all the needs of these travellers, and wayside inns really came into their own, springing up at strategic points between the monastic guest-houses. Some were under ecclesiastical jurisdiction, others secular—in so far as anyone or anything could, in those religious times, be purely secular.

Not all pilgrims were as ascetic as might have been wished. The whole concept of pilgrimage was debased as the years went on, and progress towards the major shrines often took on the character of a modern trip to a football match or race meeting. More austere souls accused the rabble of singing wanton songs and creating vulgar uproar in the places through which they passed with a cacophony of drums, bagpipes and bells.

Inns catered also for those on their way to the fairs and markets of the Middle Ages. Such functions provided what was often the only chance each year for inhabitants of provincial towns to buy fineries from afar and to sell their own wares to strangers visiting their market. Inns grew up around market-places for the benefit of visitors wishing to drink during the day and lodge there a night or two. And when the brief cosmopolitan uproar was ended, there was still the regular local function of the market—cattle, butter, wool, or whatever it might be—and a continuing need for these hostelries.

By now our wayside inn has probably acquired a name of its own. If its existence owes something, if only in tactful deference, to religious foundations of the region, it may have chosen a sign depicting the Seven Stars of the Virgin Mary's heavenly crown. Later this may change to the Pack Horse, declaring a more mundane allegiance to those beasts whose itinerant merchant owners drop in so regularly and profitably.

Drink and accommodation are offered. Comfort is not guaranteed. Sound commercial practice involves packing as many folk as possible into a room regardless of age or sex, with little more than rushes or straw to sleep on. One difference between monastic and secular establishments is that the latter do not invariably offer solid as well as liquid food. Also, though dormitories are shared, the inn rarely provides a communal refectory. You are well advised to bring your own food with you; and you eat it alone. Even when landlords begin to see the chance of additional profit from the sale of victuals, their prices are often so exorbitant as to bring curses down on their heads.

By the middle of the fourteenth century, abuses had become so widespread that Edward III had to introduce a statute constraining 'hostelers and herbergers' to sell food at reasonable prices; and again, four years later, tried to put an end to the 'great and outrageous cost of victuals kept up in all the realm by innkeepers and other retailers of victuals, to the great detriment of the people travelling through the realm'.

Landlord, fill the flowing bowl

Although all classes of society enjoyed their regular tipple, the business of brewing and selling the product was regarded as not altogether respectable. Those inferior mortals who worked in the trade were harassed by piecemeal national or local legislation, and in the cities found it necessary to band together and speak with one voice. In 1446 the Hostelers of London were granted guild status for their 'craft and mistery', only to plead 30 years later for the amendment of their title to the supposedly superior one of Innholders. In 1501 Henry VII granted a charter to the Coopers of London so that they too could proudly be incorporated as a guild.

The text within the photograph reads:

THE
TAR INN
AR PARK

HISTORIC
STAR
INN
LUNCHEONS
DINNERS

2 The Star at Alfriston, Sussex, a fifteenth-century monastic inn once under the control of Battle Abbey. The red lion figurehead is thought to have come from a seventeenth-century wreck on the coast nearby

In smaller communities far from major centres, one brewer might supply his neighbours in the same way that the butcher and baker supplied them. The actual brewing was usually left to his wife. Innholders and tavern-keepers were accustomed to produce their own ale behind the premises, and again it was customary for the host's wife to take charge of the process: hence the term 'ale-wife'.

Century after century there bubbled up innumerable enactments against inns and their keepers, and against tipsiness on the part both of clerics and of the laity. The repetitiveness of these statutes and religious denunciations shows

3 A wayside inn—the Waggon and Horses at Kingston Market

how small was the lasting effect they could hope to achieve. Over and over again there would be local ordinances forbidding labourers to spend time in inns or ale-houses on working days. Penalties were framed for publicans who allowed customers to drink on their premises on Sundays or holy days. If every regulation had been obeyed to the letter, it is difficult to see how any publican could ever have made a penny, or any thirsty soul ever have downed a pint.

When Henry VIII's Dissolution of the Monasteries freed inns from all ecclesiastical control, there were few choruses of celebration at this new freedom. The loss of the pilgrims' custom was far more crippling than the most Draconian increase in the price of petrol in our own day. Canterbury, of all places, was soon grovelling to Thomas Cromwell, the 'hammer of the monks', asking for the revenues from a mill once belonging to St Augustine's abbey in order to ease the hardship suffered by innholders and victuallers since the demotion of St Thomas Becket.

Nevertheless in Tudor times our highway inn finds ways of surviving. Henry VIII's descendants maintain their grip on the kingdom by extensive travelling on the part of messengers, officers and administrators, and in Elizabeth's case by personal appearances designed to capture the people's loyalty.

Many a private building comes partially into service as an inn. Just as local schools are often held in one chamber of a private house, so the front room or hall of such a house can serve as a bar. Favoured visitors are offered the domestic comfort of the parlour. Whatever additional amenities may eventually be added, the concept of tap-room and bar parlour will last a long time.

The ordinary house owner may content himself with running a snug little ale dispensary. Our latest acquaintance in the Pack Horse, however, is more ambitious. Pilgrims and their hangers-on may have faded away, but there are other horses and riders to cater for, and a fair number of produce wagons make overnight stops. A second storey is added to provide bedrooms, and although travellers are expected to share such accommodation, there is no longer the huddle of the rush-strewn dormitory, and they are at least provided with reasonable pallets. New building extensions embrace a courtyard with stabling for horses and space for parking wagons. Occasionally a passenger coach may appear; but these are rare, used reluctantly by those hardy enough to survive the discomfort caused by hard wheels, hard seats, and no springs— used, in general, only by men and women of a status which would more likely qualify them for a night's lodging in the nearest mansion of some noble friend or relation.

In one wing of the building there is now a kitchen, for since the Dissolution the traveller can no longer rely on finding food in a monastic hospice; and since monastic breweries have been suppressed, there has to be room for a greatly expanded, self-contained brewhouse. Perhaps in the bar and dining-room can be found seats which later generations will not find too unfamiliar. A remarkable number of twentieth-century inns seem to have found a use for discarded church pews. In the sixteenth century, while stones were torn from abbeys and monasteries to make stately homes, there must also have been a shareout of surplus seats.

During his short reign between those of his father and his sisters, the young Edward VI declared that there were far too many inns and their numbers must be cut down. In London the total was reduced to 40, in York to nine, and few other towns were allowed more than two or three. But out in the country it was difficult to enforce what was in any case an unpopular law. Less than a quarter of a century later in Hertfordshire, for example, more than 500 licensed premises were recorded, obviously run by and for every stratum of society, since it was stated:

As we find some of the keepers of those inns and ale-houses of good wealth so do we find the greatest number of them very simple houses and the inhabitors of them very poor.

Royal messengers in Tudor times were empowered to impress any fresh horses which might be needed *en route*. This led to a number of abuses and sometimes, thanks to the natural reluctance of local owners to part with their best mounts at a moment's notice, to what one might call instant non-availability. During the reign of Queen Elizabeth I it was found wiser to establish posting houses on inn premises along the major highways. The Crown paid chosen innkeepers a small salary, in return for which fresh horses were guaranteed whenever royal couriers should require them. The royal warrant for this service was eagerly sought after: not merely was there the benefit of the regular salary, but extra custom was brought to the inns, and the stabling facilities could be used for the private hiring out of other horses. Also carts could be hired out to merchants, or a sort of parcels service offered to those not needing to send a full cart-load.

Passenger wagons plied their trade as well, but were as yet pretty crude vehicles, without springs and without comfort. Most travellers preferred to make their own way on horseback rather than be jolted along in a primitive carriage, crowded in with others—just as a twentieth-century tourist may prefer his own car to the congestion of a long-distance coach.

Whatever the drawbacks to the actual journeys, inns were building up a reputation for hospitality, tempting the passer-by to seek refuge within. Fynes Morrison, who travelled widely in England and on the Continent during Elizabeth's reign, wrote after her death in *An Itinerary*:

The world affords not such Inns as England hath, either for good and cheap entertainments at the guest's own pleasure, or from humble attendance on passengers. For as soon as a passenger comes to an Inn, the servants run to him, and one takes his horse and walks him till he be cold, then rubs him and gives him his meat. Another servant gives the passenger his private chamber and kindles his fire, the third pulls off his boots and makes them clean, and when he sits at table, the Host or Hostess will accompany him, while he eats, he shall be offered music, which he may freely take or refuse, and if he be solitary, the musicians will give him the good day with music in the morning.

For my own taste, there is far too much so-called music—jarring, insidious, interminable—in pubs and inns and cafés. But perhaps a quiet aubade on lute and flute would go better with morning tea than does the latest pop tape or disc.

Not all his contemporaries would have agreed with Fynes Morrison. In the eighteenth century John Byng expressed other views in *The Torrington Diaries*:

The innkeepers are insolent, the hostlers are sulky, the chambermaids are pert, and the waiters are impertinent; the meat is tough, the wine is foul, the beer is hard, the sheets are wet, the linen is dirty, and the knives are never clean'd!

An early enactment of James I laid down that inns and victualling houses were obliged to lodge wayfarers if requested. Tavern-keepers, on the other hand, were not only under no such obligation but were expressly forbidden to do so. It was a difficult distinction, and one which local authorities found it difficult to administer.

By the end of James's reign, when the population of the country was in the region of five million, there were known to be over 13,000 inns and taverns, and no sign of their numbers decreasing.

Posting houses attracted increasing custom as the carrier trade expanded. In the late seventeenth century a famous service was started between the Bell on Bishopsgate, London, and the George in Cambridge, which stood between the Bull and St Catharine's college. The University carrier was one Thomas Hobson, who insisted that customers patronizing his livery stables at the George should take the first horse which came to hand: whence the phrase 'Hobson's Choice'.

On his crossroads near two increasingly populous market towns, the great-great-grandson of one of our landlords of the Pack Horse is suddenly presented with a ticklish problem. Parliament has finally decided to discontinue negotiations with the evasive Charles I. Civil war breaks out, and reluctant armies lurch towards each other. The monarch himself spends a night in our friend's inn, and in a fit of patriotic fervour the signboard is repainted as the King's Head. Not so many months later, the king's son seeks refuge on his erratic route into exile, and after his departure the sign is hastily taken down.

Although many diversions such as music, dancing and the theatre are officially frowned on during the Commonwealth interregnum, the taverns suffer surprisingly little. Inn signs of religious significance are removed, just as 'superstitious pictures' and statues in churches have been removed or smashed; but otherwise trade goes on much as before, with the added presence of argumentative sectarians. John Taylor, the 'Water-Poet' and eccentric traveller, complains that 'Religion is now become the common discourse and table talk in every tavern and ale-house'. Levellers, Ranters and other splinter groups meet in bars, sing revolutionary and often blasphemous songs to well-known hymn tunes, and debate fine or blurred points of doctrine. One of these 'malignants and sectaries', as a more orthodox Puritan preacher calls them, declares that drunkenness is no sin but enables one to see Christ better.

On Charles II's return to his throne the inn's earlier hospitality is remembered, and it is renamed the Royal Oak in memory of the fleeing monarch's sojourn in an oak tree at Boscobel. Much is made of a sliding panel in the ingle-nook: visitors are regaled with stories of the hours His Majesty spent hidden in a niche within, breathing through a tiny hole while the landlord made sure the fire was not allowed to smoke too much.

4 A coach leaving the Turf, Newcastle-upon-Tyne, from a 1783 woodcut by Thomas Bewick

Similar tales will later be told about fleeing Jacobites after the Hanoverians put paid to the hopes of Bonnie Prince Charlie.

Throughout the Cromwellian period the coach trade has continued to grow. By the time of the Restoration, London and Durham are linked by regular services, there is a steady traffic between Newcastle and Lancaster, and new routes reach down to Exeter and Plymouth. Our innkeeper, like many of his fellows, sees chances of hitherto undreamt-of independence.

Coaching days

The coaches and coaching inns shown in so many framed prints in so many bar parlours, and on so many Christmas cards, automatically call forth the adjective 'Dickensian', as if Charles Dickens had invented the whole scene rather than been inspired by it. It is impossible to step into any bar, snug, lounge or parlour without instinctively comparing or contrasting it with the archetypal nineteenth-century picture painted by the novelist.

Serialized in monthly parts and published as a book in 1837, the *Posthumous Papers of the Pickwick Club* were originally conceived as a set of sporting sketches, but ultimately developed into a lurching pilgrimage from one hostelry to another, filled with the smell of roast beef and any number of potations. The indefatigable Charles Harper calculated in a 1926 publication that 'no fewer than 55 inns, taverns and places of refreshment are mentioned in *Pickwick*'; and without going to the effort of checking his calculations I see no reason to doubt his conclusions. Other books, too, feature Dickens's favourite or least-favoured inns. Although I was born in south-eastern England, I came late to his Bull at Rochester—now much modernized and what might be called Dickensified. But I have known much longer, and enjoyed his opinions on, certain other places.

In Tavern Street, Ipswich, is the Great White Horse, where the young man stayed while reporting on election campaigns for the *Morning Chronicle*. When it came to writing the saga of the Pickwickians, his memories were so dismal

5 The coachyard of the Old Bull and Mouth, St Martins-le-Grand, London

that the landlord threatened a libel action:

'The Great White Horse' is famous in the neighbourhood, in the same degree as a prize ox, or county-paper chronicled turnip, or unwieldy pig—for its enormous size. Never were such labyrinthine uncarpeted passages, such clusters of mouldy, unlighted rooms, such huge numbers of small dens for eating and sleeping in, beneath any one roof, as are collected together between the four walls of 'The Great White Horse' at Ipswich.

Who would then have predicted that it was largely the disparaging author's connection with the establishment that prevented its being demolished only a few years ago?

What a change when the Pickwick Club tourists reached Bury St Edmunds! 'The nicest town in the world', declared the not easily pleased William Cobbett. 'And this', said Mr Pickwick—one can almost hear the sigh of anticipation—'is the "Angel"! We alight here, Sam.'

To forewarn the reader not so much of my personal prejudices as of what I like to call postjudices—in other words, a conviction born of experience rather than predisposition—I confess that it would take a major cataclysm to rid me of my doting affection for Bury and for the Angel. After my wife and I had stayed there some years back, followed by a stay in a much more expensive and much less amiable hotel in Derbyshire, we felt the contrast so keenly that, having expressed our displeasure clearly in the latter place, it seemed only fair to express our pleasure in the former. I wrote a paean of praise to the manager, assuring him that no reply was necessary; but in fact received such a friendly response that on subsequent visits I have not liked to make myself known in case it was suspected I might be in search of a free drink! If between the time I write these words and the time the book is published the Angel proves to have deteriorated, I shall personally ensure that it suffers the fate of the great abbey across the road: just as those vast buildings were torn apart by the townsfolk and their stones used in walls and local houses, so I swear to tear the Angel down stone by stone.

Not that I think this will be necessary. This book is not meant to be a hotel guide, and is not sponsored by any business organization or hotel chain; but I am happy to record that the experiences of friends visiting this cherished establishment have, up to now, been just as happy as ours.

What, then, of our temporarily neglected friend on his bustling crossroads? What would Cobbett, or Pickwick, or the modern tourist, make of that hostelry since we last saw it in the company of remoter ancestors?

Improvements to roads and vehicles have forced improvements on his premises. Food and service are of a higher standard, and accommodation for both travellers and horses has been upgraded. The enclosed, sheltered stableyard is now a common feature, with a high arch to admit the coaches in from the main road. To make sure that profits do not all end up in the pockets of metropolitan combines, our landlord has joined a consortium of fellow publicans who run their own coach services to and from London termini and between important provincial towns.

Coaches now boast better springing and suspension. Outside passengers, once left to cling to the roof or flounder among the baggage, are provided with safer seats and limited in number by law to avoid danger to the balance of the vehicle. The coachman no longer bullies these cheap fare passengers into getting down at the foot of each hill and walking up in order to ease the strain on his team.

Such refinements in vehicle design would be of only marginal value without a corresponding improvement in the carriageways themselves. All through the Commonwealth period there were demands for a national policy in road building and maintenance. Local authorities could not cope on their own with the demands of increasingly heavy traffic. If in summer they repaired a main through road—which did not necessarily bring their own district any trade or profit—it could be ruined by winter rains and frosts. Among business on the Parliamentary agenda just before Cromwell's early 1658 dissolution was a Bill for Repairing of the Highways and Improving the Public Roads. A Surveyor-General of Highways was to be appointed and provided with all necessary finance.

Not until three years after the Restoration of Charles II do we get an Act introducing a new method of funding road maintenance. Gates are set up to control specific stretches of the highway, at each of which every rider and every driver of cattle, sheep, wagons or coaches must pay a toll. These become known as turnpikes, a term later applied to the subsidized stretch of road itself.

Inevitably there is now a great deal of profiteering and corruption. Administration, at first in the hands of local magistrates, is soon transferred to bodies of trustees who find devious ways of creaming off profits rather than applying them to repair work; and even before such profits reach them there has been widespread petty pilfering on the part of the gate-keepers. Squabbles break out over the division of expense between the trustees and relevant parish councils.

Nevertheless the system has brought substantial advantages, and in spite of cumulative dishonesty the improvement in road surfaces and the provision of bridges where once there were muddy fords has helped to lower the cost of transport, since heavy loads can safely be drawn at higher speeds.

Echoes linger on into the future from these toll roads, in inn signs such as the Gate, the Falgate, the Talbooth, and the Toll House near Bridport in Dorset.

But in the matter of moving goods in larger quantities and at increased speeds, there is now a new threat to coach services, their termini and wayside halts. At first derided, the railways will within very few years spell ruin for many an innkeeper and 'lightning flyer' operator. Weaving a web over the landscape, they establish new junctions and new stopping-off places. Traffic through the crossroads by the Royal Oak dwindles. After a clash over land sales nearby, the engineers choose instead a valley route ten miles north of the crossroads. There a new railway town grows up; the Railway Tavern does business at the end of the station approach. Our neglected roadside inn tries to compete, its half-timbering partially bricked up and partially plastered over to make it look smart and modern. All to no avail. Travellers use the Railway Tavern and its new rival across the street, the Engineers Arms. Nearer the cities, a new breed of daily travellers who come to be known as commuters will soon be crowding the bars for a quick drink or two every evening before going home to face their wives.

Longer journeys by the iron road soon bring a demand from passengers for overnight accommodation, and ornate hotels are built beside or over the main stations.

Not until the invention of the internal combustion engine and the return of individuals to the highways in their motor cars do the old roadside inns perk up again. Many have been lost forever: though the shape of a roadside building here and there, the positioning of its doors, and occasionally a name carved in stone on a wall panel, betray its original function. Of those that struggle back to life, a number go all out for modernity, becoming roadhouses and then motels, while others aim at a nostalgic atmosphere by fashionably remodelling half-timbered frontages, buying horse brasses in large quantities from Birmingham, and training creeper round their latticed windows.

Still some of the old terminology survives into this brasher world. When inns were still basically private houses making spasmodic profit from the sale of home-brewed ale or beer to passers-by, the phrase 'tap-room' distinguished that room where beer was drawn from the front parlour in which it was served. We rarely speak of a tap-room nowadays, but the parlour has remained as the bar parlour. When an inn has blossomed into a plushier hotel, there may have been added a residents' lounge and a cocktail bar. But there are few old-established hotels which do not preserve their public bar, no matter how poky, in which the locals still huddle and ignore temporary guests—some of whom make a point of being hearty and showing themselves 'one of the lads'. I remember, a few decades ago, a small town inn whose landlady, an excellent cook, decided to open a bistro-style restaurant in the public bar. She was well ahead of her time in this, and was viewed with dark suspicion by a little group of regulars. The bar itself could not be shifted or abolished, so these stalwarts huddled dourly close to the counter while food was served on chequered table-cloths across the rest of the room. A few evenings after its inauguration, my wife and I sat down at a table and were approached by a young and wary waitress with a strong local accent. 'Did you want a meal', she asked dubiously, 'or was you just sitting there?'

Many a time since, while waiting for service in a large impersonal, over-staffed and under-organized hotel, I have watched gossiping waiters and waitresses assemble in remote corners and have murmured under my breath '. . . or was you just sitting there?'

Uses and abuses

The Hotel Proprietors Act of 1956 defines a hotel or inn as an 'establishment held out by the proprietor as offering food, drink and, if so required, sleeping accommodation . . . to any traveller presenting himself who appears able and willing to pay a reasonable sum for the services and facilities provided and who is in a fit state to be received'.

What constitutes a reasonable sum is often, in the eyes of the said traveller, a matter for some cynicism. From the authorities' point of view, what constitutes fitness to be received, and the fear of lapses from this state, have conditioned the framing of laws over the centuries. Some reformers complained that the unrestricted service of alcoholic refreshment at all hours of the day was the cause of chronic inebriation throughout the kingdom. Others have declared that too stringent a limitation of permitted drinking hours results in many a drinker putting back more than he really wants, at a greater rate, before the grim moment of 'Time, gentlemen, please'.

During the sixteenth and seventeenth centuries, licences distinguished between sellers of wine and sellers of ale; and there were special clauses for the sale of spirits. Licences for selling wine in inns were hard to come by. There was some relaxation in the following century, but still too many restrictions for the tastes of seller and buyer: many establishments purveyed wines and spirits when they had no licence to do so, and many a tavern-keeper made the odd penny from letting odd rooms when legally he was forbidden to do so. Then and until well into the nineteenth century, the issuing of such licences was in the hands of local magistrates in some regions, and even, in others, the hands of the parish constables. Attempts now began to be made to establish some kind of uniformity.

In 1839 London public houses were ordered to close at midnight on Saturdays until noon on Sundays, and it was not long before this regulation extended to the rest of the country. In 1854 the sale of liquor on a Sunday was permitted only between 1 and 2.30 p.m., and again between 6 and 10 p.m. After that time it was forbidden to serve further drinks until 4 a.m. on the Monday morning. Following a campaign of protest it was agreed that hotel residents might be allowed refreshments outside these hours; and the somewhat unreliable concept of a thirsty 'bona fide traveller' has survived in Scotland into our own time, producing some strange perversions of the truth and some remarkably energetic trots from one hotel to another on a Sunday.

During the First World War there was puritanical concern over the tipsiness of young men away from home for the first time and thrown into rough company. Under the first Defence of the Realm Act in 1914 it was made an offence to get soldiers or sailors drunk while they were serving on railway or harbour installations. Then came the turn of the civilians: munitions and other industrial workers were losing too much working time because of drunkenness, so local licensing authorities were empowered to regulate opening hours within their area. A Central Control Board established in 1915 had by the following year introduced strict classifications for the types of liquor which might be drunk in specific areas, and gave itself powers to close taverns or clubs when this was considered justifiable, to issue or suspend licences, and to inspect premises whenever and wherever it felt so inclined. One of its main achievements was the restriction of opening hours from noon to 2.30, and 6 to 9 p.m., with a few minor variations to take into account the needs and problems of different districts. Acts and amendments since then have been largely built around this basic pattern. The Licensing Act of 1964 confirmed our contemporary timetable in general as 11 a.m. to 3 p.m., and 5.30 to 11 p.m., on weekdays; noon until 2 p.m., and 7 p.m. to 10.30 p.m., on Sundays. In country districts there can be shifts of a half-hour or so in one direction or another; coastal holiday resorts are often granted summer extensions; opening is allowed right through the afternoon on market day;

and City of London premises have been granted concessions allowing them to cope early with the evening rush-hour, followed by almost total desertion later in the evening.

Throughout history inns and taverns, especially those in rural areas, have offered many services not expressly covered by the terms of their licence. Some have been authorized to accommodate part-time post offices on their premises, and post boys with their strapped leather bags were once a familiar sight. Others have provided a room for the tithe collector or tax inspector. One village inn I know still opens its door as the local bank two afternoons each week. Turnpike trustees found the atmosphere of roadside inns congenial for their meetings, and many a coroner's inquest was held in bar parlours until the Licensing Act of 1902 forbade this 'if other premises have been provided'. Justices administered the law in local pubs such as the White Hart at Welwyn, where petty sessions were held regularly until 1900. The earliest reference to the George and Dragon in Baldock concerns the convening there in 1591 of an archdeacon's court. And of course the inn of the local market town was usually the centre of semi-private auctions of land worked out between farmers, builders and agents.

Election campaigns were fiercely waged in the bars of town and village. There were few restrictions on the bribery a candidate might exert in the way of 'treating' electors until the Parliamentary Reforms of the nineteenth century. Even after this practice had been declared illegal—and in one town a citizen incredulously commented 'A brewer standing, and no free beer?'—it continued for quite a time in various underhand ways.

In July 1852 a scheming candidate for Parliament told an investigatory committee that a lavish dinner for local worthies in the George Hotel, Rye, had been paid for by his predecessor and therefore he could not himself be accused of any impropriety. It was discovered after further inquiry that the meal had in fact been paid for by this candidate, Alexander McKinnon, who had left £230 under a bench in the Red Lion Inn for collection by an intermediary, who passed it to McKinnon's string-pulling election agent, one Jeremiah Smith, who in turn then paid the bill.

In addition to the formal dinner there were lavish treats for lesser mortals:

Public houses were opened free to all and the scenes of dissipation were disgraceful. There were men and women, boys and girls, drunk. Some were brawling drunk, some crying drunk, some singing drunk, some fighting drunk, some stupid drunk, some cunning drunk, some crazy drunk and some merely dead drunk.

After attacks in the national press, the conniving Smith was tried at the Old Bailey and sentenced to 12 months. Within no time at all he had persuaded the jurors who convicted him to sign a petition declaring that they had misdirected themselves and that he was innocent. More strings were pulled, and he was granted a free pardon.

At the end of this chapter I would like to issue a word of warning to researchers who, like myself, may rely on loyal, helpful friends to take them round local hostelries. Every inn of real character takes months, even years, to understand fully. Praise heaped on one public house because of its wonderful landlord may turn out to be misplaced because that landlord has left. Others take time to grow on one and convey their unique flavour. It's impossible to use them all regularly; but there is lasting pleasure to be derived from the memory of a sudden attractive vision here, a laugh there, a tang of locally brewed beer in this place or that one. Advertisements can prove misleading, too. The glowing brochures do not mention that on picturesque premises the staff have the habit of Hoovering round one's feet all through breakfast, or

6 Electioneering as seen in 1757 by William Hogarth, himself a noted painter of inn signs

that the garage is an expensive extra and closes at 9.30 p.m. At one beautifully restored house in which I stayed, the hall ceiling fell down one afternoon, and workmen hammered away throughout the night. When I complained, the landlord said, 'We've got to think of guests arriving tomorrow.' I asked him what about his present guests, who could not sleep; but we were already trapped on the premises, and of little concern to him. Then there was a widely advertised 'Tudor-style' hotel with solar heated swimming pool and mouth-watering amenities, offering attractive terms for short breaks in autumn, winter and spring. Tempted, I booked in for several days in what was, I admit, early summer rather than late spring. Half the place was being repaired, the swimming pool was dirty and cold, and service was minimal. When I commented on this, I was airily told, 'Oh, we concentrate on the winter conference trade—the summer's our slack season, when we have to get repairs done.'

And of course there will be the historic building listed in every evocative book on English inns, which no longer offers any accommodation at all: 'Not for a hundred years, sir. But Mrs Jones up the road has rooms.'

Never mind. In spite of tribulations and the excesses of Puritan, Philistine and profiteer, the essence of the English inn is miraculously preserved in so many delightful buildings in so many delightful settings. Behind the braggarts, the expense-account boomers, the Jag-and-gin shriekers and show-offs and the noise-drugged addicts of the juke-box, can still be heard the eternal murmur of the true regular and the unfussily appreciative visitor.

William Langland's fourteenth-century tavern has survived many trans-mutations, but its occupants are still familiar to us, even if some trades and professions are no longer as common as they were. Tinkers and hackneymen are rarely to be found these days, though the local butcher and gamekeeper may well appear in their chosen corners. As for others:

> An haywarde and an heremyte, the hangeman of Tyborne,
> Dauwe the dykere, with a dosen harlotes,
> Of portours and of pyke-purses, and pylede toth-drawers. . . .
> Ther was lauhyng and lakeryng and 'let go the coppe!'
> Bargeynes and bevereges, by-gunne to aryse,
> And seten so til evesong rang.

Their talk and their song, their bargains and beverages, could not have been too unlike those exchanged today.

Needing no Bush

Not more distinct from harmony divine,
The constant creaking of a country sign.

William Cowper

The bush of ivy or vine leaves outside a Roman tavern might have been necessary until the place established its reputation, but once that was secure the drinking public knew where the best vintages were to be had: 'A good wine needs no bush.'

Similarly with the later ale-stake. In times when few of the populace could read, such a simple announcement was essential, as with the easily identifiable trade signs of hatters, farriers, bakers, apothecaries and others. But as the population increased and as people travelled more freely about the country, so competition for their custom increased. One local tavern might not be enough to assuage local thirsts, and a rival might open up down the street, or even next door. Patrons would come to prefer one brew to another, or the hospitable atmosphere of one building to the other. So now there had to be some individually distinguishing board outside; and, as literacy was still rare, it had to be pictorial and immediately recognizable. In due course Richard II commanded that all inns should carry such signs.

Some announcements became wildly ambitious, extending ornamental arches from one side of the thoroughfare to the other with such a profusion of decoration that they threatened high loads on vehicles, or wrenched themselves away from their fastenings and fell on passers-by. Local authorities introduced a number of ordinances to limit these extravagances, and by Charles II's time it had become necessary to rule that in London streets 'no signboard shall hang across, but that the sign shall be fixed against the balconies or some convenient part of the house'. In spite of such decrees, many establishments continued to pride themselves on the elaboration of their signs. One which collapsed in Fleet Street in 1712 brought down a large section of the inn's façade and killed four pedestrians.

Three-dimensional figures of animals or other motifs leaned or leapt from inn frontages. In defiance of regulations, many a 'gallows' sign still stretched across city and town streets, such as the bar carrying a lively representation of the Four Swans at Waltham Cross, the famous George at Stamford, and what must have been the most staggering sight of the White Hart at Scole in Norfolk—later renamed the Scole Inn—more like a triumphal archway spanning the road, covered with allegorical figures, and costing over £1000 in the seventeenth century.

The record as the longest sign still surviving in England is claimed by the Coach and Horses at Chislehampton in Oxfordshire, over eleven feet across and six feet deep. The mail coach in the painting is based on one which ran

from London to York between 1827 and 1860 and is now in the collection of the Science Museum, London.

7 A 'gallows' sign at Barley, Hertfordshire, recalling a day long ago when a hunted fox took shelter in the inn

As literacy improved, actual names were added to the pictures, a tendency which strengthened when large breweries began to supply numbers of houses with their product and, in due course, to buy them up and administer them from a central office, promulgating the name and trade mark of the brew alongside the name of the building.

Saints and kings

On the earliest pictorial signs, ecclesiastical and regal themes predominated. Nurtured in the first place as monastic offspring, it was only natural that inns should pay tribute to their upbringing and to the widespread influence still exerted by abbots, priors and their brethren.

One of the oldest representations is that of the Star. A sixteen-pointed star was in fact adopted as the emblem of the Innholders' Company, but had appeared as the Star of Bethlehem on hostelries long before that guild's foundation. The Star at Alfriston in Sussex, for example, was already in existence in the thirteenth century under the governance of Battle abbey; the present building dates back to the middle of the fifteenth; and its name and sign have remained unaltered over the years. Another celebrated house bearing the Star is at Great Yarmouth—though, old as the building itself is, it has been an inn only since 1780.

The Seven Stars, as we have noted, relate to those in the Virgin Mary's celestial crown. The sign of the Angel honoured the Annunciation: one of the oldest recorded is in Grantham, later linking the holy with the secular (but

regal) as the Angel and Royal. St Peter is associated with the Cross Keys or
Crossed Keys.

Another sign which, despite confusing variations and animal attributions,
may be of religious origin is that of the Bull, which could derive from the seal of
the parent abbey, a bulla. What, then, of the Bull and Bush? The Bush survives
on its own as a common enough designation, familiar through the Middle
Ages at places such as Barnstaple, Devon, where anyone wishing to profit from
brewing and selling ale during the three days of the annual fair had merely to
display a pole and broomhead outside his house to be a short-term publican.
Thus the Bull and Bush may in some localities be a combination of this
basically Roman marker with the later monastic licensing seal.

There are, however, other explanations of the Bull and Bush. During Henry
VIII's campaign against the French in 1544, Boulogne was captured after a
battle at the Boulogne Bouche, or mouth of Boulogne harbour. Two plausible
corruptions are at once obvious: the Bull and Bush, and the Bull and Mouth.
The most famous one using the first version is that near Hampstead Heath,
somewhat unimaginatively rebuilt after the Second World War; and the
second usage appeared in the historic Bull and Mouth by St Martin's-le-Grand,
rebuilt in 1830 as the Queen's Hotel as coaching fortunes were on the decline,
and ultimately demolished in 1887.

Of course there are innumerable straightforward identifications of the Bull
purely and simply as an animal. The Black Bull at Sleaford, Lincolnshire,
preserves a bull-baiting stone relief from 1689. The Bull's Head at Barnes, on
the site of what was a farmhouse before suburbs crawled out over the fields,
appropriately sports the arms of the Worshipful Company of Butchers of the
City of London on one wall. And one of the worthiest inns in East Anglia is the
galleried Bull at Long Melford.

The Long Melford house also displays in its lounge a remarkable carving of
a green man clad in girdle and ivy wreath. The Green Man is in itself a familiar
inn name, though not one which would have been approved by monastic

administrators. Its significance may well stem from before the days of Christian influence in this country. Known also as wild men—there is a Wild Man public house in Norwich—these figures often featured in pageants and fairs, decked with foliage from local woods, playing the fool and dancing wildly, sometimes identified with Robin Hood but really echoing ancient pagan beliefs and rites, as when one such might be welcomed into the village at springtime for the maypole ceremony and its symbolic undertones of witchcraft and phallic worship. My own favourite for quite some time when we lived near the top of Putney Hill was the cheerful Green Man just across the road from the edge of Wimbledon Common.

From religious devotion the next obvious step in signboards was homage to the king. As owner of lands vaster even than those of the monasteries, and after Henry VIII's time as ruler of the Church also, he commanded obeisance. But since in medieval times very few of his subjects ever saw him face to face, there was little point in painting lifelike impressions of his features—especially as he might be overthrown by a usurper, which would necessitate taking the board hastily down and declaring another allegiance. To be on the safe side it was best to adopt the image which is in fact the commonest of English inn signs: the Crown.

Many of these were impersonal. One monarch might follow another, by right or by force; but there would always be a Crown. A few, however, are associated with specific rulers. Soon after Mary Tudor had raised her standard at Framlingham castle in Suffolk and marched on London to become queen, a shrewd local worthy built an inn, called it the Crown, and profited from the regular return visits of Bloody Mary when she chose to hold court in Framlingham and so drew suppliants and sycophants to the town. The building is still there, altered in the 1950s but preserving its old yard, once a thoroughfare right through the hotel for coaches.

The Crown and Treaty at Uxbridge began life in the sixteenth century as a country mansion. In 1645 representatives of Parliament and of King Charles met in what is now called the Treaty Room to find some way of halting the Civil War which had already begun. They failed. Another one-time manor house near which there was a Civil War encounter is the Three Crowns at Chagford, Devon, in whose porch a Cavalier bled to death after being severely wounded in the leg.

In London, Dean Street in Soho has the unique Crown and Two Chairmen. This recalls days when Queen Anne visited Sir James Thornhill in the house opposite to have her portrait painted. She was carried to and from the sittings in her sedan chair, and while Sir James proceeded with his task the two chair-men took their ease in the tavern.

King's Head and Queen's Head crept into popular usage, and there were also the King's Arms and the Queen's Arms. These, too, could be kept non-committal if desired, and the 'Arms' were often represented by the royal crest or the two heraldic beasts which in some places achieved distinction in their own right as the Lion and Unicorn. Oddly there seems to be only one example of the Royal Standard of England in the country (though there are several shortened to the Standard)—at Forty Green near Beaconsfield in Buckinghamshire. Even this was once known as the Ship, and would appear to owe its advancement to help given by the landlord to Charles II during his flight across country.

But individual attributions are not too hard to find. A brief skim through English history can be made with inn signs doubling as signposts.

Obviously we must be wary of the authenticity of any name or picture related to kings and nobles before the medieval spread of pictorial boards.

The White Horse was a Saxon emblem; but if there is still an authentic Saxon ale-house surviving anywhere in the realm, I don't know of it. Depictions of The White Horse are more likely to be associated with the earls of Arundel or, later, the Hanoverians. The Raven was the Danish royal emblem for some time before and after Canute, but its frequency along the Welsh marches is usually associated with the crest of local families. William the Conqueror appears outside quite a few houses near the Channel shore, but such a christening came centuries after his death. And throughout the conflicts of rival lineages, allegiance to a particular monarch was often allusive rather than assertive.

Among his personal insignia Edward III adopted both a Golden Lion and the Rising Sun. In 1346 his eldest son, the Black Prince, distinguished himself at the battle of Crécy and seized as his own the ostrich feather crest and motto, *Ich dien* (I serve), from the fallen standard of John, blind king of Bohemia. The Feathers, symbol of every Prince of Wales since that time, are to be found in all parts of the country. Perhaps the two worthiest bearers of the sign are at Ludlow and Ledbury. One has a notably personal reference: in 1739 Frederick, Prince of Wales, father of the future George III, leased Cliveden House above the Thames, which is why the inn just outside its walls loyally became the Feathers.

The Black Prince's son, succeeding to the throne as Richard II, took both the swan and the antelope as emblems. A mere ten years of age at his accession, Richard came under the influence of the powerful John of Gaunt but later antagonized him. Richard's antelope had become transmuted into a White Hart; Gaunt's emblem was that of a Red Lion, and against a lion the hart stood little chance. In struggles against his Parliamentary enemies, Richard granted his badge of the White Hart to militant groups who would swear loyalty to him. But Gaunt's son, Henry Bolingbroke, deposed him and proclaimed himself king as Henry IV. Richard was imprisoned in Pontefract castle and, it was soon reported, murdered there. Supporters who refused to believe tales of his death went on meeting secretly at establishments labelled with the figure of the White Hart. By now such signs were nothing out of the ordinary: it was, after all, Richard himself who had ordained that inns and ale-houses should all display identifying boards. There is a direct association with the king in the 600-year-old White Hart at Witley in Surrey, which was built on to one of his own hunting lodges.

The Wars of the Roses followed, one of whose most bitter battles was fought in 'Bloody Meadow' outside Tewkesbury. Stained glass in 20 leaded lights of a finely preserved window in the Olde King's Head, Aylesbury, include the arms of Henry VI, his wife, and their son Edward, Prince of Wales, who died in the fighting at Tewkesbury. The king whose head is referred to in the name, however, was of later origin: Henry VIII often visited here when the lord of the manor was Anne Boleyn's father, and his image was added to it after he dissolved the monasteries and so freed it from the suzerainty of the Franciscans, whose guest-house it had hitherto been. Whether Henry would have approved of a later guest on the premises, Oliver Cromwell, is open to question.

Henry VI, virtually mad towards the end of his confused life, was used and misused by Warwick 'the King-maker', whose badge of the Bear and Ragged Staff is still to be found all over Warwickshire and into neighbouring counties. Many inns which have dropped the full title and call themselves simply the Bear nevertheless retain the ragged staff in their design—as with the Bear at Berkswell, near Coventry. There is also a famous Black Bear at Tewkesbury, after which battle Henry VI was probably murdered by the Duke of Gloucester, later to become Richard III.

Richard's emblem was a White Boar, which could easily be changed after

Market house &c at Hoddesdon, Hertfordshire.
B. May 4th 1832.

his death by swift repainting as the Blue Boar, crest of the earl of Oxford, Henry Tudor's supporter. It was at the Blue Boar in Leicester that Richard slept the night before the confrontation at Bosworth, only to return there naked the following day, his corpse thrown across his horse's back for display in the Town Hall down Blue Boar Lane.

His conqueror, Henry VII, made haste to marry the eldest daughter of Edward IV, a union symbolized by a sign marking the end of the Wars of the Roses – the Rose and Crown.

Henry VIII, Bluff King Hal, is probably the most frequently portrayed monarch on signs of the King's Head, the King's Arms, and so on—and was adopted, I recall, as trade mark by a northern brewer with many houses in Lancashire and along its borders. In his destruction of monasteries and the dismissal of abbots and monks from their homes and even from the country into exile, Henry also destroyed shrines and the reputations of those who lay therein. Among others, he ruled that Thomas Becket was no longer a saint. Unfortunately the Brewers' Company had selected Becket as one of their patron saints, and one half of their coat of arms contained his emblem, the other half featuring three barrels and three sheaves of barley. Now they had to expunge all reference to the martyr and substitute a helmet and a female figure holding ears of barley.

Henry's sister Mary, who married the duke of Suffolk, has also given a not immediately attributable name to a few inns. She had such a great appetite for artichokes that her head gardener dubbed his house the Artichoke, a name which was carried on when it became an inn. Among other East Anglian mementoes of the lady is the Artichoke on the outskirts of Norwich; and there was once a tavern called the Queen's Head and Artichoke in London.

Queen Elizabeth I, who travelled in her kingdom more widely than her predecessors had done, was none too pleased with representations of herself on inn signs, and finally issued one approved portrait which had to be faithfully copied: all other versions 'by unskilful and common painters should be knocked in pieces, and cast into the fire'.

When Charles I was followed by Oliver Cromwell there were fewer proscriptions against the jollity of tavern life than might have been expected, but objections were raised to certain signboards with religious connotations. St Catherine's Wheel, incorporated in the arms of the Worshipful Company of Turners, had to discard its saintliness and become the Catherine Wheel, in some cases even corrupted to the Cat and Wheel.

After the Restoration it was a long time before any references to Oliver Cromwell were permitted in names and signs. There are a few examples of his son's nickname to be found: Tumbledown Dick, at Wortham in Norfolk for one, and at Farnborough in Hampshire. This latter is sometimes explained by legendary visits from Dick Turpin, but such an attribution seems mistaken.

When Scotland and England were at last united during Queen Anne's reign, a number of taverns inevitably celebrated by calling themselves the Union. During that period there also appeared portrayals of the Prince of Denmark, Anne's consort.

In the time of George III, yet another act was introduced forbidding shops to display obtrusive signs liable to endanger passing riders or coaches; but inns escaped many of these prohibitions, or simply ignored them.

Queen Adelaide begins to feature after 1830, when her husband came to the throne as William IV and made his own appearance on signboards, usually in naval uniform. After them the Queen's Head, for long the virtual monopoly of Elizabeth I, became more frequently that of Queen Victoria—usually portrayed later in life, though some recent versions show her young face on one side of the board, the older one on the other.

There are those who maintain that the Elephant and Castle also has a royal connotation, being a corruption of the Infanta de Castile, a Spanish princess with whom it was hoped to arrange an English prince's marriage. Others relate it to the Infanta Castille, a ship lying in the Thames at the time when the original tavern in south London was completed. Yet another theory ascribes it to the discovery of an elephant's skeleton during excavations in 1714. Perhaps the most prosaic explanation is the correct one: that it derives from the Cutlers' Company arms and the company's involvement in the ivory trade.

Among other foreign royalties, real or imaginary, Oliver Goldsmith tells the tale of one switch of allegiance in the eighteenth century:

An Alehouse keeper near Islington, who had long lived under the sign of the French King, upon the commencement of the last war pulled down his old sign and put up that of the Queen of Hungary. Under the influence of her red nose and golden sceptre, he continued to sell Ale, till she was no longer the favourite of his customers; he changed her therefore some time ago, for the King of Prussia, who may probably be changed in turn for the next great man that shall set up for vulgar admiration.

Names of great military commanders often date an inn, a street, or a whole residential development. The Duke of Marlborough became England's darling after his victory at Blenheim in 1704, and was celebrated in many places, including Dedham in Essex, where a clothier's workshop converted that year into an inn became predictably the Marlborough Head. The Marquis of Granby may not have been such a great national figure, but he was a hero to his own troops. When the turmoil of the Seven Years' War was over in 1763 he, unlike so many kings and commanders, did not immediately forget the men who had served under him. He made himself personally responsible for settling disabled NCOs as landlords of inns throughout the country—and they needed no persuasion to perpetuate his name on their premises. Granby was son of the third duke of Rutland, and the family crest is to be found on one of the most celebrated hotels built just after Waterloo— the Rutland Arms in Newmarket, favourite residence of owners and devotees

during race meetings—and on others about the family's expansive estates in Derbyshire.

A whole cluster of Victorian streets and street-corner pubs in Kentish Town dates them from the time of the Crimean War. The battles of Inkerman and the Alma are commemorated here and in many a Victorian provincial town, as is the commander-in-chief, Lord Raglan. He was also given belated command, as it were, of the Raglan in Aldersgate, though these London premises had existed long before his day: as the Bush, it was one of the earliest established taverns in the city, with cellars still revealing sections of Roman wall. After Charles I's execution it became the Mourning Bush, its signboard painted black by the doggedly Royalist host.

Turk's Head and Saracen's Head recall men who went on Crusade; and later there was to be many a Volunteer and Spanish Volunteer. Some warriors did not fare too well, as the comment on the sign of the Soldier's Fortune at Kidderminster bears out:

> A soldier's fortune, I will tell you plain,
> Is a wooden leg, or a golden chain.

Souvenirs of more recent conflicts include the Red Beret at Chelmsford, the Battle of Britain at Northfleet in Kent, and the Douglas Bader on Martlesham Heath in Suffolk. This latter was opened by the wartime ace himself on the eve of Battle of Britain Day in 1979. Being himself a teetotaller, Bader admitted the irony of his performing the ceremony by pulling the first pint. Asked if he often flew nowadays, he observed that finding one's way was so much more difficult than it used to be: the old method of navigating by the railway lines below was now impossible because Beeching had torn up so many of them.

Near Harpenden in Hertfordshire the sign of the Malta features a George

10 The Rutland Arms, Newmarket

Cross, awarded to the island and its people for their part in the Second World War.

Sports, trades, pigs and puzzles

Not all haunts of the horse-racing fraternity are as grandiose as the Rutland Arms in Newmarket, and names of many others have more direct reference to the sport itself rather than its wealthy patrons. Near Towcester race-course is an inn pessimistically called the Folly; and at Hereford and Newbury, the Starting Gate. Famous winners include Master Robert near Isleworth, and Little Wonder at Harrogate.

Older diversions which had achieved recognition on signboards included bull-baiting, bear-baiting, and cock-fighting. The pitting of one infuriated cock against another had been a great craze from the time of the Romans onwards, and by the reign of Edward III involved such ruinous gambling that in 1366 it was banned. Royal households did not always pay much respect to their own edicts, and the bouts flourished up to Tudor and Stuart times— 'the royal diversion' long before race-tracks offered 'the sport of kings'. Oliver Cromwell made another attempt to suppress the savage pastime, but it regained favour under Charles II, after which most towns had at least one cockpit and often more, whilst inns declared their interest under the sign of the Cock or even the unequivocal Fighting Cocks. The famous inn at St Albans was one of the last to feature such duels, while the last house in Great Yarmouth of that nature was—for different reasons, but with rather disturbing appositeness—called the Feathers. In 1849 the sport, if that is the word for it, was prohibited by Act of Parliament, though there are records of it continuing at clandestine meetings for some time afterwards.

It may be mentioned in passing, though, that not every inn bearing the sign of the Cock should be shunned by those afraid of a haunting by hundreds of maltreated birds. Some were so named because the wooden spigot used for regulating the vent of a barrel once it had been broached was for several hundred years commonly called a cock, and the sign thereby advertised the presence of draught beer. Maybe our contemporary Campaign for Real Ale enthusiasts should consider adopting this as one of their symbols, especially when operating their own premises in the interests of good traditional drink?

The Horse and Hounds or the Hare and Hounds bring us to those other sports in which men on animals' backs urge other animals on in pursuit of yet another sort of animal. It seems logical that inns called the Fox offer some solace to the most frequent prey, or some encouragement to its pursuers, but this is not always so. The Intrepid Fox in Soho has nothing to do with some imaginary huntsmen racing through the fields crying 'So-ho', though this is what they did when there really were fields between the city of London and Westminster, but commemorates Charles James Fox, whose supporters used the tavern during the election of 1784. When the pro-Whig landlord was on his deathbed, Fox himself hurried to the scene with his own physician.

I have frequently had my own doubts about the Fox in that lovely stone village of Barnack, whose quarries provided the Barnack Rag to cover the frontage of the eighteenth-century inn. They also supplied stone for the construction of the great Burghley House just up the road. William Cecil, later ennobled as Lord Burghley, was known to Elizabeth I as 'my spirit' but to his enemies as 'the fox'—so isn't it a bit of a coincidence that the local inn should carry that name?

The Pig and Whistle would seem straightforwardly rural if it were not for the inexplicable presence of the whistle. A theory has been advanced that the

phrase is a corruption of the Danish 'Pige-washail'—'here's health to the girls'; but the pig might be related to the Saxon 'piggin', a pail, surviving from days when ale was served in buckets and customers dipped their own mugs, or pigs, into it.

Another animal with an odd companion is the Goat and Compasses. A religious origin has been suggested for this: 'God encompass us.' But there are those who point to the arms of the Worshipful Company of Cordwainers in which, between goats' heads, an ornamental chevron could easily be distorted by amateurish sign-painters into a pair of compasses.

Surely we need no complicated explanations for the Falcon, the Old Dun Cow, or the Dog. Crops and vegetation, too, have their obvious rural place: the Barley Mow, the Wheatsheaf, the Oak, the Cherry Tree. Embracing both livestock and produce there are the Jolly Farmers—though, in truth, most such folk I have met would more appropriately deserve the sign of the Gloomily Prosperous Farmers.

One not so common name is perhaps not as innocuous as it appears at first. The Hempsheaf all too often marks a decline: as the wool trade left East Anglia for the Cotswolds because of the swifter running waters which drove fulling machines there, and then moved on to the industrial mills of Yorkshire, desperate attempts were made to preserve some local spinning and weaving trade, based on the growing of hemp. Still the trade was unable to survive.

Different regions, different trades—though in due course some spread into new settings. The Butchers Arms, the Ordnance Arms, the Horseshoes . . . all speak of neighbouring crafts and industries. Crests of merchant guilds, too, were adopted by inns serving members in particular locations. The Ram and the Lamb represent the Drapers and the Merchant Taylors. After 1480 the

12 This inn at Bretton in the Peak District might well be called the Cat and Barrel!

arms of the latter were definitively registered as the Lamb and Flag, though some researchers postulate a largely religious significance in this. There is an odd contradiction between the picture of a lamb either as a potential supplier of wool or a Christian symbol, and the nickname of the well-known Lamb and Flag near Covent Garden—the Bucket of Blood, derived from its association with bare-knuckled prize-fighters.

The Compasses (without an attendant goat) represent the Carpenters' Company. The Skinner's Arms in Hexham, Northumberland, recalls the town's past renown as a centre of leather work. In the Midlands, the Golden Fleece at Hinckley is associated with local stocking makers; hats are a speciality of Atherstone, so there is a Hat and Beaver; and the Glover's Needle comes as no surprise in Worcester, famous for its manufacture of gloves.

A 400-year-old steelyard, once used for weighing wagons and their loads of produce, projects from beside the Fountain at Soham, Cambridgeshire, a dull-looking place from the outside but enclosing one surviving oak-panelled sixteenth-century room, all that lived through a fire at the turn of our own century. And thrust over the street from the Old Bell and Steelyard at Woodbridge in Suffolk is a similar device, in such good condition that it was removed to London for an exhibition at the end of the nineteenth century and then restored to its present position.

Mention of a Bell or Old Bell, or any number of bells, strikes other chords. In olden times the English were great devotees of handbell ringing, and of course pioneered the art of change-ringing in church belfries. Many an inn far from the sea may seem at first glance to have nautical associations with its Four Bells or Six Bells; but the chances are that these refer to handbells or the numbers of bells in the local church tower.

Among strange but evocative titles we find the Live and Let Live, frequent in industrial areas as a dismal memento of times of slump. The Little Barrow at Lichfield has much older resonances of an ancient burial ground which was enclosed, like the cathedral, within fortifications guarding the slopes above the city.

The Punch Bowl is not, as one might readily assume, a simple reference to one sort of beverage supplied by an inn. At the end of the seventeenth century the popularity of punch was promoted largely by the Whigs, so that establishments which they frequented hung out the sign. The Tories in defiance made a point of demonstrating their loyalty to old-fashioned drinks such as claret, sack, and port.

Wariness is essential. A Magpie is a bird is a Magpie. But a 'magpie' was once a colloquialism for a half-penny or a half-pint. The Marlow Donkey has nothing to do with the animal, but remembers a little steam train which once plied between Marlow and Maidenhead. Nicknames can all too often confuse the issue—and the traveller. Between Dudley and Gornalwood in the Black Country is a pub called the Glynne Arms, which a stranger might have difficulty in finding, since everyone locally refers to it as the Crooked House: not surprisingly, since the presence of mine workings below has caused the place to sag alarmingly. A drinker unsteady on his feet might well fear, on leaving the premises, that he was about to plunge into some infernal shaft and disappear forever.

One of the bars at the George, behind Langham Place in London, is labelled as the Gluepot. Near what used to be the Queen's Hall before the Nazis bombed it, this was frequented by orchestral musicians and bitterly referred to by conductors and managers as the Gluepot because of the difficulty in getting these players out of it for a performance.

The First and Last offers a friendly warning. If the traveller is striking out into less populous parts of the countryside, he will be well advised to fortify himself with food and drink before proceeding. It was the equivalent to the contemporary signs of 'last services for 50m' or 'last petrol station before motorway'. If you and your horses don't stop for replenishment now, don't say you haven't been warned!

The Rocket, on the outskirts of Liverpool, commemorated the winner of the Rainhill railway engine trials in 1830, and stood at such an important road junction that to this day the whole region of shops and suburban houses, now

entangled in a mesh of dual carriageways and flyover, is known locally as the Rocket. We have seen the Railway Inn flourish . . . and fade. Of more recent date is the Horseless Carriage at Chingford in Essex, where a Brighton Belle dining car has been converted into a static restaurant, with an entrance in imitation of a ticket office. And one Railway Inn demonstratively gave up the ghost when Evercreech station in Somerset was closed: the inn became the Silent Whistle.

An interesting personal sign is that on the Five Arrows at the gates of Waddesdon manor. Baron Ferdinand de Rothschild completed his great mansion in 1889, displaying on both the house and the inn a crest of five arrows and a crown in testimony to the original five Frankfurt brothers who founded the Rothschild fortune.

Wry humour creeps into some pictures. The Honest Lawyer sets out to raise a laugh; or there's the Triple Plea, with a dying man being subjected to parson, doctor and lawyer wrangling over which has prior claim . . . while the Devil waits patiently in the background. The Man with a Load of Mischief carries his wife on one shoulder, a monkey on the other, and round his neck a chain labelled 'Wedlock'. The Quiet Woman or the Silent Woman are invariably headless. In the face of such libels will there, one wonders, ever be a lady publican who dares display the signboard of the Male Chauvinist Pig?

Let us nod respectfully to one of the most characteristic signs of all English themes: the Bat and Ball at Hambledon, Hampshire, commemorates the birth of the game of cricket on nearby Broadhalfpenny Down in 1774.

Names and signs are as important as the names of innkeepers, and usually live longer. At their best they somehow impose their own standards and traditions. It is salutary to note that even under the austere régime of Communist countries, where personal names have long been banished from shops to make way for bare announcements of Vegetables, Delicatessen, Shoes, and so on, the inns and wine cellars are allowed to retain their own personality: in Prague, for instance, it is much more fun to meet friends not just at a bar or kavárna or vinárna but at the Three Fiddles, at the Green Frog, or at the Golden Lane.

3
Taverns in the Town

Souls of poets dead and gone,
What Elysium have ye known,
Happy field or mossy cavern,
Choicer than *The Mermaid Tavern?*

John Keats

By the time the City of London had assumed proportions and features we might still recognize today, the tag that all roads led to Rome had ceased to be true. The capital of the Romans' lost Britannic province suffered ups and downs during the conflicts of Saxon chieftains aspiring to kingship and during the Danish disorders, and there were times when centres such as York and Winchester were of greater importance. But when an English nation with a central government was moulded into shape, it became true that the most important roads led to and from London.

As a capital city, port, trading centre and meeting-place of all kinds and degrees of men, it needed a wide range of inns: places to stay, places where merchants might meet and philosophers wrangle, and above all places where residents and traders could rely on the quality of the food and drink.

Again we find contenders for the oldest and most historic premises. In Bishopsgate, just outside the gate demolished in 1760, is an inn with the date 1246 set into its stonework, and improbably claiming an even more ancient lineage from the fifth century. Originally named the White Hart, it once catered for travellers who had arrived at the gateway too late in the evening to be admitted. Later it became simply 'No. 199' and is still so referred to although its actual street number is 119.

It is hard to give a ruling on pioneer establishments within the City proper, since all save one were wholly or substantially destroyed by the Great Fire of 1666, and rebuilding confused or overlaid many sites and frameworks. The sole verifiable survivor of what sixteenth-century records numbered as a thousand taverns is the Old Wine Shades in Martin Lane, near the Monument and perilously near the outbreak of that fire. Its splendidly sombre, panelled interior has secretive cubicles, old advertisements, and bottles and mirrors whose dusty appearance is due not to neglect but to an admirable wish that everything should be in keeping with the old, cobwebby atmosphere. One of the place's treasures, token of its authenticity, is a pre-conflagration lead cistern dated 1663. The name has changed a few times: early records give it as Sprague's Shades, but for a while in the middle of the nineteenth century it was known as Henderson's Shades.

Innumerable inns and taverns, in the metropolis and elsewhere, claim that Charles Dickens visited regularly or stayed on their premises. In London alone he could scarcely have managed to patronize them all, since at the height of his fame there was an average of one tavern to every 60 houses. He does seem, however, to have been a genuine habitué of the Old Wine Shades and also of

15 Ye Olde Cheshire Cheese, off Fleet Street, in 1896

the Cheshire Cheese in Wine Office Court, Fleet Street, which did succumb to the Great Fire, preserving only the great medieval cellars over which it was later rebuilt. Among its other literary visitors were Thackeray and Jerrold, and great play is made of associations with Dr Johnson and Boswell. In fact, although the Great Cham's chair is on display, it was brought here from the Mitre, which Johnson did frequent but of which all that remains is a blue memorial plaque in Fleet Street; and although Boswell lived at 6 Wine Office Court, there is no reliable record of either him or his mentor having ever been through the portals of the Cheshire Cheese.

When it comes to literary echoes, there can surely never have been a more resounding rendezvous than another victim of the Great Fire—the Mermaid, south of Cheapside. Here in about 1603 Sir Walter Raleigh founded the Mermaid Club, sometimes referred to as the Friday Street or Bread Street Club because of the streets into which its side doors opened. Among members at one time and another were Ben Jonson, John Donne, Thomas Carew, Shakespeare, Beaumont and Fletcher. Specialities of the house were fine Canary wine and fine conversation in which, according to Beaumont, was displayed:

Wit enough to justify the town
For three days past—wit that might warrant
For the whole city to talk foolishly
Till that were cancelled; and when that was gone,
We left an air behind us, which alone
Was able to make the next two companies
Right witty; though but downright fools, more wise.

In self-indulgent moments I like to imagine that the eager, voluble gatherings of our early generation of science-fiction enthusiasts under the tolerant eye of landlord Lou Mordecai, first at the White Horse in Fetter Lane and later at the Globe in Hatton Garden, had the same sparkle; but don't we all have such gleaming memories, enhanced by the passage of time? Anyway, Arthur C. Clarke did use our first meeting-place imaginatively as the setting for a volume of short fantasies under the title of *Tales from the White Hart*.

Many inns had strong ties with local trades and the markets or fairs associated with them. In the Middle Ages both Flemish and native clothiers congregated around the street still called Cloth Fair, on the edge of Smithfield, and settled many of their disputes over weights and measures in the Hand and Shears—some amicably or grudgingly through the summary Court of Pie-powders (*piepoudrous* or 'dusty feet', signifying an itinerant seller), some doubtless more violently as the day wore on and the ale flowed. It was from the door of the Hand and Shears that every St Bartholomew's Day the Lord Mayor declared Bartholomew Fair open by cutting a measure of cloth.

Off the Strand is the Coal Hole, taking its name from nineteenth-century coal heavers along the Thames. The Nag's Head in Covent Garden started life as a hotel, largely for the benefit of performers in the nearby opera house. It then began to serve the morning needs of fruit and vegetable porters from the market; but even before that market was shifted to Nine Elms it was once more engaged in an equally profitable evening trade with opera-goers. North of Covent Garden, the White Hart in Drury Lane has little to show of its old lineaments, but is said to date from the early thirteenth century and is known to have been a favourite (if that's really the word in such desperate circumstances) stopping-place for criminals' last refreshment on their way to Tyburn. The highwayman Jack Sheppard was among those who took their final draught here.

The favours of Fleet Street journalists and barristers from the Law Courts are distributed among so many establishments that it would be hard to point to one as archetypal. The Wig and Pen Club, just over the City boundary, is a private eating and drinking place shared by the two professions. Also on this Westminster side of the boundary, on land once belonging to Elizabeth I's beloved and then beheaded Earl of Essex, the Essex Head was converted in 1975 into the Edgar Wallace, marking the centenary of the birth of the journalist and thriller writer who revelled in every aspect of Fleet Street life.

Those who seek a tribute to an earlier and more distinguished writer of thrillers—or, rather, detective stories—can move west towards Northumberland Avenue, down which will be found the Sherlock Holmes, with a mass of framed material on the bar walls dealing with Arthur Conan Doyle and his inimitable creation, and a facsimile of Holmes's study upstairs behind a sheet of glass.

Leaving the City northwards is the City Road, at whose junction with Shepherdess Walk stands a modern public house on the site of a famous tavern with other trade associations—in this case, the leather workers. Even those who have never visited it, or those too young yet to consider doing so, must be familiar with its jingle:

> Up and down the City Road,
> In and out the *Eagle*,
> That's the way the money goes;
> Pop goes the weasel.

The song seems to have existed in very much this form around 1780, but there are hints that it dates even further back. This is odd, since it was only in 1825 that Thomas Rouse bought the Shepherd and Shepherdess and renamed it the Eagle, from which the lyric is supposed to derive. In Nile Street and in other neighbouring workshops the saddlers used a tool called a 'weasel' to punch holes in their leather. Some of them made a habit of pledging their implements with the landlord of the place when they were short of beer money, so that the phrase 'popping the weasel' came into the language.

There was another shift of name, or at least an addition, when a music-hall was opened on the premises. As an extra rather than a substitute, the Moorish Pavilion offered variety turns, music and dancing in the open air beside the tavern. These entertainments, accompanied by liberal refreshment, took place in a pleasure garden much resembling a miniature Vauxhall Gardens until a later owner, Robert Conquest, made a bad mistake. Setting up what he called his Grecian Theatre, he took out a full drama licence in 1851. The Theatres Act of 1843 had allowed music-halls to continue serving drinks in the auditorium; but theatres licensed for drama were not permitted to do so. By 1882 the Grecian Theatre had failed, and the entire complex was taken over by the Salvation Army as a citadel and temperance hotel. Demolished in 1900 but then rebuilt in its present form, it now has illuminated vignettes of past variety stars and old song sheets above the bar, and some interesting relics in a glass case, including a miniature re-creation of the Grecian Theatre in its prime.

All the great entertainers of Victorian times must have appeared on those boards, including Marie Lloyd. Among other souvenirs of the boisterous or more restrained performers of that era and later ones we have the George Robey in Finsbury Park; the Gilbert and Sullivan in John Street, not too surprisingly near the Savoy Theatre and garnished with posters and model stage sets; many yellowing signed photographs in a number of Drury Lane and Shaftesbury Avenue pubs; and a rather touching array of old photographs in the Lamb, in Lambs Conduit Street, where it is hard to distinguish politicians from actors, but where from the high-backed padded benches one can make one's nostalgic choice between the beauties of Ellaline Terriss and, more formally, Miss Bloomfield, Miss Forsyth, and Miss Fortescue.

In the middle of the seventeenth century a rival diversion had sprung up in the City to threaten the livelihood of innholders. A London merchant who had acquired a taste for coffee while working abroad set up his Greek servant in a coffee-house off Cornhill. The new fad soon caught on, and competing establishments flourished, condemned by some for the 'evil smells' of roasting, but praised by others:

Whereas formerly Apprentices and clerks with others used to take their morning's draught in Ale, Beer, or Wine, which, by the dizziness they cause in the Brain, made many unfit for business, they use now to play the Good-fellows in this wakeful and civil drink.

Literary and political clubs were formed in certain favoured coffee-houses, becoming such venues for outspoken criticism of royalty and lawmakers that at one stage Charles II tried to have them all closed down. He failed. By the end of the century there were almost twice as many such houses in the City as there were taverns. The most famous surviving name is that of Lloyd's in Lombard Street, whose proprietor began to handle shipping advertisements,

43

16 & **17** On the fringe of London, two famous Hampstead taverns: *(right)* the Bull and Bush on a Sunday morning in 1903; *(facing)* the Spaniards, with an old toll-cottage on the other side of the road

produce his own gazette, and draw under his roof the leading marine insurance underwriters.

Not until the beginning of the nineteenth century were there signs of a decline. Residential hotels were becoming fashionable, with their own tea and coffee rooms; and tavern bars made a comeback. Some proprietors of coffee-houses abandoned the newer beverage for older ones. The Horn Coffee House, catering to practitioners in Doctors' Commons—courts whose Doctors of Civil Law operated in the fields of Admiralty, Probate and Divorce until these were amalgamated in the Probate Court of 1857—duly became the Horn Tavern, still to be found in Knightrider Street behind the College of Arms. It honours Charles Dickens with a bust of Mr Pickwick, who during his spell in the Fleet prison sent his friends here to obtain bottles of wine for him.

Victorian puritanism resulted in many restrictions on public houses. In 1869 the introduction of a law requiring a justice's licence to be issued for any sale of beer and cider put some out of business. But others continued to flourish despite the strictures, and proliferated in suburban areas for the benefit of those employed locally and for the growing number of commuters. In 1837 the outlying borough of Camberwell had 138 public houses and 96 beershops. By 1902 these centres of social life and relaxation in an otherwise drab area numbered 307, and there were over 130 off-licences. Figures for 1903 show an average of one public house to every 845 inhabitants.

Riverside moorings

When slave-driving masters begrudged their apprentices more than a few hours' leisure each week, it must have been a great treat for a youngster to escape from cramped working and living conditions to spend those few hours on or beside the Thames, seeking fresh air and brief amusement. There are many delectable riverside inns along the Thames's course from the Cotswolds to the sea, but for a short inexpensive outing from London a reasonable limit would have been Isleworth. Here on the bank stands the London Apprentice, which in the early eighteenth century used to stay open all night for the pleasure of visiting roisterers, if not for the pleasure of anyone so ill advised as to take up temporary residence. Loftier mortals who are said to have

patronized the place included the ill-fated Lady Jane Grey, and Charles II and Nell Gwynne. Its present attractive form is the result of an eighteenth-century rebuilding, with a fine stucco ceiling in the first-floor lounge and generously proportioned windows giving attractive views down the river.

At Strand on the Green we find references to two modes of transport: the Steam Packet and, of older repute, the City Barge. This house has stood here since the fifteenth century near moorings for the mayoral barge, supplying the needs of visiting dignitaries and others. The first substantial building recorded, however, was founded in the time of Elizabeth I, who granted it a charter for 500 years. It has survived many perils, including extensive bomb damage during the Second World War, from which some of the original fabric was salvaged and incorporated in the present restoration. A recurrent danger is that of flood water, against which defensive boards are kept ready for slotting across the door and wedging into place with clay. Customers still eager for sustenance then have to get in from the garden at the back. Inside, a Parliamentary clock with an open face recalls Pitt's revenue-raising dodge of taxing windows and clock faces with hinged glass covers. There is also a copper pan for mulling beer on winter evenings.

Another sufferer from flooding has been the Doves near Hammersmith Bridge, where a marker in the bar records the height of a 1928 tide. The building was once joined to the house next door, and for a while functioned as a fashionable coffee-house. When this was split into two, No. 17 became a smoking-box for the Duke of Sussex, one of Queen Victoria's uncles. The original name of the Dove was transformed into the plural by a nineteenth-century signwriter's mistake. In its time the inn, with its verandah overlooking the water and its grapevine which actually bears fruit, has been frequented by Charles II and Nell Gwynne, by James Thomson—who according to legend composed the lyric of *Rule, Britannia* within these walls—and by William Morris, who lived close at hand and brought many of his friends here. In our own day it has associations with the late A. P. Herbert, who used it under an easily penetrable disguise in his novel *The Water Gypsies*.

Favoured customers can watch the Boat Race from the verandah of the Doves; but the buildings most obviously associated with that annual event are the Star and Garter on the opposite bank at Putney, close to the starting line, and the Ship at Mortlake, near the finishing line. The Star and Garter has been a starting place since the golden days of the Thames regatta, and accommodated crews during their training and preliminary heats. Well-to-do oarsmen made the most of the 'Dinners and Old Wines' offered by the management. Others, less affluent, took private lodgings and fed more cheaply in the Refreshment Rooms next door.

The banks soon cease to be green as we continue down-river past Chelsea and Westminster. At the eastern end of Westminster bridge we may nod to a relic of past beer-making. Until demolished in 1949 to make way for the 1951 Festival of Britain, the Red Lion Brewery near Waterloo provided a celebrated South Bank landmark in the shape of a mighty red lion made of Coade Stone— a sort of terra-cotta admirably resistant to wind and weather, made between 1769 and 1837 in a nearby factory from a secret formula belonging to the Coade family. They took their manufacturing mystery with them to the grave, but the lion was fortunately saved during the brewery demolition and set up to watch over Waterloo station approach, only to be moved again in 1966 to its post by Westminster bridge.

Below Blackfriars is another salute to the oarsmen of the river. This, fairly recent in construction, is Doggett's Coat and Badge, commemorating the seventeenth-century actor Thomas Doggett, who presented a scarlet coat with silver badge to be rowed for by Thames watermen each July between Chelsea and London bridge. The inn displays a replica of this prize, as well as paintings of City livery company barges.

Under the rattle and rumble of Cannon Street railway bridge nestles the Anchor, at the junction of Bankside and Park Street. It stands trim and cheerful in a setting of crumbling warehouses with windows smashed or bricked and boarded up, and gaps of wasteland. A newish factory behind the inn is already dusty with the dissolving fabric of its neighbours. In the shadowy precincts of the bridge once stood Winchester palace, south London residence of the bishops of Winchester, and the Clink prison, together with the bars, brothels and bear-baiting pits of a notoriously sordid area. There was also a large brewery which at one stage in its career covered almost ten acres. In the eighteenth century this came into the possession of the Thrale family, who then sold it to a Mr Barclay and a Mr Perkins. Rooms within the Anchor, on different levels and split levels, glimpsed cosily down a few steps or at an angle through stair rails and half landings, sum up a great deal of this local history.

Dr Johnson's room reminds us that the great lexicographer worked on his dictionary in a room set aside for him in the brewery through the good graces of his friends Henry and Hester Thrale. His own preferred tipple was said to be a porter specially brewed for the Empress of Russia, thereafter achieving wider distribution as Russian Imperial Stout. There are inevitably a Mrs Thrale room in the Anchor; a Boswell restaurant upstairs under the exposed roof beams; and delineations of Johnson in Barclay Perkins bottle labels and old advertising plaques.

The Globe bar has an impressive model of the Globe theatre, in Shakespeare's time standing some 200 yards away, though there is nothing to substantiate claims that the Bard himself used the Anchor. The Bear Garden recalls another less edifying diversion in the locality. And the Clink room displays disquieting old pictures, documents, police truncheons and rusted gyves in memory of Southwark debtors' prison, which added two phrases to our language—'in Clink' meaning 'in prison', and 'on the fiddle' to denote malpractice, derived from the sign of a violin which hung outside the gaol.

One room has five doors, and through the centre of the inn runs a vertical shaft wide enough to hold a man, reaching up to a skylight in the roof. Most likely there were ways of getting out of the Clink and bribing the landlord of the Anchor to hide one—though if a prisoner had been committed to a debtors' gaol in the first place, how would he be capable of raising the cash? Another explanation is that the hiding-places of the Anchor were designed to help those threatened by sudden raids from the Press Gang.

In 1876 the old Anchor was destroyed by fire, but was soon rebuilt in its present form. In 1939 it was threatened with demolition but, unlike so many other features in the riverside landscape, was saved by the Second World War. The view from here of London's second great fire, during the Blitz, must have been awe-inspiring. The modern view of rebuilt London can best be observed —by those masochistic enough to enjoy it—from a viewing platform on the other side of the cobbled lane, jutting out above the water.

An even wider prospect, offered to a truly water-borne spectator, was provided until early 1980 by the Caledonia, a former Clyde paddle steamer converted into a floating pub with bars, a restaurant, and a cafeteria. Having emerged successfully from war service during the D-day landings, it fell victim to a fire in May 1980, raging from the stern through the bars and setting the entire stock ablaze. More than a hundred firemen were rushed to the scene, and got the blaze under control. The vessel is still afloat, but I doubt if it will have been refitted and reopened for custom by the time this book is finished.

Further downstream we can steer in right under two celebrated rivals. Which one of them is the original of the Six Jolly Fellowship Porters in *Our Mutual Friend*? Argument has ebbed and flowed for many a moon; but one is tempted to think that a novelist as accomplished as Dickens would happily have taken a feature from this, a nuance from that, and blended them to his own recipe.

The Prospect of Whitby stands on the site of a timbered tavern built in the time of Henry VIII, when its immediate backing consisted of marshes and a few gardens. For long it was nicknamed the Devil's Tavern because of its regular use by the worst riff-raff of the river. A memorial stone in adjacent Shadwell park recalls the departure of many courageous navigators from this reach, among them Sir Hugh Willoughby, who in 1553 set out to open up a north-east passage to Muscovy—a venture ending in his crew and himself

being frozen to death on the Murmansk coast. Samuel Pepys was such a frequent visitor that in due course the Pepys Society made their regular assembly room upstairs, and a contemporary chart of the Harwich approaches inscribed to him is given a place of honour.

Judge Jeffreys was not merely a sadistic persecutor of the Duke of Monmouth's defeated followers, but a great gloater over the agonies of other wretches. In Execution Dock, between here and the Town of Ramsgate inn, many a malefactor was hung in chains until three tides had ebbed and flowed over him; and Jeffreys, resident in the Wapping street now appropriately called Butcher Row, made a practice of taking meals on the balcony of the inn so that his appetite might be quickened by the sight of the bloated bodies. It was equally apposite that when he tried to flee the country after the collapse of James II he should be captured in disguise on Wapping Old Stairs below the taverns and despatched to the Tower of London to rot away in his turn.

In 1777 the premises acquired their present name as the consequence of a ship from Whitby, the *Prospect*, being moored for a long period beneath their windows. The picturesque decrepitude of the setting attracted artists such as Turner, Whistler and Doré, and there are mementoes in the bar of other distinguished and lesser-known patrons—spears, skulls, shoes, and wine bottles. A fine vinicultural tradition is maintained in Wapping High Street behind, which boasts a number of importers unshipping their wines from the

wharves at one end of the warehouses and selling them cheaply out of the other.

19 The Trafalgar Tavern at Greenwich

In Narrow Street, Limehouse, is the contender for Dickensian immortality. The Bunch of Grapes also has a balcony, and a conglomeration of bow windows offering an equally fine prospect of, if not Whitby, at any rate the Thames. A ladder much used by watermen for direct access to the tap-room is kept in place; and there are grisly old anecdotes of those same watermen luring tipsy customers down that ladder late at night to be drowned and then sold to eager anatomists.

Teetering on stained, weed-strung piles on the other side of the river is what before the Reformation was known as the Salutation, altered to the slightly less evocative name of the Angel. It offers a vista of the reach just as admirable as that from its opposite numbers, and the trap-doors in the flooring indicate that it, too, had its fair share of villains—smugglers and other such rogues. Here, too, Samuel Pepys was a regular visitor. He used to collect cherries from a Rotherhithe garden to take home to his wife, doubtless in the hope of assuaging his conscience after having visited the merry Mrs Bagwell, his 'Valentine' in the vicinity.

At Greenwich we may choose from any number of houses with maritime ascriptions. The Admiral Hardy stands beside the entrance to a covered market, from which there is a door direct into the bar. The Ship, known to Dickens as Quartermaine's Ship, disintegrated under enemy bombs in the Second World War, providing a site for the now landlocked *Cutty Sark*, queen of all clipper ships; while the seventeenth-century Union on the quay has been renamed the Cutty Sark in deference to its towering neighbour. One side of the Gipsy Moth signboard portrays the de Havilland biplane in which Francis Chichester made his solo flight to Australia in December 1929; on the other, one of the boats which he named after it. *Gipsy Moth IV* herself lies preserved nearby, and within the pub are souvenirs, maps and photographs relating to Chichester's circumnavigation of the globe in 1966, at the end of which Queen Elizabeth II knighted him at Greenwich with the same sword which her namesake had used to create another Sir Francis—Drake, bringing his *Golden Hind* into Deptford.

The Greenwich meridian runs right through the 300-year-old Yacht, which has an agreeable and inexpensive glassed-in verandah restaurant overlooking the water or, according to the state of the tide, the mud flats. Rubbing shoulders with it, and offering a restaurant with similar outlook but decidedly higher prices, is the Trafalgar Tavern of 1837, replacing the earlier George ale-house. Here Dickens and Douglas Jerrold dined together for the last time. Designed by Joseph Kay when he was Surveyor of Greenwich Hospital, the inn made a feature of whitebait suppers so appetizing that Gladstone and his cabinet were known to travel down in a bedecked ordnance barge specially to indulge in 'Ministerial Suppers'. In 1915 the building became a merchant seamen's institute and then a working men's club. Half a century later it reclaimed its licence and also its old Nelsonian name, the subsequent restoration—moulded ceilings, gilt and pastel shades, superb glittering chandelier in the Nelson room—winning it a Civic Trust Award in 1967. The award was well merited; but did its donors know that the admirable setting was going to be contaminated by the most inappropriate babble of canned music?

Arrivals and departures

In his *Carrier's Cosmography* of 1637 John Taylor listed the more important wagon and coach services of his time, with arrival and departure points, routes, and frequency of service, together with comments on the hostelries favoured by various 'carriers, wagons, foot-posts and higglers'. The route between London and Winchester, for example, had its main station at the Swan in the Strand, and other inns set themselves up as the Kings Cross and Paddington of their era.

It appears that carriers from the north-west tended to operate in and out of the Swan with Two Nicks (later with Two Necks) in Lad Lane, now swallowed up by Gresham Street. Also it was served by a mail diligence from Bristol and Bath, and increasingly by passenger coaches, until an early nineteenth-century landlord found it worth his while to invest in other properties and

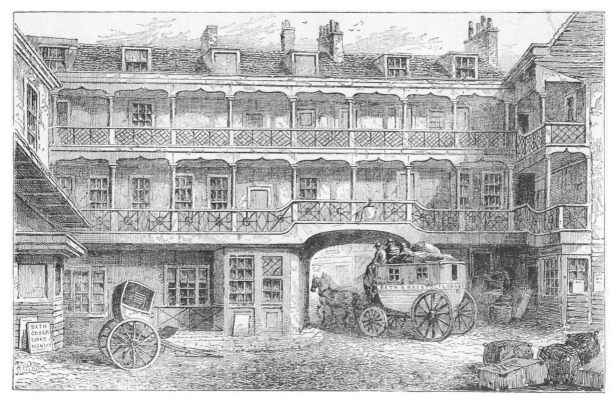

stabling, including the White Horse in Fetter Lane with its regular timetables to and from Norwich. Many a long-distance traveller arriving after an exhausting journey from the provinces would take a room in order to rest before setting out on business or pleasure in the capital, and might even use one such place as a base during his entire stay. In his diary Parson Woodforde records having booked in at the Swan with Two Necks but, finding it not to his taste, transferred to the Bell Savage on Ludgate Hill.

From the time of Henry VI onwards this was one of the most celebrated of City inns. Through several reigns it was known as the Bell on the Hoop, until in Elizabethan days it was taken over by an Isabel Savage, who built up trade by encouraging the production of plays in its galleried inner courtyard, and offering other diversions such as cock-fights and bear-baiting. Her name and that of the inn were later corrupted rather fancifully to the Belle Sauvage, misleadingly implying some derivation from a beautiful native girl, which in fact became the colophon of a well-known English publisher whose offices were built on the site of the demolished inn—to be themselves demolished during Second World War bombing. After opening its own coach service to Bath in 1667, setting out at five o'clock in the morning towards its other terminus at the White Lion, the Bell Savage acquired a considerable reputation for its services to Salisbury, Bath, Exeter, and the West Country. But it had a competitor on this route and others, as the George in Aldersgate instituted fast runs (that is, two-day journeys) to Salisbury, and expanded northwards towards Birmingham, Doncaster, and even as far as Edinburgh.

When 'railway mania' swept the country in the 1840s it was clear to all save a few diehards that the stage coach was doomed. Critics had once argued that coaches travelled too fast and too dangerously. Now a later generation of critics condemned the speed and risks of steam engines and their carriages.

20 The inner courtyard of the Belle Sauvage on Ludgate Hill

Nevertheless manufacturers, postal authorities and the general public transferred to the iron road. Every time a new line was opened, it took only a few months for local coach services to go out of business and the coaching inns to face bankruptcy.

In 1835 the annual ceremonial parade of the principal mail coaches was led by six vehicles belonging to the most prosperous operator in the field, Mr Chaplin of the Swan with Two Necks, the rear being brought up by a single coach from Mr Nelson of the Belle Sauvage. In the middle were four more of Chaplin's vehicles, based on the Spread Eagle in Gracechurch Street. But Chaplin was not a complacent man. Quick to scent danger from the railways, he began selling off surplus carriages to European buyers, offered the services of remaining vehicles for freight, passenger and luggage transport in conjunction with the railways, and succeeded so well that he ended up as Chairman of the London and South-Western Railway.

Now there arose new termini. And to serve incoming passengers or those waiting for a train, the railway companies began to build their own hotels, mightier than the most imposing inn. Florid assurances were offered to patrons in the prospectus and advertising of the Great Western Hotel at Paddington:

Passengers by the Trains can pass between the Platforms and the Hotel at once, without trouble or expense, and proper persons will be always in attendance to receive and carry the Luggage to and from the Trains.

Whatever happened, one wonders, to those 'proper persons'? And one also wonders how, if such a one could be found today, he would react to the ruling on the tariff:

Hotel servants not allowed to receive any Fees or Gratuities.

It would be many years before those old inns which managed to survive could find a new rôle in serving the motor traffic of the twentieth century. Unfortunately many were lost forever: the Golden Cross at Charing Cross, loved by many if not by Dickens, who complained that his bedroom 'smelt like a hackney coach and was shut up like a family vault'; the Bull and Mouth in St Martin's-le-Grand, whose spacious galleried courtyard became a railway goods siding after one last attempt to cope with its new world by rebuilding and changing its name to the Queen's Hotel, finally giving up the struggle in 1887; and so many great Southwark inns.

Among the 'many fair Inns for the receipt of Travellers' which the Borough boasted when John Stow produced his *Survey of London* in 1598 were the Spur, the Christopher, the Boar's Head, the Old Pick my Toe, the White Hart—associated with Jack Cade's arrival at London Bridge with his Kentish rebels—and the George. A couple of decades after Stow's publication, an official paper records that the inhabitants of the Borough consisted chiefly of innkeepers.

The route from the City over London Bridge was for centuries the only traffic highway in and out of Kent and Sussex. When the bridge was closed at night, delayed travellers had no access to the north bank and had to seek their accommodation in Southwark. It soon dawned on local entrepreneurs that incoming traders ought to be dissuaded from even bothering to cross the river with their produce. A market was regularly held on London Bridge itself, and the Borough Market which developed from it at the southern end can now claim to be the oldest fruit and vegetable market in London. Well on into coaching days this was one of the capital's busiest junctions, and its inns the most numerous and prosperous in all London.

Now the sole survivor of those establishments is the splendid, galleried

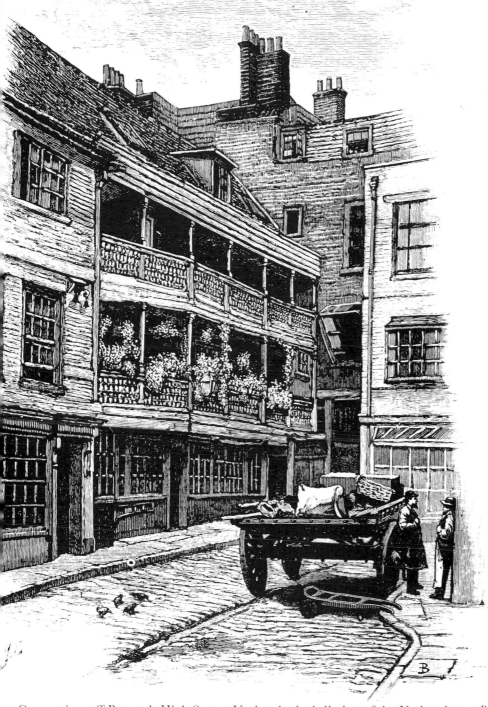

George, just off Borough High Street. Under the jurisdiction of the National Trust the future of the George should be subject to fewer threats than its past has been. Considerable alterations have been made since, according to tradition, Shakespeare frequented the inn, and in 1677 the whole building had to be rebuilt after the devastating Southwark fire. It once had galleries round three sides of its courtyard to give access to tiers of bedrooms, but only the south side now remains intact, the others having been encroached on by railway sheds. Even the entrance is not the original, having been introduced

21 Remaining galleries of the George, Southwark, in Victorian times when the railway company's expansion around London Bridge station threatened to choke the whole yard off altogether.

In spite of the advance of the Philistines, the inn preserves much of its old atmosphere, and without too many gimmicks and affectations. A winding staircase serves the galleries and bedrooms, and we can still locate the tap-room where drivers of stage coaches rested between journeys. It is easy to imagine ostlers busily at work in the yard and stables, as mail, goods and passengers rolled in from Kent and Sussex. In its palmy days the George could cope with up to 80 coaches weekly, serving Dover, Folkestone, Hastings, Brighton, and many intervening stages; and there was a steady traffic of carriers' carts and wagons.

Somewhere along the line a coffee room with high-backed partitions was introduced, perhaps to vie with the coffee-houses which once threatened the trade of so many inns and taverns.

In his little book on the George, published in 1918, B. W. Matz tells of a small dining club formed by nineteenth-century Southwark businessmen who met daily at four o'clock—hours for lunch and dinner having, like so many other things, varied throughout our history—and not unnaturally called themselves the Four O'Clockers. The room set aside for this daily ritual was in the north wing, and when this was demolished in 1889 they voted to abolish the club rather than shift to the other side of the yard. A later club was that of the Old Chums, formed by City businessmen who dined together on the first Saturday in each year. During the First World War, when many of the group's stalwarts were absent for obvious patriotic reasons, one member and his wife came here on each anniversary to keep the tradition alive.

What remains of the galleried courtyard still makes a fine summer auditorium for Shakespearean plays, and there have been occasional Dickensian productions. Some devotees of the place have tried to claim the George as the inspiration for the White Hart in *Pickwick Papers*; but although Dickens undoubtedly patronized the George, and mentions it in *Little Dorrit*, his White Hart is surely the establishment of that name, now demolished but still recollected in White Hart Yard and in Shakespeare's *Henry VI*.

Other old echoes stir in an opening to the far side of the George. There has often been a confusion between Talbot and Tabard on inn signs. Some show a now extinct hunting dog known as a Talbot after the old English family of that name, who became earls of Shrewsbury and adopted the animal in their heraldic device. But there has been a two-way corruption between this and another name with heraldic connotations: the Tabard, a sleeveless surcoat worn by knights or heralds. In Southwark there has certainly been an alteration. What is now Talbot Yard once sheltered that 'noble hostelry known as the Tabard, hard by the Bell', whose host was 'large, bold, well wrought, had protruding eyes, and was a very merry man', from which Geoffrey Chaucer dispatched his oddly assorted group of pilgrims resolved to ride or trudge the road to Canterbury and the shrine of Thomas Becket.

From this fabled spot one can still follow the course of that fictional pilgrimage; but in modern traffic conditions it might be safer to drive than ride, and certainly better to drive than walk.

And yet . . . isn't it the dedicated walker who stands a better chance of appreciating to the full the most attractive surviving hospices converted into village taverns, the most snug and traditional and unflurried inns beside lanes and pleasant by-roads, than the motorist speeding along swathes of main road and motorway?

22 *Facing* The George, Southwark, as it looks today

4

Pilgrims' Ways and Dover Road

But first, quod he, her at this ale-stake
I wil bothe drynke and byten on a cake.

Geoffrey Chaucer

At the time when Chaucer began the narrative of his *Canterbury Tales* at the Tabard, its merry landlord was a friend of his, Henry Bailly, whose family had provided several bailiffs of Southwark and who had himself twice represented Southwark in Parliament. Much of his financial security must have been owed to the hiring of horses to travellers along that ancient trackway on which the Romans built what was to become Watling Street.

It is now declared by experts that the designation of the route to Canterbury as 'The Pilgrims' Way' is a misnomer, and that the only considerable numbers of genuine pilgrims were more likely to have followed the other track of that name from Winchester to Canterbury. But even from a city as dissolute as London there must have been a fair number of the devout wishing to visit Becket's shrine, and even if they did not cling strictly to the ancient track they would scarcely have strayed very far to one side or the other. In Chaucer's own lifetime there are records of a bicentennial celebration in which food and drink were provided all the way along the road from London to Canterbury, the supplies being in fact so lavish that the pilgrims began to wax even more boisterous than was customary. Simon Sudbury, Bishop of London, was so enraged by the jollity of the crowd that he thundered: 'Better hope might ye have of salvation had ye stayed at home and brought forth fruits meet for repentance!' To this one of the intemperate travellers retorted: 'I will give up mine own salvation if you yourself do not die a most shameful death!' This was, if not in the circumstances a charitable utterance, at any rate a prophetic one: as Archbishop of Canterbury, Simon was murdered by Wat Tyler's rebels on Tower Hill in 1381.

The Tabard itself was originally part of an ecclesiastical guest-house built some 30 years before Chaucer's birth by the Abbot of Hyde, near Winchester, for himself and attendants when staying in London. The Bishop of Winchester himself had a palace nearby on Bankside, as we have already noted when visiting the Anchor. The Tabard survived numerous changes and extensions, including a major rebuilding in Elizabeth's time, until gutted in 1676 by a fire which broke out between itself and the George. After restoration the change from Tabard to Talbot took place, and it bore this name until demolition in 1874.

The first stretch of Roman road which led pilgrims out towards the North Downs and the shrine was known as Tabard Street. Once they had torn themselves away from the fleshpots of Southwark, the more determined among them usually aimed to reach Dartford in the first day. There were temptations

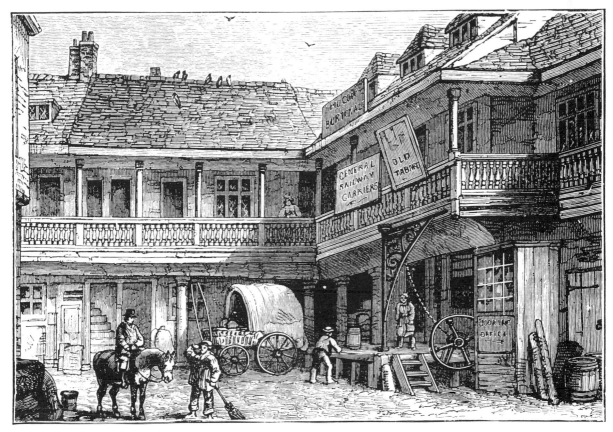

along the route: indeed, the number of inns and taverns across Kent which were, or claim to have been, old refreshment houses for pilgrims lead one to suppose that such pilgrims must have been permanently pot-valiant rather than pious.

Nothing remains of the old Dartford hostels, but the Bull occupies the site of one, and in the middle of sprawling, dusty industrialization preserves a galleried Georgian elegance.

Proceeding eastwards, the pilgrim would soon reach Cobham, which later attracted the acolytes of another English religion—cricket. In the nineteenth century Cobham Hall, now a school, was often visited by W. G. Grace, and it was from here that a great eleven was sent on its way to confront the Australians in 1882. Today, Cobham cricket is played on a pitch designed as the village war memorial. It was in the park of Cobham Hall that Charles Dickens one afternoon in 1870 took his last walk. He was fond of the half-timbered 'clean and comfortable village ale-house', the Old Leather Bottle, which in *Pickwick Papers* he had made the scene of Tracy Tupman's attempt to blot out the memory of his jilting by Rachel Wardle. Visitors should spare some minutes from the admirably maintained inn for a stroll to the local church, whose chancel has perhaps the finest display of brasses in the country.

We are still in Dickens country as we enter Rochester, on whose outskirts he lived out his last years in the house he had coveted for so long, Gad's Hill Place. The garden chalet in which he wrote his very last words after returning from that Cobham Hall walk has been removed and lodged in the grounds of the city's Eastgate museum.

In the early thirteenth century the Rochester monks grew jealous of

23 The Old Tabard, Southwark, from a sketch made shortly before its demolition in 1874

24 & 25 A remarkable restoration: the Leather Bottle at Cobham, Kent (*left*) as it was earlier this century and (*right*) after its original timbers were revealed again

Canterbury's attraction for pilgrims, and desperately tried a bit of canonization on their own account. A Scottish pilgrim who had been murdered here on his way to the shrine of Thomas Becket was pronounced a holy martyr and became St William of Perth. He did not prove as profitable a draw as St Thomas, but for a while there was custom for a number of guest-houses around the cathedral, and of course those who persisted in heading for Canterbury often required lodgings at this stage of their journey. Then and later, Rochester relied for trade and income on its strategic position on the Medway crossing.

The George in High Street was an important inn during coaching days, but its original lineaments were disguised in 1972 by an uninspired reconstruction. What has not been destroyed, however, is the vaulted crypt below it, most probably a thirteenth-century survival of a monastic guest-house.

Journeying on to Ospringe, we find ourselves on the fringes of fields—or, according to other regional usages, gardens or yards—which have for several centuries contributed a key ingredient to the favoured tipple in the most truly English inns and taverns. Queen Court Farm at Ospringe was once the centre of the manor, which belonged after the Conquest to William I's half-brother, Bishop Odo of Bayeux. The present building, embodying part of a fifteenth-century structure, controls the working of a hop farm which supplies the needs of Shepherd Neame's Faversham brewery. Today many hops have been stripped out in accordance with EEC regulations, and replaced in the brewing process by imported mash from the Continent; but on this road in Kent we ought to pause in our pilgrimage and look back for a short time on the people and processes which have so strongly influenced our drinking habits.

Bring us in good ale

Flemish weavers had been establishing settlements in eastern and south-eastern England since the time of King Stephen, but there was an especially large influx when Edward III invited them to bring the 'mysteries' of their cloth-making here to stimulate English manufacture. Religious persecution brought many more in the sixteenth century, and by the end of that century there were about a thousand such foreigners settled in Canterbury alone.

As well as importing the skills of their 'new draperies', these immigrants also brought with them the cherry—and the hop. The bitter flavour this added to ale was not at first acceptable to the English palate, and for a while the Flemings were the sole brewers of what came to be called beer, as opposed to ale. The word comes from the Old English 'beor' which, paradoxically, seems to have referred originally to a sweet-tasting wort and even to mead.

How far back can we trace the existence of such drinks, and the development of an identifiable public taste?

The earliest reference to such a product in the British Isles is probably that of Dioscorides, a Greek physician who around the first century A.D. wrote of a drink which,

made from barley and often drunk instead of wine, produces headaches, is a compound of bad juices, and does harm to the muscles. A similar drink may be produced from wheat, as in Western Spain and in Britain.

26 The Red Lion at Herne Hill, Kent, was a fourteenth-century rest house for pilgrims, older than the neighbouring church built by local people in thanksgiving for the return of their menfolk from Agincourt

In the same century Pliny the Elder is to be found declaring:

Western nations intoxicate themselves by means of moistened grain.

The Romans imported wine into Britain and tried to cultivate grapes in the province itself. Grape pips thought to have been left over from local pressing have been found at Silchester. By the time Pliny was sneering at the ale swillers of the west, vineyards occupied so much working time in the Roman Empire that Domitian ordered the demolition of all plantations outside Italy itself, probably not merely in an austerity campaign but also to ensure a monopoly for the homeland. This prohibition did not last. Probus was later to grant Spain, Gaul and Britain permission to establish or re-establish their own vineyards. Even the ale and mead swilling of the Saxons could not entirely have swept wine from the table, since William the Conqueror's Domesday Book in 1086 refers to nearly 40 vineyards in Somerset and East Anglia. Wine continued to be produced until Henry II's marriage to Eleanor of Aquitaine brought the Bordeaux trade under English control. Imports of cheaper and tastier wines meant the decline of home industry, though many monastic foundations kept going until the Dissolution: the open space known as The Vines in Rochester, for example, was the priory vineyard. In our own time there have been serious attempts to revive production, with some admirable successes in Hampshire, Sussex, and East Anglia.

But for ordinary folk, from as far back as we have reliable records, the everyday drink seems to have been ale, deriving its name from the Danish 'øl'. Its ingredients were water, yeast, and malt made chiefly from barley but occasionally from other grain. The law did not allow the introduction of sugar in the process until halfway through the nineteenth century.

Medieval monks were as adept at brewing ale as at making wine, and the job of Cellarer was always a coveted one. These monastic brewers devoutly marked their barrels with the sign of the Cross—and when they had achieved finer and stronger brews they advertised the fact with a proud XX or XXX. One of the foundations with the highest reputation for its ale in Richard I's time was the abbey of Burton-on-Trent; and although the abbey crumbled with the rest, Burton's reputation has remained sound.

Many functions in the Middle Ages were built around a supply of ale. The ale-house being usually near the parish church, it was reasonable for it to offer comfort at weddings and funerals. On a wedding day the bride's parents laid on a supply of ale for which the guests were expected to pay, so contributing to a bridal gift. These were known as bride ales, taken with such liberality that the Church often made scandalized protests: in 1223 Bishop Poore issued a stern injunction that marriages

be celebrated reverently and with honour, not with laughter or sport, or in taverns or at public potations or feasts.

He would have frowned on the Danish saying that 'It's better to sit in the inn thinking about the church than to sit in the church thinking about the inn.'

The word 'ale' itself came to mean an occasion on which the liquid was drunk. A bede ale was a drinking party designed to raise money for some local character or family fallen on hard times. Realizing that out-and-out prohibition was not going to work, the Church was soon organizing its own approved ales. The lord of the manor, not to be deprived of valuable revenue, exerted his privilege of taxing home-brewed or inn-brewed liquor, and laid on his own local money-raising functions, rather like some contemporary local squire's garden party or bazaar to raise funds for an election campaign: if attendance was not exactly compulsory, manorial residents found it not

WHITBREAD

Cardinal's Error

27 This sign on the outskirts of Tonbridge, Kent, ruefully recalls Cardinal Wolsey's promise to use profits from a dissolved priory to give the town a grammar school—a promise not kept because of his fall from favour with Henry VIII

exactly tactful to stay away.

And so, slowly and reluctantly, from ale to beer . . .

When the new technique of using hops in the brew showed signs of spreading, a London petition was presented to Parliament asking that these intruders should be forbidden

in regard that they would spoyl the taste of drinks and endanger the people.

Even when the brewing of both ale and beer was allowed, the Masters and Keepers or Wardens and Commonalty of the Mystery or Art of Brewers of the City of London denied membership to anyone who introduced hops into his ale. Henry VIII's royal brew was commanded to be kept free from such contamination. But palates changed; tastes changed; the tang of hops appealed to more and more adventurous drinkers.

Whether one favoured unhopped ale or the bitterness of beer, there were still standards of quality to be maintained within each category. Henry VII authorized local justices of the peace to close down establishments which they felt were supplying a poor product or encouraging rowdyism, 'and to take sureties of keepers of ale-houses in their good behaving'. Edward VI strengthened these powers and also ruled that no drinking house could be opened without a licence. Brewers and ale-house keepers may have grumbled at these restrictions, as they grumble nowadays at far more complex legislation, but they continued to prosper:

Men of good Ranke and place, and much command
Who have, by sodden water, purchast land.

Control of quality was a local issue. Craft guilds or magistrates appointed ale conners to make spot checks for strength and purity. One accepted procedure was for a quantity of ale to be poured on to a wooden bench, on which the conner would then sit. If within 30 minutes his breeches had stuck to the bench, the ale was pronounced fit for human consumption. An adverse judgment could result in the brewer being ordered to drink his own mistake until he was fit to burst, when the remainder would be poured over his head. Once in every ten years a formal ceremony takes place in London to commemorate these old procedures. At the Tiger Tavern near the Tower of London—said to be the successor to the tavern which supplied Elizabeth I with meals when she was prisoner in the Tower—the Lord Mayor and a company of sheriffs and aldermen bring along an expert who goes through the old routine of pouring beer on a stool and sitting on it. There have been no reports in recent decades of a failure to satisfy the conner, and at the end of the session the landlord is presented with a garland round his neck and a bouquet of laurel leaves for his door.

Charles I was not one to miss a chance of raising taxes, and on one thing at least he and the Parliamentarians agreed: as the Civil War loomed, they both imposed excise duties on liquor . . . and both declared, with the solemn sincerity of modern political parties locked in electoral struggle, that this was a temporary measure only and would be rescinded once the conflict was over.

We know the sequel. Indeed, we see every sign of such taxes and duties and variously named imposts on conviviality being increased throughout every generation rather than abandoned. Still our thirst is insistent, and shame-facedly or defiantly we echo Boniface in *The Beaux' Stratagem*:

I have fed purely upon ale; I have eat my ale, drank my ale, and I always sleep upon ale.

The Way from Wessex

Another so-called Pilgrims' Way converges on the London to Canterbury route from the direction of Winchester. This, too, was a prehistoric trackway long before the days of Christianity.

Pilgrims from abroad appear to have favoured Winchester as the starting-point for their penitential journey to St Thomas's shrine, along with native worshippers from the west and south. As one-time capital of England, it had almost as much to offer at the beginning of the route as Canterbury had at the end. The Hospital of St Cross, founded in 1133, is the oldest surviving charitable institution of its kind, catering for pilgrims, wayfarers and the needy. To many a traveller passing through or setting out on pilgrimage it offered a Wayfarer's Dole of bread and ale, a custom which is still observed from the porter's doorway.

Later indulgence, or self-indulgence, is recalled on one of the Cathedral tombstones. In 1764 a Hampshire militiaman came to an untimely end:

Here sleeps in peace a Hampshire Grenadier
Who caught his death by drinking cold Small Beer.
Soldiers be wise from his untimely fall
And when yere hot drink Strong or not at all.
An honest Soldier never is forgot
Whether he die by Musket or by Pot.

The humble wanderer of medieval times would surely be taken aback by the sight of Winchester's dominant modern hotel, the Wessex, cheek by jowl with

the cathedral. It is a comfortable, indeed luxurious place, and the evening view
from some of its windows of the floodlit cathedral is superb; but, with all due
deference to the hotel's excellent service and cuisine, one cannot say the view
of it from the cathedral is altogether in keeping with its setting.

Pilgrims leaving Winchester would head for Alton and on to Farnham,
just across the Hampshire and Surrey border. But deviations were not
uncommon. The village of Chiddingfold is some way off the obvious route,
yet its beautiful inn, the Crown, is thought to have been built somewhere
around 1285 for the benefit of organized parties of Cistercians plodding their
way from Winchester to Canterbury. Its history as licensed premises has been
unbroken since 1383, when as the Hall it was let to a brewer, Thomas Gofayre.
By the 1550s it had become the Crown, and offered its services to Edward VI
when he and his retinue were on their way from London to Cowdray House
outside Midhurst. The building then consisted of only one storey, but this was
provided with a second floor containing four bedrooms. The original access
to these can still be detected in one of the present bars. This rebuilding featured
a characteristic timbered framework filled in with wattle and daub, later
covered by attractive but inappropriate tile-hanging. Yet another restoration
in 1951 removed the tiles and revealed the old half-timbered façade.

Veering back towards Farnham, we cannot escape paying tribute to a
splendid Englishman born long after pilgrims had ceased to trudge this way.
In 1762 William Cobbett was born in the ale-house which expanded into the
Jolly Farmer inn, and now respectfully bears his name and portrait. Tireless
pamphleteer and disputant, he never forgot his countryside upbringing, and
during his *Rural Rides* unforgettably recorded the splendours and miseries of
the land and its exploitation, always eager to hurry on from a stricken hop-
garden which made him angry to something else which might whet his appetite
for further generous rage. He sometimes grew impatient with the slow tenor
of tap-room tittle-tattle; but at other times envied the talkers their warmth
and placidity. In this very region, having misguidedly set out from the Holly
Bush at Headley in driving rain and lost his way, he took a much mellower

view of another inn on which he stumbled at last:

It is odd enough how differently one is affected by the same sight, under different circumstances. At the Holly Bush in Headley there was a room full of fellows in white smock frocks, drinking and smoking and talking, and I, who was then dry and warm, *moralized* within myself on their *folly* in spending their time in such a way. But, when I got down from Hindhead to the public-house at Road-Lane, with my skin soaking and my teeth chattering, I thought just such another group, whom I saw through the window sitting round a good fire with pipes in their mouth, the *wisest assembly* I had ever set my eyes on. A real *Collective Wisdom*. And, I most solemnly declare, that I felt a greater veneration for them than I have ever felt even for the *Privy Council* . . .

In the agricultural collection of the Old Kiln open-air museum three miles or so south of Farnham is a well-planned display of brewing processes, including a hop press.

From Farnham the pilgrim is soon in Guildford, where the Angel retains not merely its religious name but a thirteenth-century cellar with two vaults, one on each side of the street. In spite of theories that these might have been the basements of medieval merchants' houses, it strikes one as being much more probable that they formed part of the Carmelite monastery known to have been here and that the Angel was originally the monastic guest-house.

Another guest-house a few miles further on was the 600-year-old building now trading as the White Horse in Shere. It has cosy ingle-nooks and a remarkable fireplace enclosing a smaller fireplace; but its most interesting features are the beams, which, in spite of the distance from the sea, are unmistakably ships' timbers. The inn literally leans upon them, thrust directly into the ground with no properly supportive foundations. Their likeliest source was the barge traffic which plied between here and the coast when the neighbourhood was given over to the manufacture of gunpowder. In Elizabeth I's time the Evelyn family were charged 'to dig and get' saltpetre for the production of gunpowder, and operated mills between Ewell and Godstone. In 1636, when they had lost the royal favour, other mills were opened at Chilworth and for a time worked as the only authorized gunpowder makers in the land. Even after the end of their monopoly they continued to function until the end of the First World War. Powder was taken to naval bases on the coast by river barges, which loaded old ships' timbers as a return cargo.

Dorking, too, has its White Horse. It started life as the Cross House when the Knights of St John of Jerusalem, granted the site in 1278 by the Knights Templar, built here and displayed their emblem of the Maltese Cross. The old cellars survive, and some of the interior timbering is of a great age; but the frontage was rebuilt in the eighteenth century. Some confusion was been caused by the debates of avid Dickensians: one school identifies this house with the 'Markis of Granby' in *Pickwick Papers*, while another says this was clearly the King's Head, now vanished.

Daniel Defoe refers to the town during his *Tour Through the Whole Island of Great Britain* as Darking, and records goings-on in a secluded cavern on Box Hill which became the haunt of an 'abundance of gentlemen and ladies from Epsome' driving here in their carriages to meet, walk, talk, 'divert, or debauch, or perhaps both'. One local innholder saw the chances of profit from some outside catering:

A vintner who kept the King's-Arms-Inn, at Darking, taking notice of the constant and unusual flux of company thither, took the hint from the prospect of his advantage, which offered, and obtaining leave of Sir Adam Brown, whose manor and land it was, furnished this little cellar or vault with tables, chairs, &c. and with wine and eatables to entertain the ladies and gentlemen on Sunday nights, as above; and this was so agreeable to them that it increased the company exceedingly. In a word, by these means, the concourse of gentry, and in consequence of the country people, became so great, that the place was like a little fair; so that at length the country

1 Stage coach arriving at an inn yard, c. 1820. James Pollard

2 Stage coach travellers at breakfast, c. 1830. James Pollard

3 The Elephant and Castle on the Brighton Road, 1826. James Pollard

began to take notice of it, and it was very offensive, especially to the best governed people; this lasted some years, I think two or three, and though complaint was made of it to Sir Adam Brown, and the neighbouring justices; alleging the revelling and the indecent mirth that was among them, and on the Sabbath Day too, yet it did not obtain a suitable redress. Whereupon a certain set of young men, of the town of Darking, and perhaps prompted by some others, resenting the thing also, made an unwelcome visit to the place once on a Saturday night, just before the usual time of their wicked mirth, and behold when the coaches and ladies, &c. from Epsome appeared the next afternoon, they found the cellar and vault, and all that was in it, blown up with gun-powder; and so secret was it kept, that upon the utmost enquiry it could never be heard, or found out who were the persons that did it.

The 'certain set of young men' may, one suspects, have been not puritans but the hirelings of other local innkeepers who resented one of their number having stolen a profitable march on them.

Below Box Hill, where the Pilgrims' Way crosses the river Mole by way of stepping-stones, stands the Burford Bridge hotel, smart and expensive and much modernized—but very comfortable and welcoming, as I can gladly attest. It was in earlier premises here that Lord Nelson finally parted from his wife in 1800. Another 'final touch': at the George and Dragon in Westerham,

General Wolfe stayed in December 1758 on his last visit to the town of his birth.

Pilgrims spending the night in the church of All Saints at Boughton Lees may well have passed an hour or two in the nearby inn, the Flying Horse, which is thought to be a good four centuries old. There used to be an annual fair on the village green facing it, and its comparatively recent name may have been inspired by the colourful roundabout horses.

The non-flying animal in Chilham is the White Horse, providing a perfect corner-piece for perhaps the most photographed village square in England, with the church in admirable traditional balance. A former vicar of this church once discovered human skeletons in the inn, and now his own ghost is said to be seen at certain times warmly ensconced in the ingle-nook. Down the street is a dazzlingly timbered and plastered house with a bell-cot, called Pilgrims' Cottage. Less immediately appealing from the exterior than the White Horse, even a bit laughable with its flourish of Victorian battlements, but proving delightful inside with dark planking in the bar, a huge old fireplace, and a long dining-room ending in a spacious bay beneath those battlements, is the Woolpack. This was used as an illicit collection point from the fifteenth century onwards when wool was carted in woolpacks (or woolsacks) to the Kent coast and smuggled across the Channel.

The last stage along this route is Chartham, making good use of the river Stour in its long-established paper-making industry. A little way outside the village at Chartham Hatch, the Chapter House or Chapter Arms is a one-time farmhouse standing right upon the Pilgrims' Way. Its original inn sign was Canterbury Priory's coat of arms—azure on a cross argent, the letter IX in pale sable—which was adopted after the Reformation by the Dean and Chapter of the Cathedral. In a beautiful setting, the inn has an always lovely garden and a wonderful view from every window in the place, encompassing a gentle valley, woods, and orchards.

And so we make for the outskirts of the city itself, with the fifteenth-century Bell Harry tower looming ahead.

Canterbury

It would be impossible to trace the existence of each and every one of the pilgrim hostelries which once flourished within the walled city. A few, however, have lived on in history long after their physical transformation or destruction. The whole course of history, in fact, was affected by a meeting in one of the most celebrated, the Fountain, before there were such things as pilgrims to Canterbury. It was here that the four knights who planned to confront Thomas Becket took their final decision, and from here that they set out to murder him. Thereby, however heinous their crime in the eyes of the Church and the appalled public, they brought considerable prosperity to Canterbury itself.

In the thirteenth century a German ambassador lodged in the Fountain while in this country attending Edward I's marriage to his second wife, Margaret of France, and wrote of it:

The inns in England are the best in Europe, those of Canterbury are the best in England, and the Fountain, wherein I am now lodged as handsomely as I were in the King's Palace, the best in Canterbury.

Both charity and commerce expanded rapidly within a very short time of Becket's martyrdom. One of the earliest foundations for providing food and lodging to pilgrims was the Eastbridge Hospital, or Canterbury Pilgrims'

Hospital. Its refectory, chapel and undercroft are still open to the visitor, but the provision of refreshment ceased long ago: the building was neglected after the Reformation, until incorporated with neighbouring almshouses. Other names evoking memories of past hospitality are those of St Thomas's Hospital and the Poor Priests' Hospital.

Right on Watling Street, and within the arena of the largest Roman amphitheatre in Europe outside Rome itself—in which, despite city congestion and planning problems, excavations have been going on for several years recently—is the Queen's Head. In the thirteenth century the land belonged to St Gregory's Priory, and the building may have served as a guest-house before becoming a fully-fledged inn during the fifteenth century. In 1600 it was known as the Three Tuns, changed in 1797 to the Queen's Head. The first queen to be depicted on the sign was Bertha, wife of King Ethelbert of Kent, who converted her husband to Christianity in 597. A priest-hole in the dining-room leads to cellars and a tunnel which is said once to have reached as far as the Cathedral. On the road junction outside once stood the Tierne Cross, where citizens met to air their views. It would be too dangerous a corner today, and even in the late nineteenth century the ground floor on that corner had to be rounded off to ease the entry of traffic into the stableyard.

The sign of the Sun Hotel in Sun Street tends to mislead the visitor, since there is no longer a hotel there. A fine building with two successive steps of oversailing upper storeys, like so many in Canterbury, its importance was once such that the street was named after the inn rather than the other way round. But it did not even begin life here. In the early thirteenth century it was established beside Christchurch gate to cater for servants of the monastery there, and one end of it served as stables to a house belonging to canons of Canterbury. Somewhere in the middle of the seventeenth century the name and the tavern licence were transferred to the building in Sun Street, whose ground floor now offers shop doorways instead of the entrance to a bar parlour.

Although there were plenty of places offering board and lodging within the walls, it soon became clear that premises were needed outside also, for those arriving after curfew. In 1403 such a hostel was built just without the Westgate, and called the White Hart. Later accounts of the churchwardens of Holy Cross refer to more than 20 inns where it was common to hold vestry meetings, one of these being the White Hart. In 1783 it changed its name to the Falstaff, and is so known today. Behind the fine gabled frontage and leaded windows are to be found great beams and heavy fireplaces, and modern carpets into which are woven figures of Henry II, Becket, and other contemporary figures. The wrought-iron sign used to be a 'gallows' sign right across the road, but double-decker buses and large modern lorries necessitated its shortening. During the Second World War a shower of incendiary bombs fell on the Falstaff, but did remarkably little damage: the one which did penetrate the roof could not manage to set those tough old beams ablaze.

On St Stephen's Green, edging out of town, is the Olde Beverlie, a mellow brick building flanked by a row of brick almshouses. It came into being in about 1570 as a house for the parish clerk, who after services at the church of St Stephen was in the habit of offering refreshments to the congregation. In due course the house acquired a licence. It has also acquired the layout of a bat-and-trap game in its nicely sheltered garden, with little alcoves set against the walls, reminiscent of the cubicles of old Vauxhall. It is claimed—whatever Hambledon in Hampshire may counterclaim—that the first true game of cricket as such was played on the green in front of the inn. On a background of four planks, which may once have been the signboard of the inn itself, are painted the 1837 arms of Beverley Cricket Club, recalling an annual festival

which developed into the famous Canterbury Cricket Week. A scene in one corner of the picture shows the entrance to Whitstable railway tunnel, the first railway tunnel in Britain.

30 *Facing* The Falstaff, outside Canterbury's Westgate

Until 1914 the house had a seven-day licence, but when the rector offered the tenancy to his manservant it was on condition that it closed on Sundays. In 1955, when England won the Ashes back from Australia, a submission was made to the authorities that an inn so closely associated with the game should again have the benefit of a seven-day licence; and this was granted.

Before leaving Canterbury it is worth paying a brief visit to the Beaney Institute museum, with its collection of inn tokens. Such exchange pieces were first struck early in the seventeenth century to make up for a shortage of coin of the realm: farthings were in short supply, and to keep their customers happy the innkeepers began to produce their own tokens as small change—which would, naturally, bring the said customers back to redeem these pieces in the form of drink. It had long been law that the use of coins in metal other than silver was illegal, and even farthings in those days were silver; but had a nasty habit of disappearing through holes in pockets or floorboards. When James I decided to legalize the production of copper farthings, he granted the monopoly to Lord Harrington, who so misused the privilege that in 1644 the whole process was suppressed by Parliament. No copper coins at all were minted during the Commonwealth, and traders of all kinds resumed their practice of issuing tokens for exchange only on their own premises.

In 1672 the production of farthings became once more a royal prerogative, and all substitutes were declared illegal. Not much more than a hundred years later, copper coinage was again scarce, and again the shopkeepers and inn-keepers offered their own reliable, redeemable tokens. It was not until 1817 that an Act of Parliament finally prohibited this private enterprise. In our modern world of credit cards and gift vouchers, tokens (plastic rather than copper) are once more on offer as substitutes for our debased currency. Even chains of wine stores issue such vouchers, though one never comes across a pub doing so; and in fact it is illegal for a landlord to allow credit of any kind, which has led to the disappearance of 'the slate' so common in the not too distant past. I have read that a hotel in Lynmouth issued gift tokens for visitors in post-war years, but the disastrous flood of 1952 removed it from the scene.

Dover road and diversions

One of the pleasanter excursions out of Canterbury to the east can encompass Fordwich, Wingham, Sarre, and other Thanet villages of some charm and character. At Fordwich the George and Dragon, noted in our own day as a provider of excellent food and accommodation, stands beside the bridge across what was once the fairly wide throat of an estuary: in Roman times and later, Fordwich was in effect Canterbury's supply port. Women who made too much noise in the bar, or anywhere else, might in olden days have been strapped into the ducking stool whose gantry still protrudes from the old town hall. Another inn associated with legal procedures is the Dog at Wingham, a building which dates mainly from the early thirteenth century and which with its neighbouring houses served until the early sixteenth as an archiepiscopal foundation for a rector and six canons. The local court was held here from the beginning of the eighteenth century to the beginning of our own, and a volume of court proceedings is still kept on the premises.

At Sarre, about halfway across the Isle of Thanet to the coast at Margate, Broadstairs or Ramsgate, is the Halfway House or the Crown—but best known by yet another name, the Cherry Brandy House. This comes from the arrival of a Huguenot refugee who became landlord of the inn and served cherry brandy made to his own special recipe. It became, and remains, a condition of the licence that the recipe shall be handed on to each incoming tenant. About this same period a wrought-iron fireplate displaying the Rose of England and the Royal Crown was set in the fireplace in honour of Charles II. The names of famous visitors are listed on boards across the frontage, including entertainers from Marie Lloyd to Tessie O'Shea.

It is possible to swing back here along another road to Canterbury, and make the return journey via Upstreet and Grove Ferry. In the story of *The Smuggler's Leap* from *The Ingoldsby Legends*, R. H. Barham tells of a wild pursuit by Revenue officers across the Thanet levels from the coast:

> *Sauve qui peut!* That lawless crew,
> Away, and away, and away they flew!
> Some seek Whitstable—some Grove Ferry,
> Spurring and whipping like madmen—very—
> For the life! for the life! they ride! they ride!
> And the Custom-house officers all divide . . .

Those heading for Grove Ferry might have stood the best chance of getting away. In those days, when the inn was known as the Ferry House, the ferryman over the Stour was in league with the smuggling fraternity and, having helped them, would hasten to moor his boat, lock the boat-house door and go to bed, pretending not to hear the hailing of pursuers wishing to cross.

From Canterbury the main road, the A2, offers few pleasures on its last stretch to Dover. This is not to speak ill of Bridge and Barham, or the orchards, woods and parkland often so close to the road; but it is difficult to contemplate the scenery when great thundering convoys of oversized lorries come grinding up from the docks at Dover or overtake one in a miasma of evil-smelling exhaust fumes.

The White Horse at Bridge was a coaching inn and looks it, with its Regency facade, but was never a main stage. Situated where it was, it served as a resting-place between stages—perhaps like the tea and beer and urinal stops of long-distance coaches nowadays. Horses could once be shod at the forge next door; and presumably it would not now be too difficult to replace a burst tyre in the vicinity.

At River is the humbler but appealingly sturdy Royal Oak, built of Downland flint and chalk, which served for 300 years as village school before being converted to a tavern around 1860.

In River we are virtually in a suburb of Dover, with its hotels and pubs of all grades and sizes catering for cross-Channel travellers delayed by gales or strikes, and for those arriving exhausted after a stormy crossing. But the ports and anchorages of the English coast deserve, I think, a later chapter all to themselves.

5

Into East Anglia

We conquered the pangs of hunger,
With Smelts and Duck and Wine,
And vow'd once more, as we'd done before,
To come another time.

*Visitors' book in the Crown and Castle
at Orford, 1887*

One Easter Sunday my wife and I were sitting just after opening time in a pleasant pub in the fascinating, haunted village square of Castle Acre in Norfolk, once the walled bailey of the castle and still overlooked by its ancient bailey gate. The landlady, chatting to one of her regulars, suddenly said cheerfully: 'It's lucky I had 50 eggs and all that bacon.' Many such a remark in a public bar has aroused my curiosity without satisfying it. This time, fortunately, an explanation was forthcoming. In mid-morning some 50 young pilgrims spending their weekend walking from Bury St Edmunds to Walsingham had broken their journey in the hope of being fed—and had been provided with a breakfast better than they could possibly have hoped.

Although East Kent offered the most prestigious shrine in the land, it was by no means the only or indeed the earliest centre of pilgrimage. St Cuthbert had long been drawing the devout to Northumbria, and other trips recommended to pietists were those to St Albans, Glastonbury, and the body of St Richard of Chichester.

In East Anglia two towns vied with Canterbury. St Edmund, martyred young by the Danes in A.D. 870, lay in St Edmundsbury. A wooden statue of the Virgin Mary brought pilgrims and prosperity to Walsingham. Perhaps some foreign visitors tried during their stay to take in all the more highly esteemed shrines in a sort of round tour. Others probably offered devotion to one chosen patron. If they did travel from Canterbury to Suffolk and Norfolk, there would then have been no Dartford tunnel to offer a short cut under the Thames.

The Angel in Bury St Edmunds, just across the road from the ruins of the once mighty abbey, dates in its present form from 1779 but is known to have been operating as one of a trio of inns side by side in the fifteenth century, the others being the Castle and the White Bear. In 1557 its owner presented its rents to the town for the maintenance of two churches and payment of the curates' stipends. This carried on a long tradition of service to the Church. The massive vaults beneath, now serving as a grill-room, indicate that the Angel was probably linked to the abbey as a guest-house. Such a link is also suggested in tales of a bricked-up doorway at the hotel end of a passage once leading to other vaults under the abbey itself. Another guest-house which became an inn under abbey jurisdiction was rebuilt in the eighteenth century and, later, further modernized as the Suffolk Hotel.

At Little Walsingham in Norfolk, the lady of the manor a few years before the Norman Conquest claimed that she had seen a vision of the Santa Casa, the

Holy House of Nazareth in which the Archangel had appeared to the Virgin Mary. A wooden statue of Mary and the infant Jesus was set in a replica of this house, and soon became an object of great veneration. In the following century an Augustine priory was established around the shrine, to be followed by a Franciscan friary close at hand. Pilgrims increased in numbers, usually arriving barefoot after leaving their shoes at slipper chapels a mile or so out of the village.

One of the hostels used by these visitors survives in the black-and-white form of the Oxford Stores, close to the main gate of the abbey ruins. Another, the Black Lion, recalls the arrival on several occasions of Edward III and his queen, Philippa of Hainault. The heraldic emblem of this powerful lady, who led an English army against the Scots in 1347 and defeated them while her husband and son, the Black Prince, were in France, was a Black Lion.

Henry VIII's emissaries destroyed the shrine and monastic buildings, and publicly burnt the wooden statue. But in 1922 the Anglo-Catholic vicar of Walsingham had a replica of the statue made from its portrayal on the priory seal. The cult of Our Lady of Walsingham had in fact been revived by Roman Catholics at Kings Lynn in 1897, but it was not until the 1930s that two factions began to revitalize the original site. A new Anglo-Catholic church and shrine were started in 1931 and completed in 1938; while, perhaps spurred on by these developments, the Roman Catholics restored the old slipper chapel at Houghton St Giles, proclaimed it a shrine, and reopened it in 1934.

So modern pilgrims tread the road to Walsingham again, while Bury—from where St Edmund's remains disappeared long ago—concentrates on more mundane things. And really, the greater number of twentieth-century travellers into East Anglia are those in search of the fleshier seaside pleasures of

Great Yarmouth and Cromer, the annual Aldeburgh music festival, or the gentle charms of the Stour valley and the cosily huddled wool towns.

Three main routes out of London feed these eastern counties, take in the Fens, and are themselves fed by any number of large and small tributaries. The A10 heads for Cambridge; the A11 strikes through Epping Forest towards Newmarket and Norwich; and the A12 describes a long arc through Colchester and up into Suffolk until it is running close to the coast between Lowestoft and Yarmouth. There is also, now, the M11 offering a speedy alternative to both the A10 and A11 for travellers to Cambridge or Newmarket. But beside the motorway there are no picturesque villages, no welcoming local inns: all of these belong to older roads and by-ways.

32 The Angel at Bury St Edmunds, Suffolk, seen from within the abbey gateway

Essex to Suffolk

Even without the motorways, one wonders how a hotel or inn fares when an
historic main road is diverted to ease traffic congestion. Inhabitants of villages
pounded by long and wide lorries or by streams of tourist traffic put in more
and more anguished pleas for a by-pass; and then, when the by-pass has been
built, find that their streets are admirably quiet, just as some of them had
hoped. But what of the others—the shopkeepers and innkeepers who find that
reducing noise and traffic by three-quarters has also reduced their passing
trade by three-quarters?

When I first ventured into Suffolk, only a couple of decades ago, what was
known as the Yarmouth road or the London road, depending on the direction
of one's journey, still wound through some tortuous villages and towns and
past some noble coaching inns. Today the A12 has ironed out most of the bends,
skirted the villages and abandoned the inns, and offers almost unbroken dual
carriageway as far as Ipswich. Even a town the size of Colchester has been
nudged to one side; but, being busy in itself, can fortunately still provide
custom for its great old Red Lion inn, from which in the eighteenth century a
'stage cart' plied to the Bell in Leadenhall Street, London, while a smarter
vehicle for first-class passengers used the Green Dragon in Whitechapel as its
metropolitan terminus.

There must have been a goodly number of Roman taverns in Camulodunum
before Boudicca set fire to the place and slaughtered its defenders, and

doubtless they were among the first essential rebuildings once a new garrison had been installed after the rebellion's failure. Roman relics show up in various parts of the town, and one section of mosaic pavement was found under the Red Lion itself, where it is now displayed. Another of the inn's relics is a trade token issued in 1668 by the then landlord.

The first traceable building, with vaulted cellars and a stone arch, must have been a monastic foundation of some kind. In the fifteenth century a half-timbered hall of the kind favoured by well-to-do merchants was set above it. Extensions in succeeding years gave it a more impressive frontage on to the street, and made it readily convertible into an inn around the year 1500. The wording of its licence in 1604 already refers to it as an 'Auncyent Inn'. The timbers of its now roofed-in courtyard, and those in the grill-room and upper lounge, are superb. One notes that in spite of its being named the Red Lion, the carvings over the yard entrance are of George and the Dragon.

The road once crossed the Suffolk border at the foot of Dedham Gun Hill, but has now carved a new route for itself. You have to turn off on to the old road to find Dedham Gun—and then to find that it is no longer an inn, though its outlines still betray its old, happier function. It is worth commenting here on a regional usage which might baffle the newcomer. Town and village names always preface the name of the inn or pub: thus, Dedham Gun and not the Gun, Dedham; Metfield Duke and not the Duke William, Metfield; and Middleton Bell, not the Bell at Middleton.

Dedham village itself, on the Essex side of the road, has mercifully been able to support two thriving establishments in its elegant main street. There is the Marlborough Head, mentioned earlier in this book, and the Sun, an early sixteenth-century building with an entrance for coaches into a still spacious yard. I remember with nostalgic appreciation one or two admirable meals I have had in its nicely proportioned, unfussy dining-room.

Come to think of it, I have also enjoyed good food only a mile away on the Suffolk side of the border. A few years after the A12 had by-passed the winding street village of Stratford St Mary, and well-nigh severed it from its church, I asked the then landlord of the Swan if he had been seriously affected by the loss of custom. The number of large inns along that one stretch of road shows what an important thoroughfare it used to be. But he said that, so far as he was concerned, things had worked out quite the other way. By maintaining a high standard of food and service, and letting people know about this, he had attracted a whole new clientele. I fancy that as well as his regulars he must have profited also from those who, like myself, find when driving from London to the Suffolk coast that Stratford St Mary is just about right for a halfway stop.

In the great coaching days along the Yarmouth road, the Swan had stabling for 200 horses. It was a regular stopping-place for farmers driving their flocks of geese and turkeys from Norfolk to the London markets, and Defoe estimated that up to 300 droves could be expected to pass this way in a season. John Constable knew this corner well. More than once he painted a view of the vale from the top of Dedham Gun Hill, and one of his greatest works is a picture of the Stratford St Mary watermill. It was by the Swan that the eighteen-year-old aspiring artist waited for the coach which would take him to London with an early collection of sketches, which in that year of 1795 aroused no interest whatsoever.

At the end of that colourful street, one road dips under the A12 embankment towards Dedham, while another rises sharply to rejoin the A12 and so resume the journey towards Ipswich. I confess that I am tempted at this juncture to swerve off the main road on to one for Hadleigh, whose long, long street offers such a wealth of richly ornamented inns—some garnished with the Suffolk speciality of pargeting, or patterned plaster relief—that it would be invidious to praise one above its fellows. From here one can choose between roads leading on into the clothiers' halls of the Lavenham district and one veering back towards Ipswich.

We have established' what Charles Dickens thought of the Great White Horse in Ipswich, but even dedicated Dickensians must grant that their idol cannot have been always right. In a town whose hostelries and restaurants I find uniformly drab and depressing, I think the Great White Horse has a lot to offer, especially since recent renovation has brightened its fading features without destroying the period character of those features. It was, after all, the first inn known to exist in Ipswich, and one course of oaken wall in the present lounge is probably a survivor of the 1518 house of the same name. The startlingly generous dimensions of the lounge, more like a Palm Court or lofty ballroom, are due to its having once been the stableyard, entered through a gateway now replaced by the main door. Long before Dickens vented his resentment upon it, it had been graced with the presence of George II, breaking a journey between Lowestoft and London, and Lord Nelson, who spent a night here in 1800. Louis XVIII, insecure king of France after Napoleon's first banishment and then again after his second, was once feasted here during his protracted exile in England. Norman Scarfe, Suffolk historian, suggests that Ipswich's old name of Gipeswic may conceivably have inspired, consciously or not, Dickens's choice of the name Pickwick.

On its north-easterly progress the A12 soon by-passes another town through which the main road meandered so few years ago, until it was decided to save Woodbridge's collection of timbered and plastered homes and inns from being reduced to dust. The Crown, on the narrow crossroads above the Deben estuary, is a friendly coaching inn whose windows once rattled from the passage of more massive coaches and trucks. There is a nice gathering of hostelries around the tilted rectangle of Market Hill, on which Edward Fitzgerald lodged above the gunsmith's, and put up his visiting friend Tennyson in the Bull, another coaching inn across the way. The 500-year-old King's Head, with its impressive oversailing upper storey, preserves carved heads credited with being those of the original innkeeper and his family.

The next stop of any consequence must be at Wickham Market, whose White Hart has been an inn since the fifteenth century, made more impressive by an eighteenth-century frontage added during coaching days. I recollect staying there a couple of nights, some years ago, being well wined and dined and provided with a most comfortable bedroom, but getting little sleep. This was because the narrow alley above which my room was situated acted as a wind tunnel for passing lorries until the small hours of the morning and once again round about dawn, each of them creating an abrupt explosion followed by an apologetic sigh. I mention this only because I can vouch for its having ceased to be such a problem, the village having in its turn been by-passed comparatively recently. An account has been kept of a sporting landlord who in 1810 was bold enough to wager 100 guineas on his ability to drive a coach and four to Norwich and back within five hours. The square facing the hotel was crowded on the great day with staff, sportsmen from all over the region, and the visiting worthies with whom Mr Keepence had made his bet. Although the most economical route must have been a tough 80 miles or so, the landlord got back with a quarter of an hour to spare.

New road junctions north of the village offer a choice of destinations: eastwards to the coast, on to Saxmundham and Lowestoft, or westwards into the Suffolk farmlands. Since I have it in mind to visit the coastal inns later, I think this is a good place to turn off and explore this world of cornfields,

exposed villages, moated farmhouses and very local 'locals'.

We have seen that the Crown in Framlingham owes its existence to a shrewd supporter of Bloody Mary. It owes its Railway Inn, previously a chapel, to the coming of a line which has since been closed; and the low-slung Castle is, not surprisingly, near the entrance to Framlingham castle, which has stood the test of many years and seems secure for many more.

It is impossible to list here the number of small inns in the villages of the region, and impossible to recommend this route or that one. Down a lane wide enough for only one vehicle at a time will be found an unexpectedly thriving pub. Others survive only in Spartan style, with no trimmings, no sign of recent repainting . . . but full of character and characters. Many are tied houses under the aegis of Adnams' brewery in Southwold and so, whatever their other minor failings, offer unspoilt, real, living beer. These are interspersed with Tolly Cobbold houses, also with strong local connections, though a few years ago the brewery was taken over by the Ellerman shipping company. Within a radius of ten miles from Framlingham can be found a galaxy of small treasures —at Swefling, Peasenhall, Huntingfield, Badingham with its White Horse complete with bowling green and garden; Dennington with its Queen's Head so close to the church and with attic rafters so ecclesiastical in style that it may once have been a part of the church buildings.

Dennington boasts another pub, but so far out of the village that only the postal address really embraces the two. This, the Dennington Bell, was so isolated that in recent years its trade—almost exclusively from local farm workers—shrank, and the building itself deteriorated. When the ageing tenants retired, the brewery decided that major repairs could never be met from takings, so sold off the property with permission for change of use as a private dwelling. A businessman setting up a factory on the far side of the A12 felt this would suit him admirably, as he and his family were fond of animals and needed a fair amount of stabling and land for their horses, dogs, and four cats. His wife, at first horrified by the state of the structure, set to with a will and, anxious for an occupation while he was away at business, decided to retain the licence and reopen the pub. Smartened up—but not spoilt—it is now a bright and sociable place: a free house with a variety of drinks and a variety of customers. There is no direction in which it can develop, nothing too grandiose it can hope to attain; but at the time of writing it's a fine place for a drink, a snack, a gossip, and an insight into the ways of the wide, often bleak, farming country hereabouts.

Another inn discarded in this decade by the parent brewers—or, rather, the inheriting brewers—is the unique King's Head at Laxfield, known locally as 'the Low House' because of its situation at the bottom of a steep, twisting hill below the church. A good 600 years old, the premises once served Laxfield as a market room for the sale of local corn and produce. Beer was brewed in the kitchen at the back and carried through to the front room as required. This custom continued when the place became an inn, and to this day it presents the most authentic possible picture of the traditional basic ale-house. There is still no bar counter: beer is still drawn from casks in the back room, and the mugs or glasses brought into the parlour. Successive generations of the same family held the licence for almost a century. When the last tenants grew too old to carry on any longer, one of the local draymen tried to calculate how many thousands of miles the wife of the house must have walked between those two rooms—and, though an energetic type himself, went pale at the thought. Again there seemed a threat of the loss of a pub and its replacement by a private dwelling. Fortunately a most enlightened local worthy bought the premises, retained the licence, and put a younger couple in to run it economically and without frills, just as it had always been run, for the benefit of the villagers and surrounding farms.

A few miles further on is the celebrated Fox and Goose at Fressingfield, another establishment clinging close to the churchyard. It was in fact once a guildhall, and bears a curious device on one of its corner-posts: a female saint stamping on a dragon. In its modern guise it has built up, under successive managements, an enviable reputation for its cuisine.

Turning away towards the west we come to Eye, with fragments of a once important castle. It is a quiet, almost melancholy little market town which long ago lost its market to Diss, and knew only brief prosperity from its lace-making trade. But it flourished just long enough to acquire a remarkably spacious coaching inn assembled, it appears, from a jumble of largely Tudor buildings given coherence only at the front by an added black and white façade. Above the archway into the yard, relief lettering proclaims that here is a Posting Establishment. One side of the yard itself offers quite a surprise: what might seem a barn or large outhouse proves to be a ballroom in Georgian style with an Adam fireplace and a musicians' gallery. The ceiling was once supplied with ornamental vents which could be opened or closed by long poles, but these have since been misguidedly painted over. A newspaper account of celebrations after a County Yeomanry review and demonstration in the last century speaks of the White Lion providing dinner 'at 2s 6d a head, including as much wine and punch as each man could swallow'.

Wool and wassail

In the cellars of Lavenham Guildhall, which once housed the wine butts of the clothiers' guild of Corpus Christi, there is now a permanent exhibition of the tools and techniques of the cooper's craft. Nearly everything else in the neighbourhood speaks of wool, and of those great days when a clothier could grow rich enough to meet most of the cost of building Lavenham's huge church.

As well as this guildhall there was in the fifteenth century a wool hall built for another guild, that of Our Lady. In 1911 it was completely dismantled, its timbers numbered, and plans made for its re-erection as an addition to a cottage owned by Princess Louise near Ascot. Strong protests resulted in the return of the timbers to Lavenham and the restoration of the building. In 1962 the hall was most agreeably incorporated in the Swan hotel, still showing some of the numbers on its beams.

The Swan, with its profusion of inner and outer timbers, oak beams and studs, jettied gables and glowing red-tiled roofs, is inarguably the most sumptuous inn which the region has to offer. From originally constricted premises on the corner of Water Street it grew apace in coaching days, not just as a fare stage but as a main station in its own right:

LAVENHAM MACHINE
in one day, SETS out June the 4th 1764
from the Swan at Lavenham

every MONDAY, WEDNESDAY and FRIDAY, to the Spread Eagle in Gracechurch Street, London; and returns for Lavenham every TUESDAY, THURSDAY and SATURDAY, at Eleven Shillings a Passenger; to be allowed 20 Pounds Weight, and all above to pay One Shilling per Score. Outsides and Children in Lap, Half-price—The Coach sets out from Lavenham at Five o'clock in the Morning, and from London at Six o'clock. *Wm.Holmsted Performed(if God permit) by Wm.Wood, and Co.*

With the ascendancy of the railways, the inn's patrons shrank in number, and a dismal Victorian frontage was added to camouflage the unfashionable timber and plaster. New fashions decreed their reappearance in the 1930s.

Came the 1940s . . . and the Second World War. Names of many American airmen who flew from East Anglian airfields—some never to return—were scratched into the bar counter, the most graphic section of which has now been removed and preserved behind glass on the wall.

The provenance of the inn's name and sign is in no doubt. The white swan was the emblem of the de Vere earls of Oxford, one of whom collaborated with Thomas Spring the clothier on the building of the church tower, and who owned the house adjacent to the Swan.

One should be chary, however, of devoting so much attention to a deservedly lauded inn that other lesser but equally interesting premises are neglected. For instance, what of the Angel in Lavenham? A fifteenth-century foundation, it was of some substance long before the Swan really spread its wings. At some stage it must have been joined to the house next door, as there are arched door-ways leading from one to the other. Its attractive Georgian plaster conceals much older features, and one of its moulded ceilings upstairs is a gem of its kind.

Tucked away in dells and crannies about Lavenham are other contributors to the history of the woollen industry—some, like Kersey and Lindsey, having given their name to specific cloths—and each has its own richly redolent inn. That near the watersplash in Kersey sported for many years a mynah bird which never ceased to imitate the squeak of the bar door, the whistles and mutterings of the regulars, and the excruciatingly phlegmy cough of one old man whom I never met but can still visualize to this day.

Bildeston has its Crown, behind a railed hummock of pavement, seemingly in perpetual danger of cracking and sliding to either side—or even, at a pinch, outwards. Here the contracts of Michaelmas Hiring were once agreed between farmer and labourer over a coin and a drink in the bar. Here, too, is a long tradition of repeated hammering noises within the building and of customers being mysteriously, fleetingly touched—experienced once by a local policeman whose immediate investigations tracked down nothing and nobody. Boxford has its White Hart, where just after the Second World War a motor-cycle 'wall of death' rider used to exercise the lion which shared his exploits in a side-car and, having died, was buried below a mound in front of the inn. And eerie, prehistoric Polstead, with its Roman remains and echoes of the murder of Maria Marten in the Red Barn, has the Cock on the hilltop village green, next to the Cock farmhouse which a hundred years ago was itself the inn.

Sudbury, which is perversely proud of having been traduced by Dickens as 'Eatanswill', has a rewarding collection of typical market-town pubs around its market-place and down neighbouring side streets. A more unusual venture is the Mill Hotel in Walnut Tree Lane, a converted water-mill on the Stour meadows, with one bar in which the recently repaired waterwheel still turns. The view from its bar, restaurant and bedroom windows towards the river is truly romantic, especially when the Stour floods and the meadows become a lake lapping the foundations of the hotel. The ghost of Gainsborough might possibly object, though, that in his own town this hotel should advertise itself as being 'close to Constable Country'. A stroll round the town should take in the sixteenth-century Ship and Star, and a glance at a fine timbered building on the corner of Stour Street, now known as the Chantry but once what must have been a splendid inn known first as the Plough and then as the Castle.

The outer northern fringe of Sudbury runs on with only a slight break into Long Melford, whose long, wide street leads to an impressively large, sloping village green, with a cluster of inns where roads diverge. The Bull began life as a clothier's home and workshop, with looms at the back of the house and then later along a side of the courtyard. This yard acquired open galleries when the premises became an inn, the proportions of which can still be easily traced. The timbered frontage was obscured in the last century and well on into this one by a brick wall, but the original black and white pattern has now been restored—together, it has to be admitted, with some modern 'Trust House Tudor', as Norman Scarfe so nicely puts it.

On the other side of the main street is the Crown, less imposing from outside but a place of great interest within. It has some unusual panels of stained glass, and a framed account of local goings-on which led to one of the last known public readings of the Riot Act from the premises. Many a landlord has, on boisterous Saturday nights, threatened to 'read the Riot Act', but few understand its full meaning. Perhaps we should be surprised that it was not more frequently read on licensed premises, which often threatened to become centres of dissent and rebellion. Local folk have traditionally assembled to air their grievances in public bars, and even without visiting radicals to stir them up have been able to voice plenty of threats. In 1853 Palmerston complained to Gladstone that such establishments demoralized the lower classes:

The words 'licensed to be drunk on the Premises' are by the Common People interpreted as applicable to the Customers as well as to the Liquor.

But Long Melford today is a peaceable place, as are its delectable neighbours with their unpretentious pubs, Cavendish and Clare—the latter with a unique, long, intricately carved sign of a preening Swan with a coronet about its neck.

Essex to Norfolk

Beside the river Lea near Tottenham Hale is the Ferry Boat, a haunt of fishermen who once sought their prey in the river itself but are now more often to be found fishing in the vast neighbouring reservoirs. In the lounge an old painting shows what the inn looked like in the time of George IV, and there are glass cases of stuffed fish. Or so I am told. And my daughter tells me it's a great, lively place to be on Friday and Saturday evenings.

I say 'so I am told' because fate has been unkind to me with regard to the Ferry Boat. In a somewhat unprepossessing outpost of London, it has a bright charm which has often tempted me off that dreary road: but what's the use of being tempted when circumstances have ordained that I shall so often pass it in the morning before opening time, or drive past in the opposite direction before opening time in the evening? How many doubtless fine inns one must have missed that way! The exteriors are so inviting, the setting so pleasant: but one is in a hurry, or it's the wrong time of day . . . and in any case, drinking and driving don't go together, and there is no pleasure to be gained from sipping a quick drink in one establishment and then dashing on feverishly to the next. Inns and pubs, like their product, need to be savoured. Still there are some places—and the Ferry Boat is one of them—which I keep assuring myself I will visit someday, somehow.

The A11 suffers nowadays from a split personality, the authorities having sadistically renumbered stretches of it in an endeavour to bewilder the traveller and force him on to the M11, which they consider is not being sufficiently used. Nevertheless those who know the route by heart rather than by numbers persist in following it; and beyond Epping are any number of pleasant roadside taverns, on the old A11 itself or on branch roads to Chelmsford and the east. Those who choose to break off at Bishop's Stortford towards Great Dunmow will find an attractive main street of fine frontages and fine pubs, though the actual street is invariably jammed by slow-moving and often stationary traffic. The Saracen's Head especially repays a halt.

Its Georgian frontage and other Georgian additions to the interior cannot conceal Tudor timbers and an original Tudor framework. The yard still has its old stables, and a mounting block. In the early seventeenth century one landlord was the father of Sir Richard Deane, a Lord Mayor of London. The whole family were supporters of the Parliamentary cause during the Civil War, and Oliver Cromwell stayed several times in the Saracen's Head.

But rather than weave a complicated route which will take us back through Long Melford, let's follow the A11 as it curves away from Cambridge and across the extreme north-western tip of Suffolk on into Norfolk. At Barton Mills there is another temptation to stray. Where the road forks near the noble old building of the Bull in its slight hollow, a sign leads one to Brandon, near the neolithic flint mines of Grime's Graves. From these mines came the flints which established the bleak Breckland region's earliest industry. A later quarry took over the supply, and for centuries flints were knapped—that is, cut and trimmed—into house and church building stone, and as flints for firearms. There is still a small but steady overseas trade, mainly with gun collectors, and the most conspicuous inn is the Flintknappers' Arms, though no longer do a couple of these craftsmen work as they used to in the inn yard itself.

At Thetford is the Bell, parts of which date from 1493. The bulk of the building is Elizabethan, and retains its long, oversailing timbered frontage along King Street. Within, what was once an open gallery over a courtyard has become an enclosed corridor but, like the other modern alterations and extensions, without in any way spoiling the historic atmosphere. The restaurant and bedroom windows in the modern wing offer a very agreeable outlook upon well-designed walkways beside the river. If you care to look out from the older side, you can smile respectfully or glare in denunciation, according to your predilections, on the gilded statue of Thomas Paine, who is also commemorated in a modern pub named after him on the industrial estate outside the town.

From Thetford runs a road which one feels ought to lead to Hastings—the A1066—but which in fact skirts Diss and, collecting a number of tributaries along its way, arrives eventually in Great Yarmouth. Just beyond Diss is the White Hart, which for a while traded as the Scole Inn but has recently incorporated both insignia. A Norwich merchant hoping for quick profits built it in 1655, when neither the village nor the passing traffic offered enough patronage to sustain it. At one time it boasted a huge round bed into which 30 or 40 people could be packed with their feet at the middle, heads to the outside. Later this was relegated to one of the outbuildings, where tramps and pedlars were generously allowed to use it. Just when the inn was at its lowest ebb there came the boom in coach traffic, and it was resuscitated by the London to Norwich services. On some days there might be as many as 40 fully laden vehicles drawing in for the refreshment of their passengers. The familiar modern sign, 'No Coaches', was unknown.

The White Hart's most famous feature, mentioned in Chapter 2, was its mighty triumphal arch of a sign. Around the figure of the hart were 25 life-sized figures acting out the legend of the huntress Diana and Actaeon, all surmounted by a weather vane in the likeness of an astronomer. The coats of arms of distinguished local families were also fitted into the design. This arch must have presented quite a hazard to vehicles and their drivers, and by 1795 maintenance had been so neglected that the whole thing had to be taken down. Nothing is known of the fate of the fragments—or the fate of the great circular bed.

Returning to the A11 we come upon Wymondham, which has a pleasant modern hotel facing the remarkable two-towered abbey church, and the much

36 The modern sign of the Scole Inn, Norfolk, incorporates its original emblem of the White Hart

older Green Dragon near the Benedictine monastery remains. A bad fire in 1615 which led to the town's rebuilding in its present mixture of seventeenth- and eighteenth-century styles fortunately spared the inn. It began life as a late fourteenth-century hostel for the monastery, to which it was still connected by an underground passage until the beginning of this century. One wall is of tough local flint; the rest is a rich blend of fine timber, darkly gleaming panels, little doors and uneven windows, with carved heads to support the oversailing.

A few miles north of Wymondham, Honingham has a pub some 400 years old. Originally called the Bell, it numbered among its landlords one John Buck, who was both village blacksmith and, according to Parson Woodforde's diary, a notorious smuggler. After the issue of its 1789 ale-house licence, the name was changed in affectionate memory to the Buck.

And so into Norwich, with its town sign proclaiming it 'a fine city'. So it is; but for such a fine city, and a cathedral city at that, built around two ancient market-places, it is surprisingly deficient in really evocative, traditional taverns. Several are pleasant enough; none is outstanding.

But at least we have the Maid's Head, the oldest inn in East Anglia, and one of the half-dozen oldest in the country. Built on the site of what had been a

LUNCHEON from 12·30 p.m. – 2·50 p.m.
DINNER .... from 7·00 p.m. – 10·00 p.m.
LAST ORDERS 15 MINUTES BEFORE CLOSING.

bishop's palace in the times of William Rufus, it became in due course a monastic hospice, and is referred to as early as 1287 as an inn. The Black Prince stayed here when visiting Norwich for a tournament, and during ensuing centuries it was a focus for the city's main entertainments and political gatherings. What was once the busy coaching yard, behind large old wooden entrance doors, is today roofed in with glass to make a pleasant, paved adjunct to the 'back bar', quite apart from the rest of the hotel, where snacks are also served in what gives the impression of being an open air setting, but without the perils of changeable weather.

The name is a constant source of argument. In view of the Black Prince's popularity during his stay, one might too glibly speculate that the Maid's Head was that of his wife, the Fair Maid of Kent. But then there is the 'demi-virgin' in the arms of the Mercers Company, engraved on brasses in the nearby church of St John Maddermarket. Other theorists point to the inn's earliest name of the Murtle Fish and suggest that this creature may have been something like a skate, for which Norfolk fishermen's colloquialism has long been a 'Maid's Head'.

Some way across the city, below the castle keep, is the Bell, once the Blue Bell. It is a building of uneven proportions and irregular frontages, its different levels and half levels adjusting to the ragged contours of abrupt slopes behind it and on two sides. Known to have been trading before the Restoration, it was for long the favourite haunt of farmers coming in to market, and of Norwich tradesmen. At the height of the cock-fighting craze it brought in even more custom. It has been a meeting-place for many clubs and groups, mostly with different persuasions from those more august types who used the Maid's Head. In the eighteenth century a number of 'Gentlemen of Principle' had regular assemblies here, but their principles were decidedly anti-social ones, dedicated mainly to disrupting Wesleyan meetings in the neighbourhood. An 'Original Club' was formed to laud the French Revolution and prepare for a similar outbreak in this country; but by the time Napoleon had risen and then fallen, views had changed, and in 1831 the Loyal and Constitutional Club had its inaugural meeting on the premises, one of its founding members being the Duke of Wellington. In recent years there was a danger of the Bell being demolished after a long closure. It was saved in time, and gradually its spacious but low-ceilinged bars and flagged passages have been reopened. One can only hope that eventually the Georgian staircase will once more be in use by guests proceeding to their bedrooms, and that the dust and cracks of neglect will be swept away or plastered over. Certainly it has already become, once again, a favourite meeting-place for Norwich folk—local businessmen in one bar, crowds of young people in the others.

The market which once spread away below the windows of the Bell is now just a vast car park. Movement of that cattle market to a more accessible site on the edge of the city was a major reason for the Bell's decline, and that of several other taverns around its perimeter. A pub called the Plough was at one stage closed down, but then given a face-lift and reopened. By this time Norwich had twinned with the city of Rouen in France, so the pub was renamed La Rouen, and the road cutting past it became Rouen Road.

From Norwich I had not intended to go straight to the coast, but a recent judicial decision in King's Lynn tempts me to suggest an afternoon excursion there. The town has plenty of pubs near its docks and the old merchant streets, and even more imposing inns around the market-place. The Globe has a painted sculpture facing out from one corner, with Atlas poising the world above his head as if to nod it down on to the market stalls below. Now a Berni Inn, it makes a commendable effort to preserve memories of Lynn's old riverside and wharves with large murals derived from blown-up photographs of cargo and fishing vessels under sail.

Dominating the square, however, is the Duke's Head. This was built in the last year of Charles II's reign and probably named in honour of the Duke of York who was to succeed Charles as James II. Sir John Turner, a vintner of the town, conceived it as a place of refreshment and accommodation for fellow merchants using the Custom House on the quay, and its front part was in fact designed by the same architect as the Custom House. Coach parties were at first discouraged: to be worthy of the Duke's Head, a gentleman was expected to roll up in his own carriage. Only later did the management succumb to the chance of profiting from the increasingly busy coaching trade.

The establishment commanding our special attention here and now is the Lattice House, a fifteenth-century establishment which was in danger of demolition until in early 1980 CAMRA, the Campaign for Real Ale organization, tried to buy the leasehold and to obtain a licence which would enable them, in the words of Judge David Moylan, to 'fulfil an unsatisfied demand for a traditional old-fashioned English pub in the town'. The local Licensed Victuallers' Association vociferously opposed this intrusion. The local licensing committee turned down the application. But CAMRA pursued the matter, and Judge Moylan, sitting with four magistrates, decided that a provisional licence should be granted. He had a few sharp things to say about local inns, their history and character, and his summing-up was followed by an even more forthright one in an *Eastern Daily Press* editorial of 1 April 1980:

Over the past fifteen years the pub scene has deteriorated. Many fine old public-houses, if not entirely torn down, have had their interiors ravaged and 'tarted up' with little care for the tastes and wishes of their customers. In the process the public has been betrayed, and one of the fundamentals of pub life, the existence of a convivial bridge between age, attitudes and income, has been uprooted and replaced by an image and an ethos more appropriate to Las Vegas. The English pub, that is to say a public-house that sells traditional English beer in an atmosphere conditioned by the English character rather than imposed upon it, is an endangered species.

It is appropriate that we should be jolted to a stop like this in Norfolk, a county almost wholly in the grip of one large brewing concern; and that, so halted, before travelling anywhere else we should consider the whole question of the ownership and exploitation of our supposedly unique inheritance—the English inn.

6
Owner, Tenant, or Manager

Here lies the landlord of the Lion,
His soul is on the way to Zion;
His widow carries on the business still
Resigned unto the Master's will.

Reputed but untraceable epitaph in
Upton-on-Severn churchyard

Most Englishmen have at some stage of their career wistfully fancied the notion of 'taking a pub'. If their wives are keen on cooking and take genuine pleasure in provoking sighs of admiration from the gourmet or the greedy, they too may conjure up a vision of a sociable, rewarding future. An inn provides a roof over one's head, jovial company, a fair number of perks and, if you work hard, a reasonable profit to put away against the day of retirement.

Or it did, once upon a time. Savage increases in rents and the innumerable petty restrictions laid by breweries upon their tied houses, whether tenanted or managed, make it almost impossible nowadays to save for that little retirement home. All you can bank on is seven days' hard labour a week, 52 weeks a year, with no security and no pot of gold at the end. Yet there are still, on average, 50 applicants for every inn which comes on the market. What leads men still to queue up for one of the most arduous and financially least promising jobs in the country?

Takeovers

Until the middle of the eighteenth century there was a great variety of owners, landlords, and suppliers. A man might run an ale-house in his own home provided he observed some simple regulations and paid a small duty. From the early part of that century until the early nineteenth, in fact, this was actively encouraged by the authorities to turn people away from the evils of cheap gin, which at one stage threatened to become the national beverage, with results hideously portrayed by Hogarth. A blacksmith might make a few extra pence by having his wife supply beer while he was attending to a customer's horse. Local innkeepers did their own brewing at the back of their premises. Breweries as separate, full-time businesses were not numerous and at first of no great size. Transport problems prevented widespread distribution: even where it was profitable for one maltster and brewer to supply a local population, the brew did not travel far from its source. It took one particular drink to provoke a far-reaching change; and that drink was porter.

This first appeared around 1720 as a ready-made substitute for mixtures of beers from different barrels which some customers insisted on. The combination of pale ale from one barrel, brown ale from another, and what was often a stale brown ale which the barman was anxious to dispose of from a third, was a nuisance to serve, and doubtless led to many disputes about the quality or proportions of the ingredients. A London brewer conceived the idea of combining three tastes into one, and brewed a new beer darkened by malt which had been roasted and browned at a high temperature, with an extra portion of hops to add bitterness to its heaviness. This invigorating concoction soon became such a favourite pick-me-up with London porters that it was named after them. But although it saved time and trouble when dispensing in the bar, it required longer maturing than other beers, which meant money tied up and additional costs for storage space, which meant a higher price.

So dawned the day of the big brewers. Unit costs fell if large quantities could be produced; and when the taste for porter declined and it became necessary to switch to paler beers, the widespread distribution of product in bulk remained of paramount economic importance. Production was more and more concentrated in large brewhouses. In London and sizeable provincial centres these manufacturers unloaded their wares on to as many licensed houses as could be persuaded to stock them. And in due course they began to see advantages in owning a chain of houses where sale of their own beer and the exclusion of others could be guaranteed. Once the proprietor of an inn had been lured into selling out, his own distinctive brew was forthwith discontinued.

Not content with local acquisitions, larger firms began with the advent of the railways to ship products farther afield or to set up kindred brewhouses in suitable parts of the country. Burton-on-Trent, whose water was ideal for making the paler beers, was a town owing its growth almost entirely to the railways.

Brand names began to appear which remain familiar to this day. A carrier in the Burton region, one William Bass, who had been supplementing his income as so many small tradesmen did by brewing his own beer and selling it to customers on his rounds, decided to go in for full-time brewing. At first he concentrated on bottling for export, but his descendant Michael Bass saw the possibilities in the home market. Buying shares in the Midland Railway company, he soon became one of its directors, and personally ensured that cellars at St Pancras station were designed for the easy handling of barrels of draught Bass.

Another family in what was enviously dubbed 'the beerage' was that of the Whitbreads, descended from the Anglo-French Blaunpaynes. In 1743 Samuel Whitbread was sent at the age of 14 from his late father's farm at Cardington in Bedfordshire to be apprenticed to a London brewer. By 1742 he was skilled enough in the trade to set up in partnership in Old Street, and in 1750 bought the brewery in Chiswell Street which was for so long to be associated with the firm. By 1761 he was sole proprietor. For 22 years he sat as M.P. for Bedford, followed by his son Samuel; and one of his grandsons also entered Parliament, and as a diversion ran the Bedford Times Stage Coach between the Swan, Bedford, and the George and Blue Boar in Holborn.

These breweries, like those of William Worthington and the Charringtons, continued throughout many years to produce real straightforward beer because there was neither the call nor the capability for anything else. Only in modern times has advanced technology made it easier to produce something which keeps longer, does not need much expert handling on the retail premises, looks consistently bright and sparkling wherever it appears, and can by insistent advertising be forced upon the public. Too many small breweries have been gobbled up by the six giants who dominate the trade. Always there is a promise that the original distinctive local beers will be retained and that this 'rationalization' will be good for all concerned: centralized accounting, well-organized transport, all the resources of the big, expert company to take

38 *Facing* Once a smithy at which Charles II stopped to have a horse shod, the Smith's Arms at Godmanstone, Dorset, became England's smallest pub when the blacksmith, regretting that he had no licence to serve the King a drink, was granted one on the spot

the burden off the smaller. In the event, none of these promises has meant anything. Once acquired, local breweries have almost invariably been closed down and their beers discontinued, to make way for characterless, mass-produced liquids so insipid that, as one critic tartly observed, they could legally have been sold in the United States during prohibition. One is reminded, too, of the two Yorkshiremen in their local pub:

'Looks like rain.'

'Aye, and it don't *taste* much like beer, either.'

There was a frightening epidemic of takeovers during the 1960s, when more than 40 per cent of individualist breweries were seized by the big operators. The full story is told in Michael Dunn's succinct yet admirably documented *Penguin Guide to Draught Beer*, a book unlikely to be superseded for a long time to come. He rightly describes these mergers as being callously planned by the giants to 'create their own demand for products which were convenient for them to produce, rather than genuinely demanded by drinkers'. The figures justify my comparison to an epidemic. In 1960 the six big-name brewers were producing a bit less than half the beer brewed in the United Kingdom. Within ten years their share had grown to three-quarters, and by 1972 to four-fifths.

This campaign of conquest has resulted not only in the loss of different beers appealing to different regional palates, but in the loss of outlets for such small breweries as hoped to struggle on. The big combines bought up pubs by the score, and when it was found that any one of them did not meet the profit criteria laid down by the all-powerful accountants, that one would be summarily closed down, even if it meant depriving a village of its only pub and social centre.

Whatever excuses may be put forward on grounds of rationalization and diversification, or whatever the current cant may be, the general tendency over the past couple of decades has been the opposite of diversification in its strictest definition. All tied houses were given the same image and fitted out with much the same fitments. Only beer provided by the controlling company could be served. All wines and spirits had to be bought through the same channels, often at prices higher than the landlord would have paid at the local cash-and-carry or supermarket. The biggest brewers put managers into their hotels and pubs, with no personal stake in the enterprise and almost no freedom of manoeuvre. Where food was served, this was often supplied through one of the group's subsidiaries, or strict terms were enforced with regard to buying and presentation, best summed up in that deadening jargon of the catering trade—portion control.

Where the landlord was a tenant rather than a salaried manager, he would lease premises from a usually medium-sized brewery on the same understanding that his 'wet stock' came from that parent company, but with a little more latitude if he and his wife wanted to make a personal profit from food. Even here, though, restrictions on tenants have grown tighter and greedier in recent years. When there are those 50 applicants for each vacancy, why should the remote owners of chains of inns, hotels and pubs bother about the goodwill of their landlords?

Moving in

I am indebted to my friends Mike and Irna Mortlock for a detailed account of some of their own tribulations in the licensed trade, and especially for their graphic description of takeover day: a different sort of takeover from those practised by the cartels. To their invaluable reminiscences I have added experiences recounted by other friends and acquaintances; and wherever any of them may be when this book is published, I hasten to absolve them from any responsibility for my own interpretation or misinterpretation of the brewer-publican relationship.

So you want to run a pub . . . ?

Free houses are hard to come by, and it's up to you to raise all the capital and take all the risk. A free house is one which has since the distant past been unattached to any brewery or holding company (a rarity) or has been sold off by such a company to anyone who can meet the asking price. The first thing you have to ask yourself is why a brewery should sell off such premises. Are they in a lonely spot, with no local trade to speak of; or has trade been lost to a newer and smarter place half a mile away; or has a new road scheme ruined the whole scene? If the inn were profitable, the brewery would surely keep it on. If they have been losing money, what leads you to suppose you can, all on your own, make a profit? Maybe the price is such that you can just raise it. If you want the building to be mainly a private dwelling, you have no need to go through the rigmarole of applying through the authorities for change of use: you simply make yourself so objectionable to the few regulars that they cease to come. If, on the other hand, you fancy making a small income just to keep things ticking over, you can run the place amiably but unadventurously. Or, of course, you can go all out to show the world that your free house, offering whatever variety of ales, wines and spirits you can persuade suppliers to

deliver, is better than any tied house with its limited range.

If you prefer to be the employed manager of a house in one of the major chains, you will have to work your way up through their own ranks or produce a track record of some kind which will convince them of your competence in performing exactly the tricks they require. Managers are appointed by the owning brewery, and that's that.

The best way into the trade for an aspirant of talent and determination is as a tenant landlord. Where long-standing tenants have had leases on premises taken over by the big combines, those new owners have usually found ways of forcing them out and installing their own brain-washed managers. But still there are local breweries, revivified after the gallant campaigns of CAMRA and other anti-monopoly elements, who will accept tenants willing to buy their way into the bar.

As a starter you get in touch with a broker, who plays much the same rôle as an estate agent does in the finding and purchase of a residence. When a pub is on offer for a new tenancy, neither the present tenants nor the owning brewer advertise it themselves but put it in the hands of such a broker. In some cases, in small local concerns, word may get round without any such inter-mediaries, and I have known the case of one aspirant being accepted by a local brewer merely on the strength of a remark made in the street. This is rare, though, and for most applicants the road leads through the broker's office.

These middlemen advertise their services in the trade paper, the *Morning Advertiser*, growing especially poetic about properties which have proved hard to get rid of. When you feel you are ready to run the gauntlet, you arrange an interview with such a broker, who will probably represent a number of breweries or management chains. You may apply for one specific pub which appeals to you, or simply put your name on his list and wait for him to come up with something. After he has questioned you for anything up to two hours, he will decide if you are the right type for such an establishment. If you fail to impress him, you'll get no further. If he thinks you are at any rate tolerable, you will have to supply him with photographs of yourself and your wife to make it clear that you won't disgrace the general décor. From then on you will receive regular lists from him, as you would from an estate agent. If there's nothing you fancy, you sit tight and wait for subsequent lists.

Then, through his notifications or because of some tip-off you have been able to pass on to him, something crops up which looks promising. Now you start playing it clever with existing tenants, just as one fine day someone will play it clever with you.

Let us suppose the inn is called the Crown and stands at one end of an attractive village which you visited on holiday two years ago and have since remembered as quite a beauty spot. You make another visit, and drop into the Crown for a pint of bitter and a glass of white wine. Under no circumstances do you let on who you are. But a shrewd tenant may guess, especially if he has an unusual number of strangers in that day, all covertly sizing up the seats, the wallpaper, the locals, the state of the fittings, the general atmosphere. If you like the place, you dash off and report to your broker; telephone the landlord, come clean, and make an appointment to be shown round. Tenants must let all applicants make a detailed inspection, but have no say in the ultimate choice of their successor.

This is the time when you need to be on your guard. The smell of polish on the bar and all the way up the stairs may disguise the stench of dry rot. The crowd of free-spending leather-jacketed motor-cyclists in the public bar may be the very reason why the present tenant is anxious to retire early. And there are things which the tenant who is matily showing you over the place may not so much falsify as simply not mention. I know of an incoming tenant who carefully assessed the bar and restaurant takings, worked out the profit on five letting rooms, and was quite happy with the turnover declared on the statement provided by his predecessor. All in all, a small but reasonable profit was possible. But what the outgoer had not mentioned, and the incomer had not thought to check, was that the outgoer had not lived on the premises but had bought his own private cottage next door, in which he now intended to spend his retirement. This meant that the new tenant, with a wife and two adolescent children, did not after all have the income from five letting rooms but only from two; which meant that the viable margin of profit ceased to be viable, and that he was going to have to find other ways of supplementing his income.

Having made your own assessment, appraised the toilets and assessed the hazards of carrying food through a door on the other side of which is the dartboard, you decide that this is what you want, and notify the broker accordingly. He goes through your application, along with a batch of others, and makes out his own short list. Again you are at the broker's mercy. If he doesn't like your manner, your eyes or your accent, you may not even get to the brewer's final selection.

Then comes the brewery interview. After this, when you have put on your old regimental tie and your wife has removed her spectacles and substituted contact lenses through which to blink sexily at the interviewer, you may be in luck and find yourself on *their* short list. The district manager will want to put you through another grilling, and you'll appear on an even shorter list, usually of three couples.

A week or two later you hear from the brewery that you've been accepted . . . or that you haven't.

If you've got the job, the immediate whoops of joy are subdued when you realize that now is the time when you have to put the money down. The outgoing tenant has prepared his inventory through a friendly valuer, and you must pay whatever he wishes to dispose of in the way of trade fixtures, fittings, furniture and effects. Your own valuer, hastily summoned, argues with the outgoing tenant's valuer over the price for each item. A cracked plastic lampshade, for instance: 'That's worth something, it's ancient' . . . 'I'd say it was old and battered rather than ancient.' But, however you may wrangle over the price of these discarded bits of rubbish, you may not refuse them. I have before me the inventory prepared for a somewhat run-down inn by a reputable firm of Licensed Trade Valuers, and have compared its phraseology with the actual items involved. 'Cable electric light pendant with bulb and plastic ribbon shade' was a frayed piece of flex ending in a bare bulb and draped with the scorched remains of a pink transparent shade which would never have been accepted in the sleaziest of billiard parlours. A 'sponge filled cushion' was a sponge-leaking blob. And who would dare to put a price on three wire coat-hooks? 'Heavy duty red inlaid lino' meant a worn and cracked strip of lino whose furrows would bring even the most mildly intoxicated regular to his knees. And when you find you are expected to pay for every length of flex from every ceiling, and are tempted to say that you don't want the flex and why don't they take it with them—thereby fusing every light in the place and conceivably setting fire to the building via its already rotted wiring—you are told that you have to accept, and have to pay. Who's for a plaster wall plaque? Or a wooden mask? And what about a wooden mallet . . . one screwdriver . . . and (I still want to know more about this) a tickler?

Among such items for which they felt little enthusiasm, my friends the Mortlocks on one occasion were only too willing to pay for fitments in an inn they were taking over. There on the bar were some beautiful porcelain hand pumps. But the brewery exercised its right of first choice, and chose to pay the outgoing tenant for them. The pumps remained in place; but they belonged to the proprietors and not the tenants.

When the price has been agreed, you must give your broker the money a month before you propose to move in. In fact you usually pay him more than the agreed figure, to allow for adjustments on the morning of takeover. With a bit of luck the adjustments may be in your favour, and you get a refund.

So the great day arrives. You show up at the Crown at nine in the morning to meet your broker. The outgoing tenant's broker is also there, and the two of them set off round the premises, mumbling and arguing over the inventory. Every single item is re-checked in case of damage, deterioration or disappearance in the short time since the inventory was drawn up. At ten o'clock you and the outgoing tenant go to Court together to obtain a protection order for the licence: the changeover is always done on the day when the local Court is held. In your absence, the outgoing tenant's wife opens up at the usual time and sells beer as usual, and the money going into the till is still theirs. The moment you return, the place is yours. All their money has to be removed from the till and replaced by yours. If you have forgotten to come amply provided with small change, you'll soon be in trouble.

Your wife is expected to provide food at midday for all those on the premises in any way involved in the transaction: brokers, people from the brewery, and reps who can't even wait for you to settle in before urging their wares upon you. All the local publicans for miles around drop in to size you up. All drinks are on the house. The outgoer has run his stock down as far as possible, but there has to be a last-minute calculation of what remains. This you buy from him, and there will be two lots of VAT to sort out. In addition you will have put in your own order to the brewery; and the draymen are outside right now waiting to deliver.

In the middle of all this, one lot of furniture is being carried out to a removal van, and another van is waiting to unload your own furniture. You have no time to supervise this operation and must leave the removal men to get on with it, unless you are as lucky as my friends the Mortlocks were. A landlord for whom they had once worked took a few days' holiday, ensured that a refrigerator full of food left their old home last thing, was plugged in at the removal firm's depot overnight, and came first off the van at their new home; and coped with every awkward problem which threatened to distract them from their prime task of keeping the pub going. In the afternoon he and a couple of relatives bottled up, and made up the beds.

You hope to have a little time to yourself in the afternoon and to sort things out. One rule is that the outgoing landlady leaves curtains up in your private accommodation. You will probably have had to pay for them anyway, no matter what condition they are in or however much the pattern revolts you. But certainly you will have no time to hang your own bedroom curtains for that first night.

In the evening all the locals come in to inspect you, and again it's drinks on the house for each of them. And the phone will ring, you'll be asked if you have two single rooms, bed and breakfast, for three nights from next Monday on, and you have to decide if you're ready for coping with residents yet. The outgoer will not have accepted any bookings during his run-down period; but if he happens to have a long-term resident, arrangements will have had to be made between you.

After a few days the panic is over. You sort out your belongings, throw away the rubbish you have been forced to buy, and adjust to the tempo of life in the Crown. The locals may have been sizing you up, but you, too, have been sizing up what you have inherited. There are the over-friendly ones, the impassive ones, the surly old man who expects his corner stool to be kept vacant for him, and the unfussily helpful couple who in times of crisis will nip round the end of the bar and help wash the glasses. In one village I knew a landlord who inherited an old age pensioner who had been coming every day for 40 years. It became the custom for a rota of well-wishers to give him a free lunch every Sunday, with the pub playing its part. On his eightieth birthday a special party and presentation were organized, and it was suggested to the brewers that they might, in the circumstances, make a small contribution. His dedication over the years, and the fact that he spent most of his pension on their product, did not seem to them to merit even a token gesture.

Morning and evening you have to come on stage smiling at acquaintances and strangers alike. You must learn who wants to be joked with, who prefers to be on Christian name terms, and who prefers to be called 'sir'. And you must smile every time at the joke or comment you will hear twice a day from now until you retire.

'Well, I suppose I'd better make a noise like an egg and beat it.'

A roar of laughter from the speaker, which you must share.

And you must look interested in long, convoluted stories from one old-timer who grows more loquacious as the evening wears on. You will soon learn to predict what's in store at any given time: one of his two-pint stories, or one of his four-pint ones.

'Last orders, please' must be called ten minutes before closing time. 'Time' must be called at closing time itself; and then ten minutes are allowed for drinking up. You will continue to marvel at the number of regulars who stubbornly insist, week in and week out, that they can buy a last drink on the dot of closing time, and that when you ask them to leave ten minutes later you are being unreasonable and misinterpreting the law. Also you will marvel at the persistence of parents who cannot see why they should not bring small children into the bar. Regulations on this matter are, it has to be admitted, fussy and often difficult to administer on certain ill-designed premises. If you do install a children's room, there must be no direct service to it from the bar. Children may have soft drinks in it, and their parents may drink alcoholic beverages with them; but those adult drinks must be fetched from the bar and not served direct. If you have a garden, there should be no hatch or other opening through which alcoholic drinks could be supplied. If soft drinks and snacks are served through a hatch direct to the garden, this hatch must be used for such service only and must not be connected to the bar.

All this and catering regulations, fire regulations, VAT records, procedures for returning bad beer and choking off aggressive reps or insurance men, you will soon take in your stride. You will know just how much beer can be written off as ullage, and how much can be written off against free drinks for the draymen. This latter calculation is a nice one: claim too much, and the VAT man will demand a readjustment.

But what you may not be prepared for is the sudden blow of being told that the brewery does not regard its agreement with you as being quite so binding as you had supposed.

Various pressures

Top pressure, the widely used system of forcing beer from cask to counter by means of carbon dioxide, almost inevitably pollutes the beer; and brewers' other pressures can ruin many a landlord.

When you have taken on the Crown on a three-year lease at an agreed rent,

4 The Boat Inn, an old canal beer-house beside the lock at Stoke Bruerne Waterways Museum, Northamptonshire

5 The rear courtyard of the Red Lion, a fourteenth-century coaching house in Salisbury

6 and **7** Two Suffolk bar interiors: *above* shelves in the Oyster, Butley; *below* the Jolly Sailor, Orford

you assume that you may rely on three years' security of tenure at a fixed rent. In those three years you will increase turnover, the brewers will be well pleased, and you can salt away some extra profits from the restaurant which you have fitted out at your own expense. But you have been in only a few months when a smart young man from head office arrives to inform you that improvements are shortly to be made. 'We'll take that wall out, and alter that ugly old fireplace for you. Oh, and we're going to put in central heating.' He beams and waits for you to thank him.

'Marvellous', you say. 'But it won't put up the rent, will it?'

Oh, yes it will. What's known as 'landlord's improvements' always pushes the rent up.

By how much?

'As soon as it's finished, we'll let you know.'

You plead that you haven't had a chance to build up trade yet, and you're not taking enough money to pay for a rent increase so soon. After a lot of argument you win the day. But it has created bad feeling, and our smooth young friend will be back. All at once your carpets and fitments are not good enough. The brewery advise very strongly on the standards they expect. It's up to you to pay for new carpets and suchlike, but you will be told what quality they demand—and usually it is more than you can afford.

Brewers like a landlord to build the place up, penalizing him for his improvements until he can stand the pace no longer and decides to get out; whereupon they have a much more desirable property to rent out to the next eager tenant, who will start at a much higher rental and then find himself being bullied, too, into accepting further alterations which will cost him yet more. One of the most contemptible—but common—of all ploys is to let a tenant smarten the place up and build up local goodwill, and then find a way of removing him and installing a salaried manager to run the place according to brewery orders. Even now it has not dawned on the big combines that managers do not have the same incentive, personal pride and personal involvement or the same affection for their customers as tenants do.

Although you have signed a three-year agreement, the brewery reserves the right to give you notice if your conduct or misconduct makes this desirable in their eyes. Their interpretation of what constitutes misconduct or incompetence is whatever they choose to make it. A landlord who has put all his savings into an inn and is increasing its turnover month by month can nevertheless be thrown out if his wife leaves him, for example. In most cases the notice to which the tenant is entitled is six months within his first year, four months in any year after that; but some breweries allow only three months right from the first year. The tenant also can give notice on the same terms.

Quite apart from the rental, there is the question of rates on the inn. These are assessed on barrelage, the number of barrels sold. The more you sell, the more they take off you.

At one time it was common for breweries to sell beer to the landlords of their own tied houses at a higher price than they supplied it to the free trade. This muddled up the accountancy, though, and it was decided to even it out. Instead, they arbitrarily increased the rents. One landlord of my acquaintance accepted this, working out that to meet this increase he would need to sell two more barrels a month, which seemed feasible. When the figures came in, he found they had been so adjusted that he would need to sell four, not two barrels, extra. In a setting such as our Crown, with a limited village trade and limited passing traffic, this could well mark the breaking point. Add to that the crippling inflation which has driven even the most loyal regulars into limiting their drinking hours and expenditure, and your daydreams of running an easy-going, gently profitable pub can soon turn into a nightmare. Reluctantly you decide you'll have to attract younger people by putting in a fruit machine. The brewers will levy extra rent. A pool table? That, too, is regarded as an improvement and therefore justifies a further increase.

And how is your restaurant or snack bar getting on? It takes a long time to build up a reputation good enough to bring in diners from further afield. Scampi and chips in the basket won't lure them halfway across the county; and you'll impress nobody by re-labelling your Scotch Egg as Oeuf écossais. I have been told of one opening night, planned long in advance and advertised in the inn and in the local press, when a number of appetizing dishes were ready and waiting . . . and not one epicure showed up. 'Have you ever', the landlady asked me plaintively some days later, 'eaten three prawn cocktails at one o'clock in the morning because you just couldn't bear to throw them away?'

If you do persevere and the gourmets begin to seek you out, be careful not to let the solid sustenance prosper at the expense of bar takings. A drop in barrelage, and the brewery will be breathing yet more threats.

The Real Ale rebellion

The assertion of the big combines that their pressurized beer was what the customer preferred had never been true, and contempt for their product grew steadily. In 1971 a few enthusiasts formed the Campaign for the Revitalization of Ale, simplified in 1973 to the Campaign for Real Ale. So much damage had already been done by the bully boys that this spurt of rebellion might well have been written off as a lost cause from the outset. Instead, it attracted so much support that CAMRA soon began to frighten the giants into rethinking their whole policy. It was shown that greater size did not lead to greater efficiency; that the combines' gassy beers were not merely weaker but cost more than the traditional brews of their smaller surviving competitors; that real beer *could* be served without difficulty by any landlord worthy of his calling, and that a high proportion of the public wanted that sort of beer. Not content with reawakening this healthy thirst, CAMRA tackled the Food Standards Committee and made representations to the Office of Fair Trading whenever there was a rumour of further monopolistic takeover bids.

Even the most dogmatic of the big six brewers found it prudent to experiment with real beers again. Pub façades which had once boasted red barrels and other such insignia now altered colour and lettering in the hope of no longer being identified with 'the baddies'.

Some splendid folk still make their own beer in their own inns. The Blue Anchor at Helston in Cornwall has maintained this tradition for many years; connoisseurs coo over the incomparable Mrs Pardoe with her Old Swan at Netherton and the newer White Swan in Dudley; and not so long ago a landlord and his wife began brewing their own beer at the Goose and Firkin in Borough High Street, Southwark, complementing it with lavish helpings of good, inexpensive food.

So perhaps we may end this chapter on a cheerful note. In what better company than the Mortlocks? A year or two back, the brewery whose tenants they then were decided to reintroduce a strong natural bitter which had not been brewed for 50 years. Landlords were invited to take part in a competition for the best promotion scheme: how could one evening best be spent putting the idea across and giving customers a good time into the bargain? Mike and Irna won this competition with the idea that for one evening the bar should be decked out in 50-year-old mood. The brewery went along with this by providing a quantity of beer and spirits to be sold (for as long as they held out)

CANNARDS GRAVE INN

ACCOMMODATION

WARBUTTON

41 Not a very welcoming offer of accommodation in Shepton Mallet. In fact the inn itself was burnt down shortly before this photograph was taken

at the prices then prevailing.

'Great scheme', approved a fellow landlord. 'I think I'll have a science-fiction evening—and charge the year 2000 prices.'

Blow-ups of old newspapers were hung on the walls. The food which the inn would have offered was represented by cottage loaves and home-made cottage cheese. Tapes of old dance tunes were played; everybody had to appear in appropriate clothes; and the fruit machine was covered up and replaced by a shove-ha'penny board.

It was an exhausting business, but one which left happy echoes. Perhaps such echoes are what persuade disillusioned landlords and their wives to go on: telling themselves they were fools ever to venture into such drudgery, they know perfectly well that if dismissed from one such place or financially crippled by it they would have but one ambition . . . to find just such another prison.

At the proof stage of this book I have to add that Mike and Irna have moved on of their own accord to build up trade in another pub as tenants of another brewery. They still look dedicated, unbeaten and unrepentant.

7

Great Roads North

Tomorrow is our wedding-day,
And we will then repair
Unto the Bell at Edmonton
All in a chaise and pair.
William Cowper:
JOHN GILPIN

John Gilpin's relegation to horseback instead of sharing the chaise resulted in his being carried further north than the inn at which he had promised to entertain his wife on their wedding anniversary, and he was lucky to have been turned around at Ware. Not that there is any lack of hospitable houses as the A10 makes its way towards Cambridge: Puckeridge, so recently freed from the dust and fumes and vibration of trunk-road traffic through its village street, has an admirable selection; and the Banyers at Royston is an excellent place to stop for lunch, in spite of the alarming proximity of lorries swinging past its corner windows. But if one plans to avoid the Wash and head north, it is necessary to leave the A10 when it veers east towards Cambridge and follow ancient Ermine Street, passing the Caxton Gibbet inn sign which echoes the gibbet replica close by, until at Alconbury it picks up one of the most historic roads in the land.

Before and during coaching days the greater part of northbound traffic left London by a route past the Angel at Islington until it reached Hadley Green, site of the battle of Barnet at which in 1471 the earl of Warwick died, yet another casualty of the Wars of the Roses. Here the road forked, one branch continuing towards the Scottish border as the Great North Road, while the Holyhead Mail from the Angel swung north-west along the Holyhead Road. This junction was a natural gathering place for inns, catering not only for passenger traffic but for merchandise wagons and cattle drovers from the north.

One survivor of those bustling days is the Red Lion at High Barnet. At the time of the Lancastrian and Yorkist battle it was known as the Cardinal's Hat, but by the middle of the following century had become the Antelope. Somewhere around 1720 it was rebuilt with an imposing porch below its main window, and at the back a capacious yard with stabling for over 100 horses. A story is told of the pressure on accommodation which the inn enjoyed in its heyday. Travelling to London to attend a funeral, an army officer and his daughter sought shelter for the night, but the place was full and it was only after some persuasion that the landlord agreed to see what could be done. Rooms were hurriedly prepared: very hurriedly, for when the young woman opened a cupboard door, a corpse fell out at her feet. Apparently some unfortunate guest who had died on the bed had been hastily bundled out of the way and might have been quietly disposed of next morning had it not been, in Charles Harper's words, 'for that feminine mingled curiosity and precautionary sense which impels our womenkind to peer agitatedly under every bed, to leave no cupboard unexplored, and no drawer not scrutinized'.

The Red Lion was largely rebuilt in the 1930s, but has preserved the elaborate inn sign with its ornamental ironwork.

Here we must make our choice between the two forks.

To the Border

What is now the A1, with sections of motorway at intervals, leads on through Hatfield, whose Eight Bells inn was used by Bill Sykes in *Oliver Twist*, past Welwyn with its old White Hart, and by-passes Baldock, through the heart of which it once twisted. Here at the meeting of the Great North Road and the Icknield Way was another prosperous cluster of long-lived inns.

A late sixteenth-century ecclesiastical court met at the George and Dragon, which in the next century was allowed to take some ground from the church-yard to expand its stables. This was an amicable arrangement, with the inn paying an annual rent. But in 1747 the hosteler fell out with the rector over a party fence. Other religious associations are with the Quakers, who made a point of staying here during their travels after George Fox had peacefully settled a dispute between two inebriated customers. The cook in 1808 was the wife of a highwayman, and brought his body to the inn on its way to burial after he had been hanged at Hertford. Early in our own century the entire place was rebuilt.

For many years the town's most highly regarded inn was the Old White Horse, but in 1864 this declined and was turned into a school, soon to be burnt down and rebuilt as a private dwelling. All that remains is a fragment which was once the tap-room of the larger inn, still calling itself the Old White Horse among Baldock's rather impressive collection of wildlife: the Cock, the Bull's Head, the Old Black Eagle, the Stag, the White Hart and the White Lion.

One of Baldock's most celebrated sons was James Ind, founder of the brewing concern of Ind Coope.

Taking another detour off the present A1 we find, in Biggleswade, the coaching inns of the Crown and the White Swan on opposite sides of the street. One wonders if each catered specifically, as modern filling stations often do, to traffic using its own side of the roadway, northbound or southbound.

In Eaton Socon is the thirteenth-century White Horse, refaced in mellow brick. Inside it is rich with black polished woodwork, low beams, spacious window alcoves, and a cosy little snug; and behind it all is a well-kept, sheltered garden. Between 1832 and 1837 the inn was run by a Charles James Fox: not the politician, but a mail guard from St Neots. When he died the premises were taken over by his sister-in-law and her husband, John Taylor, who looked after the orphaned Fox children as well as their own. The census of 1841 lists Taylor and his wife, three of their children, four of the twelve Fox children, three servants, two coachmen, and two lodgers. It is hard to believe there could have been much room for paying guests, with so many other occupants. The Taylors had a stake in several other local inns, but suffered like so many landlords from the coming of the railways.

A few miles away is St Neots, the faded Georgian glory of whose market-place is blemished by a rash of ill-matched modern signs, peeling frontages, and some jagged gaps. But there are mementoes of a rosier past: the stableyard entrances of the Old Falcon and the Bridge, and the whole of the attractive Cross Keys, provided in 1730 with a new brick front and bay windows. In Oliver Cromwell country, the Cross Keys really ought to be ashamed of the snobbish implications in its Cromwell *bar* and Royalist *lounge*! It remains,

42 The White Horse at Eaton
Socon, Bedfordshire

however, an inviting and easy-going place, with complexes of rooms on
different levels, joined and separated and propped up and latticed by beams at
all angles, like some carpentry modelling set whose owner has doggedly used
up every last little piece, filling in with every available sliver and splinter. At
the back, office work is accommodated in an unusual semi-circular room
swelling out into the old cobbled yard.

It was at St Neots that a much lauded hero of the highways once nearly came
to grief. Tom Hennesy, coachman of the Stamford Regent, was 'knight of the
crooked whip, the adored of barmaids, the idol of schoolboys'; but even in the
hands of such a paragon a coach could be a perilous means of transport. One
day when making a detour around a paper-mill on the banks of the Ouse here,
the coach rolled on to a track so waterlogged that water began to seep into the
interior. To Hennesy's horror, his coach began to float away towards the
deeper waters of the river, and it was all he could do to get his horses to hold it.

At Buckden are two rival establishments, again on opposite sides of what was
once the main road: the George, and the Lion. The fifteenth-century Lion was
once the refectory of the neighbouring red-brick palace of the bishops of
Lincoln, where Catherine of Aragon was imprisoned on the orders of Henry
VIII. Its original name when it became an inn was the Lamb, and the kitchen
has a massive carved wooden boss in the ceiling depicting the Lion and the
Lamb, which became its next title. Now it has settled for the Lion.

The story of the ghostly drummer boy in R. H. Barham's *Ingoldsby Legends*
is based on a murder which took place in Brampton in 1780. The murderer's

corpse was displayed on a gibbet near Brampton Hut inn, now incorporated in a modern hotel at the crossroads of the A1 and the main road between Huntingdon and Kettering.

Huntingdon stands on Ermine Street, once the major London-to-York road. Parts of its George hotel had their origin in the times of Charles II, including the outside stair and open gallery in the courtyard, but the wing adjoining the gallery is much older. In 1754 the George had been bought by the grandfather of Oliver Cromwell, who was born in the town, went to school here, and whose father is buried in the church just across the road. As late as 1839 there were seven regular coach services stopping here.

Many a book on pubs and inns still misleadingly sings the praises of the famous Bell at Stilton. In fact it has been derelict for many years now, facing a rival which burnt out in more recent years and so added further decrepitude to the broad street. At the time of my last visit there were local assurances of the Bell's imminent restoration, but I have heard no word of its reopening its doors yet. Also, it has to be pointed out that its reputation as the first distributor of Stilton cheese is a dubious one, since there is evidence that this trade began from the Angel, a coaching inn of even greater splendour, with stabling for 300 horses.

The village's source of fame, no matter how much disputed between its hostelers, was a cheese-maker from the Melton Mowbray district who in the 1740s began supplying cheese to the dining-room of one of the inns. Some travellers found it none too appetizing. Defoe was revolted by such fare,

43 Once refectory to a bishop's palace, the Lion at Buckden, Cambridgeshire, later became a busy coaching inn

. . . which is called our English Parmesan, and is brought to the table with the mites, or maggots round it, so thick, that they bring a spoon with them for you to eat the mites with, as you do the cheese.

Others became so addicted that they bought slices to take away with them when they left; and in due course the landlord was shipping consignments to London by carrier. Since he slyly implied that it was from his own dairy, the cheese became known as Stilton rather than Melton Mowbray or Leicestershire. In no time at all a rival across the street began to compete with '*real* Stilton cheese', presumably made on the premises.

Whether the Bell was in truth the founder of the trade or merely an opportunist pretender, it must in its great days have been a great building, in that glowing stone which one finds in so many subtle hues across northern Northamptonshire and along the border of what is now Greater Cambridgeshire. From its added eighteenth-century frontage a massive sign once thrust out far across the road. But the inn went through a succession of bad patches. In his late nineteenth-century *Coaching Days and Coaching Ways*, Outram Tristram referred to it as 'gaunt, ghost-like, deserted but half alive' with only a few memories 'locked in its old withered heart'. Although that heart did begin to beat again in the days of the motor-car, it lacked its earlier vigour and soon faltered again.

A village built almost entirely of that grey-gold local stone is Wansford, with its lovely bridge. Main road traffic fortunately no longer threatens that bridge with destruction, but skirts the village so well that without knowing the place is there you could easily miss it. Close to the river, the Haycock inn is forever linked with the legend which gave the village its full name of Wansford-in-England. There are two versions of this tale. One relates that a drunkard named Barnaby, asleep on a haycock, was carried away by a flooding of the river Nene. When he awoke, he blearily called up to a watcher on the bridge to ask where he was and, when told he was in Wansford, cried, 'What, Wansford in England?' A slightly different version, with the backing of a seventeenth-century poem, says that while being swept away downstream he found himself the butt of jokers along the bank:

'Whither away', quoth they, 'from Greenland?'
'No, from Wansford Brigs, in England.'

Defoe records a further variation, with Barnaby's return to consciousness not occurring until he was well on his way to Wisbech.

The Haycock's signboard depicts the incident, and there is an earlier picture from the eighteenth century now hanging in the courtyard, itself the oldest part of the premises, with remains of mullioned windows and stone archways. The inn buildings have existed in much their present form since at any rate 1632, as recorded on a date stone in the attractive walled garden, ablaze with daffodils in spring and rich with rose-laden pergolas. A beam in what may once have been the bar of an original tavern is believed to date from King John's time, and it has been estimated that the ingle-nook fireplace uncovered in the early 1960s must have been bricked up for at least 250 years. The great roof spans carry more than an acre of Colly Weston slates.

During its eventful life the Haycock has changed hands and changed functions a number of times, once as a wager in a card game. It has been a farmhouse, a racing stable, and a hunting box. In 1810 it was enlarged to cope with a stepping-up of coach services between London and York. Visitors in 1835 included the Duchess of Kent and her daughter, the young Princess Victoria, whose signed portrait still hangs in the room where she slept. The arrival of the railway in 1854 put an end to such good fortunes. (It might be noted in passing that this local line in its turn lost custom and was closed just

over a hundred years later; but current nostalgia for steam trains has resulted
in the reopening of six miles of track along the Nene Valley from Wansford to
the outskirts of Peterborough, and in September 1980 this was reconnected to
the main line for a British Rail shuttle service from Peterborough.) During
the First World War the Haycock played its part as an ammunition factory,
but in the age of the internal combustion engine it reverted to being an inn.
During the Second World War it became a favourite meeting-place for RAF
pilots from airfields in the neighbourhood.

Ahead we soon approach another by-pass which I, for one, never use. Who
could resist turning off down the hill for that breath-taking vision of Stamford?

The town can boast several good inns and pubs, nearly all of them beetle-
browed with sagging stone-tiled roofs weighing down on heavy yet glowing
stone walls. But there can be no denying pride of place to the George.

In Norman times a hospice of the Holy Sepulchre stood on the site, feeding
and lodging pilgrims on their way to the Holy Land. A crypt and subterranean
passage from the medieval fabric survive below the present inn, and at the
rear is what is known as the Monastery Garden, with a sunken lawn once
serving as a fish pond, though its pleasant walks are more likely to have been
used by resting pilgrims than by monks. From the gardens and from side
windows of the inn are incomparable views of the town's walls of ochre dusted
with grey and silver, of mossy slated roofs and church spires. The archway to
the original courtyard is now incorporated in the dining-room, which covers
most of the area of that yard. A minstrels' gallery and high ceiling in the west
wing recall the large ballroom which has been obliterated by bedrooms.

In 1714 the landlord, accused of being a secret Jacobite, was forced to his

45 Near Greetham, Lincolnshire, the sign of the Ram Jam Inn depicts one of several explanations of its name

knees and ordered to drink to the memory of the recently deceased Queen Anne. As he obeyed, a Hanoverian dragoon ran him through with a sabre. A mob of locals, inflamed by news of the killing, stormed the George and smashed every window in the place; but during the turmoil the dragoon made his escape.

The George has known many a royal visitor, including the consort of one George—Charlotte, George III's queen. There were Charles I, William III, and in 1768 Christian VII of Denmark. 'Butcher' Cumberland stayed here when returning from Culloden in 1745, and another traveller from Scotland—Sir Walter Scott—used the place frequently during trips to and from London.

In 1825 a brewery was established in Stamford, later developing into Melbourn's. The name is still to be found on some tied houses, but their beer is supplied by Samuel Smith of Tadcaster, the Stamford brewhouse having gone out of business in 1974. In alliance with Melbourn's, Samuel Smith's felt it would be a pity if the old brewery and depot buildings were lost forever, and between them they have opened a brewery museum complete with horse and dray, historical records and pictures, authentic equipment still in place, and—during licensing hours—a supply of beer drawn from the wood in traditional style.

Looking rather lonely beside the A1 as we speed northwards is the Ram Jam Inn, whose name has given rise to a number of authoritative explanations, not one of which accords with any other. Originally it was called the Winchelsea Arms, but changed in the eighteenth century because . . . well, let's start with the somewhat thin theory that a guest cleared off abruptly after tricking the then landlady with a tale of how to get two kinds of beer from one barrel. The *Oxford English Dictionary* defines the phrase as meaning 'crammed full', but cannot find it being so used before 1879. Yet there is a parallel in one theory, recorded a century earlier, that the inn derived its name from the habit of one landlord of offering a concoction—a cocktail, as later generations would describe it—into which everything had been rammed. And for a gloss on this, there is the story that the landlord was a retired servant of an officer who had brought him back from India and made his name with an Indian recipe which added fire to the cocktail: the native term for a servant at table being a Ram Jam, this was what the inn came to be called.

If ever an inn deserved such a bran-tub title, it was one run by a friend of mine in a corner of England whose locality I refuse to divulge. Being at the time a writer with ambitions but little capital, he thought it would be a splendid idea to take on the tenancy of a remote, run-down pub whose rental at the time was ten shillings a week. With a roof over his head, and very little in the way of regular trade, he would surely find plenty of peace and quiet in which to create his masterpiece. Unfortunately, being a most generous and garrulous character, he soon built up a thriving concern which proved an embarrassment rather than an asset. Knowing little about the handling of beer, he produced murky pints which he glibly persuaded the locals was the latest craze, until they obediently asked for 'a pint of cloudy, please'. And, having poured all the dregs of dusty liqueur bottles which he had inherited into two or three plain bottles which his wife, a brilliant artist, labelled *Brüdermacher* (their German being about as accurate as their dispensing of beer), he did very well from young women whose boy friends showed off by buying them this exclusive fire-water . . . until both the brewer and the Customs and Excise inspector came in pale and perplexed to sort out these higgledy-piggledy methods.

Pressing on, we again diverge from the new road on to the old in order to pay respects to Grantham, and in particular to the holy and regal hauteur of the Angel and Royal. As an important medieval hostel it was visited by King John in 1213 at the invitation of its then owners, the Knights Templars. A century or so later most of the place was rebuilt, including the courtyard archway which we see today with its carved, crumbling remains of the faces of Edward III and his queen, Philippa of Hainault. The oriel window above is of later date. The courtyard itself, at the back, is more like a cathedral close, warmed by added brickwork.

Behind that oriel window is the Chambre du Roi, now a dining-room running the full length of the older building, in which Richard III carried out one of his lethal tasks. The Duke of Buckingham had helped Richard seize power, but was soon caught up in the revolt against the new king's ruthlessness and shared the horror of those who believed—a story denied by many later rehabilitators—that he had murdered the two princes in the Tower. News of young Buckingham's leadership of a Welsh rebellion, ending in speedy defeat, was brought to Richard while he was staying at the Angel (as it then was) in October 1483. He ordered the Great Seal to be brought from London without delay, and there signed and sealed Buckingham's death warrant. The Richard Lounge has a portrait presented by the Lincolnshire branch of the Richard III

46 The medieval angel of the Angel and Royal, Grantham, Lincolnshire

Society to commemorate this somewhat inauspicious visit.

As the Angel and Royal, the inn expanded in coaching days, when the wings at the back were entirely rebuilt. Among earlier beauties retained in the original section are the window alcoves of the bar, with finely carved stone ceilings, one showing a pelican-in-piety feeding her young. Framed on the staircase is an old postilion's jacket found on the premises during the early 1950s, recalling days when the house had stabling for 50 horses.

Even with the coming of the railway there was still some horse traffic in the streets. Old photographs show that the George at Grantham had its own horse bus between the station and the hotel, and the Angel and Royal must surely have met this challenge with a similar conveyance.

Newark's admirably preserved cobbled market-place is joined through an archway to a modern pedestrian shopping precinct. This arch and the sketchy hint of a coaching yard behind are all that remain of the great Saracen's Head, an inn licensed in the reign of Edward III, apart from its old sign, a ferocious bust set in a first-floor niche. The Saracen's Head will also be long remembered in the pages of *The Heart of Midlothian*, where Scott's heroine, Jeanie Deans, is well looked after by the landlord before continuing on her way to London.

Next door, the Clinton Arms Motel was once known as the Cardinal's Head, becoming the King's Arms between the sixteenth and early nineteenth centuries. Lord Byron stayed here in 1806 and 1807, when two volumes of his poems were printed in Newark. In 1832 Gladstone addressed voters from an upper window after being returned as one of Newark's Members of Parliament and so entering the first Reform Parliament in the Tory cause. In the election of 1841 he was again returned for Newark; and later switched on grounds of principle to the Liberal party.

47 All that remains of the Saracen's Head in Newark marketplace, Nottinghamshire

A couple of miles off the main road some way north of Newark, but once a coaching inn of some consequence, the Bell at Barnby Moor claims to have been a haunt of Dick Turpin. But then, what inn anywhere between Epping Forest and the Scottish borders does not make some such claim?

Dick Turpin's ride to York

That a highwayman named Dick Turpin existed there can be no doubt, but the majority of his legendary exploits are an amalgam of tall tales and other men's deeds or misdeeds. The famous ride to York owes that fame largely to Harrison Ainsworth's novel, *Rookwood*, which in its turn must have been inspired by just such a ride performed by John Nevinson long before Turpin's day. Charles II was so impressed by Nevinson's feats that he called him Swift

Nick. A recent television series has put Turpin and Swift Nick together as accomplices—which, as Nevinson was captured at the Three Houses Inn at Sandal, near Wakefield, in 1685, and Dick Turpin was not born until 1705, seems as wild a distortion as any that Ainsworth achieved.

Extracting shreds of fact from a welter of fiction, it seems probable that Turpin was born at the Rose and Crown in Hempstead, Essex, where his father was landlord. During his career as a highwayman he resorted to many country inns as hideouts or places of refreshment, some in his home county and others further afield. At Woughton on the Green in Buckinghamshire he used the Old Swan as a base from which to sally forth and hold up riders or stage coaches on the Holyhead Road. One story has it that he was once chased as far as the inn, but hastily re-shod his horse so that its shoes faced backwards, thereby tricking his pursuers into riding off in the opposite direction.

In London, Turpin and his associates favoured the White Hart in Drury Lane and the Spaniard's, Hampstead, as meeting-places. The name of the Spaniard's is wrapped in mystery: one theory is that until it was licensed as an inn it served as the Spanish Embassy; another derives from two Spanish brothers who allegedly took on that licence in the middle of the eighteenth century. Today, visitors may inspect the stable in which Turpin's Black Bess is supposed to have sheltered, some keys and pistols belonging to him, and the leg-irons he is said to have worn in Newgate gaol. More authentic are the records of the Gordon Rioters who in 1780, having destroyed Lord Mansfield's house in Bloomsbury Square, stopped at the Spaniard's while on their way to burn his house in Hampstead. The landlord lavished drinks upon them until troopers arrived to seize them.

Not far out along the old Great North Road, the Roebuck at Broadwater also claims to have been favoured by Turpin. In addition it is said to be haunted, though apparently not by the highwayman.

The ride to York which followed that road in its early stages was supposedly provoked by an attempt to capture Turpin in an inn referred to in *Rookwood* as the Jack Falstaff. Leaping on to Black Bess, he headed for Tottenham and the north. Pursuers were led astray by a rumour that he had been seen outside an inn near Ware, relaxing over a tankard of ale. The frightened driver of a York coach reported that he had recognized the highwayman, but for once Turpin was too busy to stop. Resting briefly at an inn on the edge of the Burghley estate outside Stamford, he called for brandy, a bucket of water, and raw beefsteak, not for his own sustenance but in order to wash and rub down his horse. A bit off course, he was then sighted by the Black Bull on Witham Common. About this time one of his pursuers had the wisdom to abandon the hunt and resort to the pleasures of the Angel at Grantham.

Without question Dick Turpin did reach York in the end, though not in the manner he would have wished. He was captured at last in the Green Dragon at Welton, five or six miles west of Hull, which has cashed in on the incident by advertising itself as the Turpin Inn. John Nevinson, in spite of Charles II's amusement at his boldness, had been hanged at York in 1685. Dick Turpin, sentenced to death for horse stealing, followed him in 1739. The leg irons of both highwaymen are displayed in York's Castle Museum, a building combining the old women's prison and debtors' prison; and the condemned cell occupied by Turpin and other malefactors is preserved intact. Turpin's grave is to be found in the churchyard of St Denys and St George.

The highway from York to Edinburgh proceeded via Thirsk, with its Golden Fleece, and Northallerton, whose Golden Lion still has an impressive spread of Georgian frontage. Thirsk's cobbled market-place is now largely given over to parked cars, with some tricky entrances and exits, but has not

lost its bustling, traditional market-town atmosphere. Attractive bow windows look out over the square from a projecting section of the Golden Fleece, framed in a luxuriance of creeper. The inn reached the peak of its prosperity in the early nineteenth century when, as chief posting house in the town, it had up to 60 horses on call for the coach trade. In 1815 the incoming landlord and owner extended it through neighbouring houses and, at his death, handed over the improved premises to a nephew and the nephew's son. These two are still in residence, in the form of portraits hung above the stairs. Although the sign of the fleece gleams proudly outside, most of the other pictures within are of horses.

There is another appealing market-place about 15 miles away at Helmsley, though coach drivers and their horses may not have enjoyed the road: passengers must surely have been made to dismount at the foot of the 1-in-4 climb up Sutton Bank. In Helmsley the inns and pubs clustered about the square do good business with visitors to the gaunt castle, the nearby abbey of Rievaulx and its terraces, and of course with Roman Catholic parents visiting their offspring at Ampleforth college. The Black Swan has stood here for 400 years, its Tudor framework being added to in Georgian times and again in our own. From about the same era is the Crown, known for a while in the coaching years as Cooper's Posting House. Its best feature, among other attractions, is its Jacobean dining-room.

48 Ye Olde Bell at Barnby Moor, Nottinghamshire, is associated with two experts in horseflesh: Dick Turpin, and a landlord who for 40 years from 1800 combined innkeeping with breeding racehorses

The Holyhead Road

Although the modern A5 follows pretty closely the line of what may well be the most ancient highway in Britain, Watling Street, running from Dover through London and on to Chester, that highway's use had dwindled after Roman

times, and even in the coaching era was in a parlous state of disrepair. When the Act of Union of England and Ireland came into force on New Year's Day 1801, it became an urgent matter to ease the travel pains of Irish Members of Parliament between their country and Westminster. The great engineer Thomas Telford was appointed to the Holyhead Commission, surveyed the route in meticulous detail, and drew up plans which in the end were to cost the country £750,000: a large part of this resulted from negotiations and settlements with 23 different turnpike trusts along the way. The road took 20 years to complete; and at once brought increased trade to coaching houses along the route.

Splitting from the Great North Road at Hadley Green, the Holyhead Road headed for St Albans and the White Hart, or perhaps the Peahen, which has been there since the sixteenth century. At Dunstable only a 20-minute stop was allowed, during which the Sugar Loaf Inn offered:

A Boiled Round of Beef; a roast loin of Pork; a roast Aitchbone of Beef; and a boiled Hand of Pork with Peas Pudding and Parsnips; a roast Goose; and a Boiled Leg of Mutton.

Today the road through Wolverton is bordered by the vast sheds of British Rail's engineering works, appropriately faced across the way by the Royal Engineer pub.

All kinds of large and small communities hereabouts seem to have been swallowed up in the complex of Milton Keynes, and may soon lose their town and village names under references such as MK-this and MK-that. But Stony Stratford is still in reasonable trim. The A5 loops around most of it, to emerge in Old Stratford, but the traveller would be well advised to try the old road and the charms of the Cock and its proverbial rival, the Bull, both still sporting long wrought-iron signs, which with a bit of an effort might almost become gallows signs. During the Peninsular War such inflated rumours were bandied to and fro, within each hostelry and from one to the other, that the phrase 'a cock and bull story' was coined. Other old inns of the period, including the Rose and Crown, have unfortunately now disappeared behind superimposed house fronts.

At Towcester are the Pomfret Arms, mentioned by Dickens, and the Talbot, at which Dean Swift often stayed during progresses to and from Ireland. A chair still preserved here is said to have been his favourite. At Willoughby, the other side of Daventry, there once stood an inn called the Four Crosses, where Swift also stayed but not, apparently, with much pleasure. One night in 1730 he was so incensed by the landlord's wife that he scratched on a window-pane:

> There are three
> Crosses at your door,
> Hang up your Wife
> and you'll count Four.

Henry Tudor slept at the Three Tuns in Atherstone and received the sacrament in the church before defeating Richard III at Bosworth field and so becoming Henry VII. Outside the Olde Red Lion is a battered old milestone which has settled itself in mathematical harmony at a point said to be 100 miles from London, from Liverpool, and from Lincoln. Alas for its pretensions: modern calculations have shown it to be no such thing.

Avoiding Birmingham and Wolverhampton (and who wouldn't?) the A5 runs due east for many miles towards Shrewsbury. Although strictly speaking it may not fit into our category of English inns—though, after all, it does offer food, drink and accommodation—I confess to being tempted by Ainsworth's Radbrook Hall Hotel on the outskirts of the town, advertising itself as the former English home of the head of the Scottish clan McPherson. Do they offer venison, grouse and haggis on the menu when in season; and is there a wide selection of malt whiskies? I really must find out one day.

Within Shrewsbury proper are inns associated with historic names: the fifteenth-century building in Butcher Row which became the Prince Rupert as a result of the Civil War, during which Rupert made his headquarters in the town for a while when appointed President of Wales; and the Lord Hill, named after the Shropshire soldier who distinguished himself in the Peninsular War and at Waterloo, and succeeded Wellington as commander-in-chief in 1828. In Wyle Cop are the old Unicorn and a major coaching inn, the Lion. Hayward, a dashing coachman of the old flamboyant breed, used to show off by coming up the steep hill at a gallop, swinging his team round without a pause, and racketing through the stable-yard entrance of the Lion without ever making the slightest scratch on his paintwork.

Now the road has only a little way to go before it enters Wales . . . and this is a book about English inns, not Welsh inns.

Border country

North and south of Hadrian's Wall, away from the A1 racing implacably on its way into Scotland, any number of unusual inns can be found, some secretive and secluded, some filled with Geordie talk and some with echoes of ancient rivalries and conflicts on the old drove roads and invasion routes.

An interesting experiment has been carried out at Beamish, between Durham and Gateshead. It is intended eventually to re-create a complete Victorian and Edwardian north-eastern market town in this open air museum, with buildings re-assembled from various parts of the region. In the meantime there is a flourishing Victorian pub at Beamish Hall, the Bobby Shafto, open during licensing hours in the summer. Among its treasures are a symphonion, one of the coin-operated musical boxes which, sadly, opened the way to the juke-box of the modern pub.

Away from such industrial surroundings, yet the relic of even older industry, Blanchland nestles in the vale of the Derwent. The abbey founded here in 1165 provided the core of a model village built by Lord Crewe's trustees in the eighteenth century for lead miners in the locality: its gatehouse became the village post office, and the storehouse and abbot's lodging were converted into the Lord Crewe Arms. A vaulted chamber provides an excellent public bar, with little rooms opening off it, and there is a restaurant offering more ambitious fare than the monks ever dreamed of. This section of the building has memories of the first Jacobite rising, when Lord Crewe's nephew and niece by marriage backed the Stuart cause, and in one daring exploit the girl, Dorothy, managed to free her brother from Newgate and spirit him away into hiding here. It may be that he was concealed in the sixteenth-century priest's hole behind the fireplace in the former kitchen.

Hexham has long been one of my favourite northern towns, and the cheerfulness of its pubs and inns is characteristic, in spite of what Mary Russell Mitford wrote in 1806: 'We dined at a very wretched inn, for I must confess that Hexham is a shocking gloomy place.' In her day, the Royal would have been the Low Grey Bull, one of the coaching inns competing with the High Grey Bull, from which a flyer called the 'British Queen' left every morning for Newcastle. The fare was eight shillings, and the journey took four hours each way. Now the old stables are used as store-rooms. Another Bull, this one the Black Bull, once stood at one corner of the market-place, joined to a large assembly room. Judges of assize dined here when on their way through Hexham. Also on the market-place was the seventeenth-century White Horse, of which William Bell Scott, painter of the dramatic Northumbrian murals at Wallington, wrote:

This hostelry was scarcely ever disturbed by traveller, except on one day, the market-day of the week, yet the landlady, who had her cares, having lost everything sixteen years before, when her son was banished for forgery, cheerfully said the world had been very good to her; she had now something in the bank of her own again, her son was now a prosperous man, and she was looking for his return.

What a pity that it could not have been disturbed rather more frequently by travellers, rather than by the builder who pulled it down at the end of the last century and put up a row of shops in its place!

The Skinner's Arms in Gilesgate was lucky enough to be rebuilt around that time, and survives as a testimony to Hexham's great days as a centre of tanning and glove-making.

A winding road over splendidly stark countryside delivers us to Alston, the highest market town in England. Cobbled streets cling to angled slopes with houses pitched at alarming angles, looking as if they may at any moment start sliding and crashing together. No driver unsure of his brakes should ever venture up those steeps. Once there, however, he will be in no hurry to leave such a choice of inns and pubs. The number of these may be startling until one realizes that, in spite of its smallness, Alston is the warm centre of a bleak, far-flung highland community. Every bar fills up at regular intervals and for protracted periods with farmers and their extremely large dogs. And when I last sat in the bar of the Angel, built in 1611, I came across another breed: energetic types who love the town as the hub of fine, bracing walks. Such a pity that here, as in so many otherwise delectable settings, Radio 1 should be

blaring out full blast, hour after hour, day after day.

Through Melmerby, noted for the blast of its biting 'helm wind', we approach Penrith, where Dockwray Hall was reborn as the Gloucester Arms after Richard III had bestowed his custom on it. The premises in fact became his property as Duke of Gloucester, via his mother, and still display the coloured relief of his coat of arms, supported by two white boars.

From here we can dip down towards Kendal, where in the King's Arms, according to Celia Fiennes, 'one Mrs Rowlandson she does pott up the charr fish the best of any in the country'. At Troutbeck the Mortal Man, which has in fact lived since 1689, records quite a discussion on its signboard:

50 The Lord Crewe Arms, Blanchland, in Northumbria

O mortal man, that lives by bread,
What is it makes thy nose so red?
Thou silly fool, that looks't so pale,
'Tis drinking Sally Birkett's ale.

Here we are surrounded by National Trust properties, many acquired in the early years of the Trust's activities, and steadily added to since. One inn must be included in this worthy collection: the Tower Bank Arms in Near Sawrey, part of the local grouping associated with Beatrix Potter, who wrote of Peter Rabbit and other animal characters in the little seventeenth-century house of Hill Top.

Lake District farms and inns really began to blossom from the middle of the nineteenth century onwards, when William Wordsworth called on preservationists to 'share the passion of a just disdain' at the intrusion of the

51 The Swan at Grasmere, Cumbria, often visited by Sir Walter Scott when staying with Wordsworth

Kendal and Windermere Railway. Some farmers offered not merely holiday accommodation but makeshift inns, or ran little bars on the side to catch this new tourist trade. One man did not hesitate to use his daughter's misfortune as a lure for the curious: Mary Robinson of the Fish Inn at Buttermere, abducted by a man who turned out to be a forger and was executed at Carlisle in 1803, was for long afterwards featured in the local hotel guide:

FISH HOTEL, Buttermere
The Oldest-established Hotel in the Village, and formerly the residence of Mary Robinson, the celebrated beauty of Buttermere.

The rival Victoria Hotel was managed by cousins of the Fish Hotel's family in the 1880s, attracting fishermen and fell-walkers to what is now the Bridge Hotel.

At Bassenthwaite the Castle windows offer views of Skiddaw and its neighbours which might persuade the casual observer that he was in Switzerland; and those who have once patronized the Pheasant are unlikely ever to stray into the glossier tourist traps of the lakeside.

So to Carlisle, for centuries embattled on its strategic site close to the Solway Firth end of Hadrian's Wall. In the troublous times when the Young Pretender was marching towards it, the mayor was an absentee who lived out in the country and had no intention of returning, so that his functions were performed by the deputy mayor Thomas Pattinson—landlord of the Bush Inn, referred to unkindly by historians as 'a conceited windbag'. This publican was detested and frequently slandered by the powerful chancellor of the diocese, Dr Waugh, who was among those only too ready to surrender to Bonnie Prince Charlie and shared the Jacobite jibe about poor Pattinson:

O front of brass, and brain of ass,
with heart of hare compounded.

Carlisle surrendered to the first Jacobite demand for capitulation; but lived to regret this easy submission.

The Bush later gloried in the presence of the Carlisle Canal committee, which in March 1823 met to celebrate the opening of that long-delayed waterway, while beneath the inn windows a band played maritime melodies. After the formal ceremony, 14 bedizened vessels set out from Burgh-by-Sands up the canal towards Carlisle, also accompanied by brass bands and a cheering crowd. In the late afternoon the welcoming committee made its way back to the Bush to be regaled with 'an elegant and sumptuous dinner', during which 33 toasts were drunk. When the dinner was at an end, the revellers moved on to a ball at the Coffee House, now the Crown and Mitre.

This hotel today has divided its bars between the gimmicky young and the nostalgic—though the purist might say that even the nostalgia is gimmicky. It seems reasonably appropriate, however, in view of Carlisle's key position on one of the great railway lines, and the recent refurbishing of its castellated station, to devote the Railway Tavern to a display of railway prints and posters, and an impressive collection of plaques and mementoes from the Lancaster and Carlisle Railway, the North Eastern, and even the Stockton and Darlington.

Turning back eastwards along Hadrian's Wall, we find at Gilsland the Spa Hotel where Walter Scott became engaged to Margaret Carpenter; but nowadays you will stay there only if you are a convalescent miner. At Chollerford Bridge, where indeed a most graceful bridge spans the Tyne, the George is a pub which at some time expanded into a modern hotel with a beautiful paved garden along the north bank of the river. I am too fond of it to say too much about it, and thereby find it swamped next time I go.

At Ponteland is the Blackbird, produced by running a fourteenth-century defensive pele tower and a Jacobean manor house together. The initials of the house's seventeenth-century owner, Mark Errington, appear above the doorway of the gabled central section, with its mullioned windows. He incorporated the pele tower as added living space, and made its bare rooms more comfortable. The tower's ground floor has been given a new entrance and a mullioned window in keeping with the rest of the building, and a staircase leads to the first floor. As an inn it was much used by leading spokesmen for the Tory party on their electioneering travels, while their political opponents favoured the rival Green Man. Tempers ran so high that on one occasion the two licensees had to be bound over to keep the peace. There is a story that in 1771 the young wife of a much older general ran away with her husband's aide-de-camp, but was tracked down in a Blackbird bedroom, from which her lover had to escape without his breeches.

Alnwick is a grey, stony town with a warm heart. Its White Swan is close to the grounds of the castle, historic home of the Percy family. There are several likeable pubs in the town, but one threatening window is that of the Old Crosse Inn, labelled 'Dirty Bottles'. Inside its murky panes are some old bottles set there a century and a half ago by a man who at once collapsed and died. It is said that anyone daring to remove them will also drop dead at once; so there they are, untouched.

At Wooler is a coaching house which started life as an annexe for visitors to Chillingham castle when the lord of the manor had run out of spare bedrooms. This, the Tankerville Arms, is one of several now catering for fishermen and walkers in the Cheviot countryside.

Far north of Hadrian's Wall, and as far north as it is possible to get in England, stands Berwick upon Tweed, even more bitterly contested between Scots and English than Carlisle ever was. Here where the A1 enters Scotland is the King's Arms, a Georgian coaching inn with a walled garden and an interior décor owing much to reminiscences of days when the crack horse-drawn Highflyer between London and Edinburgh stopped here, before Stephenson built his Royal Border Bridge to carry longer trains of coaches flying even higher above the Tweed.

52 *Facing* The Old Dungeon Ghyll Hotel in Langdale, Cumbria

8

Great Roads West

Within this hour it will be dinner time:
Till that, I'll view the manners of the town,
Peruse the traders, gaze upon the buildings,
And then return, and sleep within mine inn.

William Shakespeare

One of the first convenient stops for travellers along the old road to Bath now vibrates not to the clatter of hoofs and wheels but to the constant thunder of Heathrow airport. The Green Man at Hatton seems in its dubious past to have catered not merely for such a respectable clientèle but also for those who preyed on them: the splayed base of the outside chimney stack provided a tolerably roomy hiding-place for 'gentlemen of the road', who in emergency could hastily disappear into it by pulling back the bar parlour fireplace. At some stage this was closed up and forgotten, until a reopening at the beginning of this century revealed the two old chairs within. These soon acquired the reputation of having belonged to our old friend Dick Turpin and Tom King, and the lane beside the inn became known as Turpin's Ride.

Only a few miles further on, a thirteenth-century landlord went one further than sheltering his guests' robbers: he robbed and killed them himself. The Ostrich at Colnbrook was originally a hospice of Abingdon abbey, its name for a time being the Ospridge, probably a corruption of 'hospice'. Foreign ambassadors and other dignitaries on their way to Windsor used it a great deal, and King John is said to have stopped here for refreshment on his way to Runnymede to put his seal reluctantly to Magna Carta. Fortunes must have declined by the time Jarman, the villainous innkeeper, began supplementing his income by murdering selected visitors. The bed in the main bedroom stood upon a hinged flap, directly above the inn's brewhouse. When the intended victim was well asleep, the flap would be released and the bed would swing over to drop him into the waiting cauldron of boiling water. It was later estimated that Jarman and his wife disposed of more than 50 unfortunates in this way.

Like many regular killers, they grew careless and too impatient. On three successive occasions they tried to manoeuvre a well-to-do clothier from Reading, Thomas Cole, into that particular bed, but each time were thwarted. On the fourth time that he stayed in the Ostrich on his way to London, all seemed to be going smoothly: Cole was in bed, the fire was burning nicely, the water was bubbling away. But Jarman felt uneasy. He tried to persuade his wife that they ought not to push their luck too far. Mrs Jarman, however, was a frugal lady and didn't fancy wasting the fuel and the boiling water. They went ahead; Cole was duly killed, and his body thrown into the nearby brook. It was quickly found, the inn was searched, and some of Cole's belongings were identified. The Jarmans were hanged.

Later the inn was burnt down. But, strange to say, landlords of an

Elizabethan rebuilding were able to show credulous guests the very room where the murder took place and the brewhouse below, into which victims were dumped. In more recent times a wooden working model was made to show exactly how the murderers operated, and displayed in the inn.

At Reading the oldest known inn is the Sun. A Norman archway in the yard, and a vault with a grim resemblance to a dungeon, suggest that the building stands on the site of the long-vanished castle. It, too, has its legend of death and retribution. Long ago one of its landlords had an attractive daughter whose

53 The Castle and Ball, Marlborough, Wiltshire

favours were struggled for by two young men, one a local lad and the other a soldier. The soldier won the maiden, but soon went off with his regiment, leaving her to drown herself. Her other admirer became a monk. A full ten years after her death the monk was in the yard of the Sun when he heard his rival's arrogant voice from within. A few minutes later the soldier came out, was attacked by the vengeful monk, and drew his dagger. The blade went in, but the monk had a grip of the soldier's throat and maintained it . . . until in his own death throes he succeeded in strangling the other.

The Bear at Hungerford was the venue for a meeting of James II's representatives with those of William III in the hope of doing a deal; but the mission failed.

In Marlborough the fashionable place to stop when on one's way to Bath was the Castle Inn. The actual castle from which it took its name was built under the prehistoric mound from which the town itself took its name—Maerl's Barrow, probably the site of an ancient hill-fort. Later the medieval castle was transformed into a mansion by Lord Seymour, who entertained Charles II here, and then passed through the hands of the Hertford family and the dukes of Northumberland until sold off in the middle of the eighteenth century to become 'an inn where the nobility and gentry may depend on the best accommodation and treatment'. One of the nobility to avail himself of this promised treatment was Pitt the elder, Lord Chatham, whose gout made him so intolerant of company other than his own entourage that he insisted on taking over the entire accommodation and on the entire staff of the inn being dressed in his livery.

When the railways came, one of the place's last landlords ended up as Richmond station-master. Abandoned, the inn was sold off to the founders of the public school now clustering around it. Today Marlborough no longer has a Castle Inn; but the old fortifications are remembered in the Castle and Ball, with a sixteenth-century interior and outside a bell which once announced the arrival of coaches and customers.

Near the cluster of prehistoric splendour between Avebury and Silbury, the road divides to offer alternative routes to Bath: one via Devizes and Melksham, one via Calne and Chippenham.

The Bear at Devizes, with its three-dimensional sign of a bear with a bunch of grapes in its mouth, has undergone quite a few transformations in its time. First licensed in 1599, it was later amalgamated with an adjoining building, became the town's head coaching inn, and has been much modernized in our own time, though without spoiling its eccentric frontage. An eighteenth-century landlord assured the public 'that no endeavour of his shall be wanting to accommodate and oblige them in a manner most becoming'. Certainly one owner was rather over-eager to oblige and entertain. This man, Lawrence, was the son of a Presbyterian minister, but the only indication he gave of religious interests was in running off with a vicar's daughter. He tried various jobs, went on the stage without success, and ultimately became a landlord, first in Bristol and then in Devizes, without achieving much in this line either. In 1780 Fanny Burney and Mrs Thrale stopped here on the third night of their journey from London to Bath. While playing cards in the evening they heard music from the Lawrence daughters in the next room, and chatted to them. The girls could talk of little else but their marvellous ten-year-old brother, unfortunately not at home at the time. They brought out various drawings which the boy had done. When he *was* at home, apparently his doting father insisted on introducing him to visitors and urging him to read poetry and generally put on an act. But then, it has to be admitted that the youthful genius did fulfil his promise: Thomas Lawrence became the most fashionable

54 One section of the double frontage of the Bear at Devizes, Wiltshire

portrait painter of his age, a Knight, and President of the Royal Academy.

In front of the Bear is the market cross, erected in memory of a woman who asked for trouble here in January 1753. She and two other women who had agreed to share the cost of a sack of grain were arguing over a shortage of threepence, when Ruth Pierce called on God to be her witness that if she had been the one to cheat she wished to drop dead on the spot. The Almighty obliged, and the missing threepence was found in her tightly clasped dead hand.

If we choose the Calne road rather than that through Devizes, we are merely emulating those arbiters of Bath's seasonal society who abandoned the old route when its alternative was improved in the eighteenth century. The Catherine Wheel at Calne replaced the Bear in their affections (or affectations), and speedily acquired some neighbouring houses to add to its

55 The Lansdowne Arms, Calne, Wiltshire, offers passers-by a free weather forecast

facilities. The division between the medieval building with its mullioned windows and these later additions can be clearly seen at the front. In the yard it had its own brewhouse, amiably advising the staff in a message on the wall to 'Welcome ye coming Speed ye parting Guest'; and on the premises still has a set of steps such as were rushed out to help passengers alight from their coaches, and a post boy's strapped leather bag. In the middle of the last century it changed its name to the Lansdowne Arms, its sign carrying the arms of the family whose country estate is just outside the town.

Another distinguished local family is to be found in Corsham, where a house known as Winter's Court became the Red Lion inn and then, around 1805, the Methuen Arms. The Nott family who owned it from the fifteenth to early eighteenth centuries have left their initials on the wall of the oldest wing; but the arms on the present sign are those of the Methuens of Corsham Court who were responsible for the Georgian frontage masking the earlier Tudor building with its brewhouse and skittle alley.

It seems almost too good to be true that this coaching road should here run past Upper Pickwick and Lower Pickwick.

Among the profusion of hotels in Bath, most try to associate themselves in some way with the lost splendours of the spa's Georgian hey-day, and many have the authentic lineaments. The Francis spreads nobly along a side of Queen Square between Royal Crescent and the abbey, but that very grandeur makes it hard to think of it as an inn. The Fernley is another Georgian building, but somewhat blurs its image by advertising among its amenities an 'entertainment pub' and a menu of Danish specialities, which would surely have surprised Beau Nash. Or would it? He, after all, did not come to Bath in search of austerity; and I have noticed that most spas to which health fanatics go to be purged and starved are well provided with the most tempting restaurants, bars, cake shops and confectioners, all intent on undoing what the masseurs and dieticians have striven to achieve.

On their way to Bath over Salisbury Plain, in bad humour because of the 'exorbitant reckoning' at the Salisbury inn they had left that day, Mr and Mrs Samuel Pepys lost their way, but

... by a happy mistake, and that looked like an adventure, we were carried out of our way to a town where we would lie, since we could not go as far as we would. By and by to bed, glad of this mistake, because it seems, had we gone on as we pretended, we could not have passed with our coach, and must have lain on the plain all night. . . . Up, finding our beds good, but lousy, which made us merry. We set out, the reckoning and servants coming to 9s.6d; my guide thither, 2s; coachman advanced, 10s. So rode a very good way, led to my great content by our landlord to Philips-Norton. . . .

In Norton St Philip stands the George, also patronized by Pepys. Built in the fifteenth century by Carthusian monks of the priory at Hinton, a couple of

56 The George, once a priory guest-house for traders at the August cloth fair and the weekly market in Norton St Philip, Somerset

miles away, it served partly as a hostel for pilgrims but more importantly as a market hall and store for wool traders: the local monastic orders, like those in Yorkshire, were deeply and profitably involved in the wool business.

Above the sturdy stonework of the ground floor, with its flight of steps up to one entrance, are two oversailing upper storeys, finely timbered and plastered in about 1500 when the market room and the rest of these upper floors had to be rebuilt after a bad fire. A section of outer gallery runs along one side of the courtyard, and there is an octagonal stair turret rather like that of a church tower.

In 1685 the Duke of Monmouth spent a night here after a preliminary skirmish which led on to defeat in the battle of Sedgemoor; and there was an attempt on his life which, if successful, might have prevented that battle ever taking place. All too soon afterwards the inn sheltered the infamous Judge Jeffreys.

The ultimate goal of pilgrims passing this way was Glastonbury, where from 1475 onwards lodgings were available in the stone-built George, also known at different stages of its career as The Pilgrims' Inn and The George and Pilgrims. Abbot Selwood of Glastonbury was personally responsible for its foundation, and may well have dictated its ecclesiastical appearance, with mullioned windows and tracery, and an entrance like a capacious church porch. From the start it was designed not for the indigent pilgrim but for those wealthy enough to pay well for their food and accommodation: rather than the abbey subsidizing the devout, the devout contributed to the abbey coffers. Those who stayed and paid here had the privilege of using a private underground passage direct from the George to the abbey itself. It is said that from one of the bedroom windows Henry VIII watched the abbey being ransacked and burnt at the time of the Dissolution.

To Exeter and beyond

As far as Hounslow the Exeter road out of London was the same as the Bath road, but then set off towards Basingstoke, Andover and Salisbury.

A few miles before plunging into the heart of Salisbury, the A30 passes the Pheasant at Winterslow, known in William Hazlitt's day as the Winterslow Hut. The long, happy periods which the critic and essayist spent here meant so much to him that his son, collecting a final batch of material written there, entitled the volume simply *Winterslow*, 'for it was there that most of his thinking was done'. Charles and Mary Lamb frequently visited him there, and it was at Winterslow that he penned his *Farewell to Essay-Writing*.

Near this spot Thomas Boulter, one of the most notorious highwaymen of the region, once held up the Exeter mail coach single-handed. In October 1816 a coach suffered a different sort of attack: just as it was arriving at the inn, the horses were set upon by a lioness which had escaped from a travelling menagerie. A dog joined in the fray but was killed by the beast, which then hid under a granary from which it had to be coaxed out by its keepers.

This next sentence ought really to start with a phrase of which I am growing weary: with the coming of the railways, an inevitable decline . . . and so on. But again it is true. Towards the end of the last century and on into our own, the place lingered on as a run-down ale-house with a labourer's cottage tacked on. Now the traffic is back on that road with a vengeance, and the inn is almost too smart and brash. Hazlitt's son wrote of the Hut in its valley,

. . . equidistant about a mile from two tolerably high hills, at the summit of which, on their approach either way, the guards used to blow forth their admonition to the hostler. The sound, coming through the clear, pure air, was another agreeable feature in the day. . . .

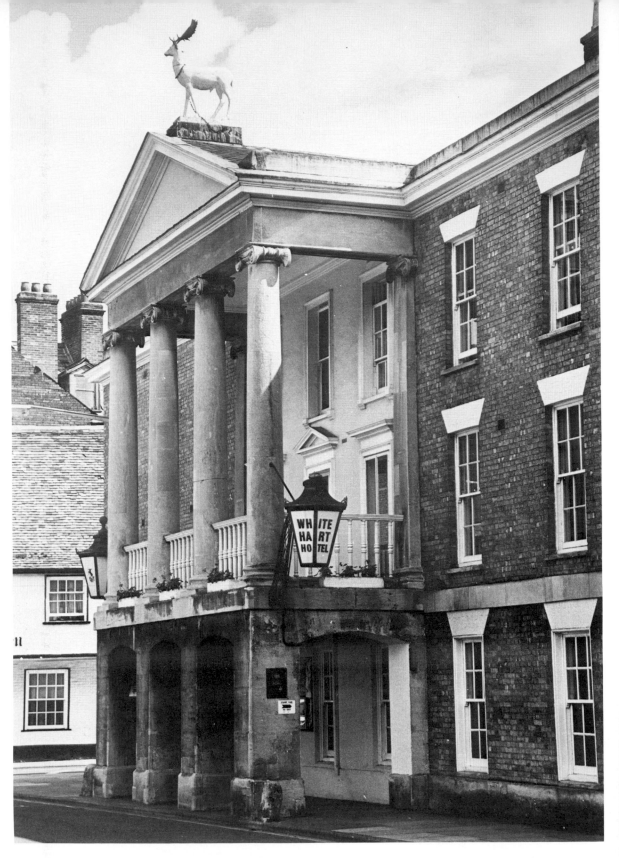

The only admonitions from horns today are likely to be those sounded by impatient drivers stuck in one of the dreadful A30 blockages during the summer holiday season.

There is another Pheasant in Salisbury which has also undergone some changes of name and fortune. The building dates from the fourteenth century, and some 300 years later is recorded as being the property of a schoolmaster who left it in his will to the Guild of Shoemakers and Cordwainers. A hall was built into it as the guild's meeting-place, and continued to serve as this even after the entire premises had been sold off in 1772 to a brewer and maltster, when it was called the Crispin Inn. By the early part of the next century it had become the Rainbow; now, as the Pheasant, it still maintains the tradition of guild meetings in the hall.

The fourteenth-century Red Lion used to be the terminus for the steel-sprung 'Salisbury Flying Machine'; and every night at ten o'clock there was a service leaving for London. The Old Plume of Feathers in Queen Street has a narrow courtyard overshadowed by the tilting upper storeys of tile and plaster, with clearly identifiable galleries now enclosed. Near the Poultry Cross, the Haunch of Venison is another bewitching tangle of stairs, steps and woodwork.

The most imposing entrance is the portico of the White Hart, carrying a statue of the creature made deliberately larger than life in 1827 in order to outshine the new sign of the Antelope, then a neighbouring rival. The older building replaced in the 1800s had entertained a variety of famous guests, including Henry VII and, in 1780, Henry Laurens, who fell into the hands of

58 *Facing* The theatrical portico of the White Hart, Salisbury, Wiltshire

59 The yard of the George at Hatherleigh, Devon

the Royal Navy while on his way to Holland to raise a loan of ten million dollars for the rebellious American Congress. Under naval escort, Laurens lodged here a night before being taken on to imprisonment in the Tower of London. Sir Walter Raleigh may not actually have stayed on the premises, but in 1618 he certainly made use of the White Hart's catering. In disgrace and afraid to face James I, who was staying in Salisbury, Raleigh pretended to be laid up with sickness in his lodging, but sent his French attendant surreptitiously to the inn to buy a leg of mutton and some bread, which he ate in secret so that his other attendants might put it about that he was too ill to take the tiniest morsel.

Shaftesbury's great coaching inn was the Grosvenor, which still has its spacious yard paved with setts, and in the dining-room a wealth of mirrors and a huge sideboard with an intricate carving of the battle of Chevy Chase.

In Exeter the Great Western Hotel makes the most of its proximity to the old G.W.R. station of St David's, featuring a Loco Bar decorated, rather like the Crown and Mitre in Carlisle, with prints and drawings of the age of steam. A little way down the estuary is another relic of that age: the Steam Packet, by the quays at Topsham; and there is an inn of the same name at Totnes. Lovers of real beer will enjoy the thirteenth-century Kingsbridge in Totnes. Near Newton Abbot there is, at Ringmore, a Journey's End, so called because R. C. Sherriff wrote part of his play while staying here.

All around the moors are squat little pubs in villages cosily huddled against wind and drifting mist, with the occasional flourish of larger places such as Tavistock. One of the most inviting establishments is the unusually imposing George at Hatherleigh. A monks' retreat in 1450, it later became an inn and in due course catered for the coaching traffic. Under its archway can still be found the stone tracks through the cobbles to smooth the passage of the coach wheels. Indoors it has unspoilt fireplaces and dark beams; and outside, at the back, once had its own brewhouse.

Cotswolds and Severnside

Nearly every guidebook will praise Broadway as the most beautiful, or most picturesque, or most famous village in the Cotswolds. Certainly its long, wide street or Broad Way is flanked by some of the most attractive and varied examples of local architecture in local limestone, in their present form largely the work of idealistic restorers at the beginning of this century. They look at their best on a bright winter's day, when there is a chance of studying the golden stonework uninterrupted by the shimmering blues and greens and puce of parked Jaguars and Aston Martins.

Dominating the street is the inn which was known in the sixteenth century as the White Hart, this reference first appearing in parish records of 1532, though in one of the bedrooms is a fireplace which seems to be of fourteenth-century craftsmanship. In 1815 General Lygon, who had been created a baron in 1806, became Earl Beauchamp and bought the estate on which the inn stood. He entrusted its running to his butler, who loyally changed the name to the Lygon Arms. The present inn sign incorporates these arms, two lions passant.

Victorian vandalism threatened the inn's character when mullioned windows were supplanted by unimaginative wooden frames, but since the Russell family took the place over in 1904 both restorations and extensions have been carried out with more care. The tariff makes it clear that this is no hostelry for the poor and needy wayfarer, and perhaps there is a certain archness about its advertising of a four-poster bed made in the year the *Mayflower* sailed, its pseudo-baronial great hall, and its Charles I and Cromwell

60 The Black Bear,
Tewkesbury, Gloucestershire

rooms. But since there is every reason to suppose the claims are genuine, why be churlish? The rooms are all luxurious, the gardens at the back could not be bettered, and there are days when the sun seems to radiate from the stones rather than shine down upon them—roof tiles like deep golden flakes, stone in the bar itself, and wistaria just waiting for colour photographers to queue up and take their pictures.

The drive over the hill from here to Chipping Campden is one of the loveliest in the region, and what waits at the other end is no disappointment. I confess I feel more at home in the Lygon Arms at Chipping Campden than in its more ambitious namesake. It is cramped in between other buildings but creates an atmosphere of expansiveness rather than constriction. A yard of cobbles, setts and chippings stretches out behind the inn, lined by old outhouses, and both inside and out there seems a never-ending, cheerful bustle. The bar is invariably full of locals, good chat and good fellowship. I will refrain from praising its lunches of Gloucestershire sausages too highly in case they are all gone next time I get there.

This is not by any means the oldest of the town's inns. That honour belongs to the Noel Arms, taking its name from the lords of the manor in the seventeenth century but known to have existed as a private dwelling for some 300 years before then. For a while it traded as the George. In the courtyard can still be seen the steps up which coachmen went to their quarters after attending to their horses.

Another veteran in the same county is the Black Bear at Tewkesbury, not just the oldest hostelry in the town but the oldest in Gloucestershire. There have been claims that it goes back 800 years, and there seems reason to believe that at any rate some kind of building stood at this entrance to the town, by King John's Bridge, in 1190. The basis of the present one, however, dates from 1308. Soon after that the manor passed into the hands of the Beauchamp earls of Warwick, whose crest was the Bear and Ragged Staff. The actual inn sign of the Black Bear derives from a fifteenth-century heraldic tile, thought to have been the work of Malvern monks, in the south transept of Tewkesbury abbey. The oldest, darkly timbered bar was originally a stable built in 1422, when the daily tariff was three horses a penny. Most of the rest of the timbering belongs to the sixteenth century.

A few miles south, where Haw Bridge crosses the Severn, stand the New Inn on one side of the road and the Haw Bridge Inn on the other, festooned with dusty guns and farm implements. A toll bridge built here between 1823 and 1825 was destroyed in December 1958 by a 200-ton vessel carried along the river in flood. The Royal Monmouthshire R.E. militia, the oldest regiment in the Territorial Army, constructed a Bailey bridge as part of their summer training; and both inns doubtless prospered from their presence. The present permanent bridge was begun in September 1959.

In 1938 this was the scene of a murder unsolved to this day. Fishermen in the river netted a male torso devoid of head, arms or legs, and further dredging produced two legs and two handless arms. Blood had already been noticed on the bridge, but a pathologist who examined it had declared it to be dog's blood. Now it was established as being human blood. Had someone hacked an enemy to death on that very spot, within such a short distance of the two inns; or had the pieces been brought here and tipped, still freshly bleeding, over the bridge? It is not hard to imagine the gossip and speculation in the public and saloon bars, or the dark mutterings about unsavoury local characters and suspicious visitors.

Bernard Spilsbury, most famous of Home Office pathologists, was brought into the picture. It was he who declared that the blood on the bridge was human, and that the arms, legs and trunk were those of the same person. In every detail they were found to correspond with the measurements and age of a Captain Butt who had disappeared from Cheltenham a month earlier. Some marks on the body led Spilsbury to conclude that the victim had been run down by a motor-car. But who had chopped him up into pieces?

It then came out that ten days after Butt's disappearance a friend of his called Sullivan had committed suicide; and under the floor of Sullivan's home was found the captain's overcoat. But the hands and head were never found, and it was impossible for the coroner's jury to return a verdict other than one declaring insufficient evidence as to identity or cause of death.

The Haw Bridge Inn seems, anyway, to have been quite a meeting-place for quarrelsome, dissatisfied folk. It retains a broadsheet published by the Grand Cock Club, founded 1 January 1821 to combat the pernicious influence of wives who disapproved of their husbands drinking and staying too long away from the fireside. Among its resolutions were:

That seeing the numerous evil consequences which take place by allowing Petticoat Government, we deem it a duty incumbent upon us to exert all our abilities in order to bring our wives to a just sense of their duty, and to check those principles that have brought so many poor men to a state of degrading starvation. And for that end we appoint the First Monday in every Month, at twelve o'clock at noon, in order that we may have time to drink our glass, smoke our pipe, and sing a good song; and that our Meeting may be as comfortable and undisturbed as possible, that if any Member allows his Wife to send any messenger or come herself, enquiring after her husband, for the first offence he shall be fined 10s 6d and for a second offence he shall be entirely excluded.

Stern injunctions were issued against the degradation of sweeping floors, rocking the cradle, and cleaning or blacking shoes—which deplorable practices could result in a club member being forever excluded.

What these henpecked, struggling male chauvinist sheep would have made of the invention of the telephone, heaven only knows. I do know a few landlords who attempt to profit from customers whose wives ring them up at the pub by displaying a tariff for evasive answers:

Not been in yet	20p
He's just this minute left	50p
Haven't seen him all week	£1
Who?	£2

I recall the wife of an elderly friend putting her head round the door of our local inn one morning and saying, 'Has Bill been in?' The landlord truthfully replied that Bill had left a mere two minutes ago. The lady having departed, Bill in due course reappeared, on his second lunchtime circuit of the neighbouring hostelries. When told by the landlord of the news which had been politely imparted to his wife, Bill went pale. 'But you shouldn't have told her that: I wasn't supposed to have been here yet.'

Near Westbury on Severn is an amiable pub with some melancholy echoes. It calls itself the Grange Court Junction: the signboard carries a picture of a steam train standing at a platform, and an actual station sign is propped up at the back of the inn yard. But where is the station, where the junction? Sadly they no longer exist. The nearby line to South Wales was the first to be converted by the old G.W.R. from Brunel's original wide gauge to standard gauge. The main line to Cardiff still runs under the bridge a few yards away; but the old one from Hereford, which formed the junction here, is gone. A couple of large sheds remind one of a fruit market which once flourished by its own sidings. Faded lettering on one of the inn's outer walls reads: The Old Junction Fruit Market. No clock or barometer was needed in the bar in those days. Trains then ran to time, and 'When you could hear the South Wales train it was going to rain, and when you could hear the Hereford train it'd be dry.'

At Newnham there were three successive churches: the first fell down, the second caught fire. Inns, too, came and went. Lots of Severnside houses were once converted into inns and taverns to supply the needs of workers in the coaling trade and the traffic to and from Gloucester docks, but as business declined so they went back to being private houses again. Some are still identifiable from their doors, windows and out-buildings.

The White Hart is one of the commonest names for an inn. The Red Hart is among the rarest. There is one at Blaisdon, and another in the village of Awre, both of them perhaps called after the red deer of the Forest of Dean. In the heart of the dark, sinister forest itself, the Speech House hotel looks incongruously smart. It makes many visitors welcome, but lays down the law to others: the Verderers' Court still meets here to administer forest laws, many of which were framed to settle bitter disputes between iron-founders and foresters. Four representatives are elected for life, and when in session sit on a shallow dais at one end of the combined dining-room and court-room. Immediately opposite the Speech House is a column marking the centre of the Forest of Dean, replaced in 1957 to mark Lord Bledisloe's ninetieth birthday and his fiftieth year as a verderer.

High up near May Hill is the Glasshouse, a cosy little pub recalling other craftsmen who were none too popular in their time. There was once a small colony of Flemish glassworkers hereabouts, using local timber for their ovens and thereby arousing the ire both of the ironworkers, who also needed timber, and the traditionalists who wanted to keep the forest as it was. They moved down to Westbury, but were driven away from there also and finally settled in Bristol, where they developed the characteristic Bristol blue glass. A specimen of their pots stands by the bar fireplace of the Glasshouse, and on the lawn are an old cider press and crushing wheel.

The Marches

After Edward II's murder in Berkeley castle there were few volunteers to take charge of the royal corpse and offer it decent burial. Only the Abbot of Gloucester was courageous enough to risk the displeasure of the Mortimer faction and inter the dead king in the abbey church which later became Gloucester cathedral. A less likely saint it is hard to imagine, but soon there was talk of miracles at the tomb, and during attempts to win the support of Rome a petition was made by Richard II—himself to die ignominiously—for Edward's canonization, backed by an assurance of Papal priority in the matter of benefices. Inevitably, where there were pilgrims there had to be guesthouses and inns. The Fleece in Gloucester still has fourteenth-century vaulted cellars known as the Monks' Retreat, though these have now been converted into a noisy Bierkeller; and proportions of the rest of the building are hard to assess because of its enclosure within a group of shops, approached from front or rear through narrow entries into a yard roofed with corrugated plastic.

The New Inn, largely fifteenth-century in construction but probably standing on the site of an earlier hospice, was said at one time to have been joined to the abbey by an underground passage. Its basic shape, around a galleried quadrangle, has survived, with its stairs and steps and fine gables, and toppling oversailing down a side alley so pinched that there once had to be mirrors angled to reflect daylight into the rooms. That enclosed yard made an even better open theatre than the George yard in Southwark for the presentation of drama by strolling players. Today it has become a Berni Inn, with table parasols and illuminated red and gilt signs to add to the trailing creeper over black and white timber and plaster. Its crest, added within recent years, sports ten cannon-balls—which, with three barrels of powder, were all that remained when the Royalist siege of Gloucester in 1643 was at last lifted by Parliamentary forces under the Earl of Essex.

The Golden Cross, brightly patterned with timber and plaster outside and weightily timbered within, offers an awe-inspiring range of real ales and an excellent buffet. Adjoining it at the rear is a modern addition once called the Dirty Duck but now the Malt-'n-Hops, with more real ale and savoury snacks. The usual inescapable canned discord comes reeling out, but the friendly atmosphere and attractive layout win one's affection in the end, more like a Continental café than an English bar.

From Gloucester I once had to make a business trip at short notice to Liverpool, and instead of taking the motorway decided on the older road which got me there in good time and in mellow mood. Its only disadvantages are the signposts tempting one to either side to visit Knighton, Clungunford, Clunbury and Clun, Wem, Wenlock Edge to the east and the Long Mynd to the west; and then, approaching Shrewsbury, there's the Wrekin humped up against the skyline. As to the inns . . . well, are you in *that* much of a hurry to get to Liverpool?

61 Galleried yard of the New Inn, Gloucester

At Ledbury there is a piquant contrast betweent the diagonal timbers of the famous market hall and the boxed chequerwork of the Feathers. This sixteenth-century inn came into existence from the amalgamation of two houses, to which a top storey was later added. As a posting house on the Royal Mail route linking Hereford, Cheltenham and Aberystwyth it did well for itself, and the lantern with red glass projecting over the pavement remains from those days. Its sign and a relief on the woodwork display the Prince of Wales's feathers, which can also be found on the Prince of Wales in a cobbled alley towards that church lauded by John Masefield, who was born in Ledbury, for its 'golden vane surveying half the shire'. In another side street, the Talbot claims that gashes in its timbers are sword marks resulting from a skirmish between Roundheads and Cavaliers.

The most imposing establishment in Hereford is the Green Dragon, a

62 For 200 years the Feathers at Ledbury, Herefordshire, reserved a pew in the church for the benefit of its residents and guests

coaching inn with a long Georgian façade, a minute's walk from the cathedral. But when I think of Hereford I have a pleasurably perverse memory of the cheerful, unpretentious, bustling little Saracen's Head across the river, right beside the old bridge, with a sociable cluster of tables and chairs on the path below its tiny but florid wrought-iron balcony, commanding a view of the cathedral rising above trees and tangled roofs on the other bank.

In Leominster, complacent in a vale of hop-yards and cider-makers' orchards, is the Talbot, here since 1470. And in Ludlow, we once more encounter the Feathers, again half-timbered, but with unusually ornate gables, carved door-posts, carved gallery, and intricately lozenged windows. Decorations within are just as extravagant: the dining-room ceiling is so heavily moulded that one expects to find chunks of it in the soup at any moment, the grape-vine curlicues threaten to throttle the passer-by, and the oak mantel-pieces seem capable of withstanding the end of the world. In 1609 it was still a private house, but became an inn just about the time when James I's son Henry, Prince of Wales died; and so took the Feathers as its emblem. It might well have done the same if Henry had lived—which would have robbed many an inn of many a legend concerning James's second son and successor, Charles I.

The A49 goes seductively on through Craven Arms (where all but the most hardly pressed traveller will stop to contemplate Stokesay Castle) and Church Stretton into Leebotwood, whose village pub has a thatched roof thought to have topped it since the fifteenth century. The Jacobean panelling in the dining-room was brought here from the rectory of neighbouring Woolstaston. During the eighteenth century the local court was held in the bar, and malefactors were put into the stocks by the village pond. Whether this gave the inn its name of the Pound, or whether there was a cattle or sheep pound in the vicinity, I have been unable to discover.

On through Shrewsbury, which we visited on our way across country on the Holyhead highway, we come upon Whitchurch, Edward German's birth-place, now by-passed. Even before the main road was swung away from its main street, the White Bear must have been inconspicuous, tucked away between sheltering houses and shops. Higher up is its cousin the Black Bear, with ornate timbering in the style characteristic of north Shropshire and Cheshire.

The discerning traveller may well decide to turn west towards Chester and the timbered Falcon or Bear and Billet; or the unpretentious little sixteenth-century Olde King's Head; or the Blossoms, of which I have some happy memories not for public consumption. I wonder, but do not intend to pursue my curiosity, about another establishment which advertises 'live folklore twice a week': whatever happens to folklore the other five days of the week?

But on the trip I mentioned a few paragraphs back, I was not allowed to start out in any discerning mood. Liverpool was my goal, and I had had in advance to make a snap choice of where I should stay when I got there. In the event it proved one of the luckiest decisions I have ever made when on my travels. Finding that there was an establishment right above Birkenhead Woodside ferry stage, and realizing that I could most agreeably travel to and from Liverpool on one of the two last remaining Mersey ferry-boats, I plumped for this small hotel, the Woodside. Birkenhead is not one of the most beautiful towns in England; the waterfront is dominated by rusting, declining shipyards; and the view of the Liverpool docks is a pretty depressing one. Yet the Woodside, in such unprepossessing surroundings, turned out to be everything that, in my view, a true English inn ought to be: unpretentious but clean, friendly, with a noisy bar for some locals and a quieter one for others, unfussy and inexpensive food, a welcoming matiness at the reception desk, neat and quiet bedrooms, and that indefinable quality which makes the visitor feel instantly at home.

The Woodside will never be on any tourist's recommended route, and will probably never get top billing in a good food guide. It will unobtrusively continue to cater for the people it knows best and who know it best. There must be others like it, in unexpected places. I am delighted to have found this one; have been back to make sure I wasn't wrong; and will be there yet again whenever I have to visit that part of the world.

9

Anchorages

For now they thought, as travellers do,
Of nought but roasted, boiled, or stew,
And beds well warm'd and comforts rare,
Which may tir'd nature's frame repair.

William Combe:
THE TOURS OF DR SYNTAX

Atkinson Grimshaw's painting of *Liverpool by Moonlight* in the Tate Gallery gives a romantic tinge to the wet, greasy setts, the ships' masts in the haze, and the reflected glow of the street corner public house. But the taverns of Liverpool throughout the nineteenth century, especially those along the quays, were not the sort of leisured, cosy places you might find in the countryside. The barbarities of the slave trade were ended, to the discomfit of Merseyside profiteers, but there were other wretches to be exploited: Irish and European emigrants, bewildered and in poverty, passing through the port on their way to a new life in America. As soon as they arrived there were runners ready to pounce on them and hustle them along to some dubious lodging-house, where they would be fleeced of whatever small savings they had managed to bring along with them. In 1848 there were 15 provision shops and 16 public houses or spirit vaults in one stretch of road past the berths of the American packets. The lodging-house keepers not merely overcharged emigrants for accommodation but sold them food at absurdly inflated prices and in many cases ran their own pubs as a sideline, encouraging the waiting voyagers to spend their time in there, as well as welcoming sailors off the Transatlantic ships. The well-appointed, sociable inn was almost unknown in such localities.

Only a short distance uphill, away from the docks, the rich Liverpool merchants had their clubs and plusher drinking-places. Visiting merchants from Manchester and other cities found accommodation in the coaching inns of Dale Street, the Fleece being the most highly regarded until history was made, and past history abandoned, with the inauguration and after-effects of the Liverpool and Manchester Railway. Today there are only a few seedy fragments to be found, and most of the old hostelries have been overlaid by modern rebuilding.

A short walk up behind the Goree, on which once stood the great warehouses and slave cellars, is a rare survivor: the Slaughter House, founded during the reign of George III. Steep steps up from the pavement lead into a bar with a long counter, more like one of the older London wine houses than a pub. There are intimate little side rooms, ledges to lean on and put glasses on, tables to sit at and dark woodwork to lean against. Businessmen and office girls form their own groups around corner tables, and many an office party or protest meeting has been held in an alcove labelled 'The Scouse 'ole'.

Connoisseurs of Victorian extravagance will find plenty to delight them in Liverpool, but few bars to match the Vines in Lime Street with its great expanses of floridly patterned glass, matched by the burgeoning ceiling

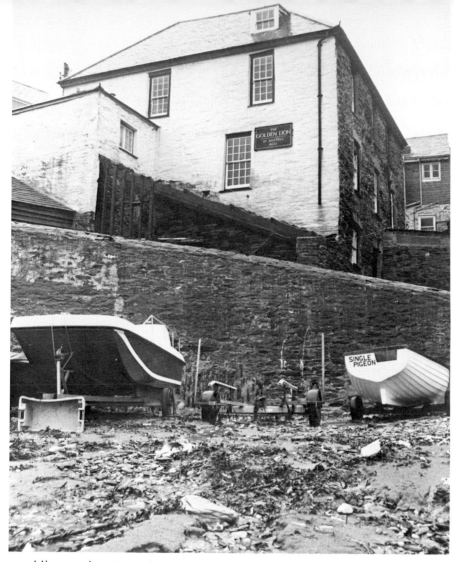

63 The Golden Lion at Port Isaac on the north Devon coast, which once had a tunnel connecting its cellar to a smugglers' cave

mouldings and patterned paper.

The showpiece of them all, though, is the Philharmonic, across the road from the Philharmonic Hall and, not surprisingly, much frequented before and after concerts or rehearsals by members of the Royal Liverpool Philharmonic Orchestra. On entering, one half expects to find a guide ready to begin a conducted tour of the building from the central bar, so much resembling a Victorian baronial hall. Room opens out of room, on and on forever it seems, in this massive eating and drinking palace. Heavy panelling is decorated with copper inlays and wooden curlicues, supporting moulded ceilings. There are silvered glass and stained glass, including a window to St Cecilia with the motto, 'Music is the universal language of mankind'. This noble precept tends to be forgotten in Liverpool when the drums and fifes of an Orangemen's procession move provocatively into earshot of a Catholic area.

Even the lavatories at the Philharmonic are palatial, with marble basins, coloured tiles, and mosaic floors and wall panels.

In 1909 Frederick Hackwood wrote about a place I should love to visit, but identified it only as 'a small inn in the neighbourhood of Liverpool', which makes it difficult to track down—even if it is still there, which is doubtful. This inn, noted for the quality of its home-brewed beer, was called the Gray Ass. Its landlord had never been happy with such a name, and after the battle of Waterloo took the opportunity of changing it to the Duke of Wellington, complete with ducal portrait on the signboard. A shrewd rival at once set up in opposition, hanging out the sign of the Gray Ass. The locals, obviously a conservatively minded lot, remained loyal to the name they knew rather than to the building, so that the publican-brewer lost nearly all his custom. In an effort to regain it he added a panel below Wellington's picture, with large letters proclaiming 'This is the Original Gray Ass'.

Seafarers and landlubbers

As a maritime nation it is natural that we should have so many inn signs relating to ships and the sea: the Ship, the Jolly Sailors, the Mariners Arms, the Mermaid, and of course the Neptune, quite apart from testimonials to great admirals such as Nelson and Collingwood. The Anchor puts in frequent appearances, linked in nautical legend with the Dolphin. From time immemorial it has been believed that the dolphin had the gift of predicting storms, and also that if it found a ship insecurely anchored it would wrap itself around the anchor to keep it steady. Brass castings of a dolphin standing on its head are to be found in admirals' barges and other craft; and it is incorporated in the arms of the Watermen's Company. The Dolphin at Southampton was the far end of the mail-coach run from the Swan with Two Necks in London, and stabled Queen Victoria's horses whenever she passed through here on her way to the isle of Wight and her beloved Osborne House.

Sennen, close to Land's End, claims that it has the westernmost church in England and also, according to its sign, the First Inn in England as well as the Old Success Inn. The Scilly Isles, much further to the west and well supplied with local and tourist taverns, might well contest any 'first in England' boast.

Whether one chooses the north or south coasts of Cornwall and Devon, the inns and taverns will show sinews and flesh—hard or soft—more distinctive than those in regions which have lost their identity under too banal a coating of stockbroker Tudor, modern brick, and plastic accoutrements. Cornish inns, like the county's indigenous cottages, shine with granite which is speckled brown in one light, hoar-frost in another, topped with slates which can look moist even on the driest of days. Devon buildings hitch themselves up higher from the ground, a mixture of red rubble and whitewashed cob, wearing voluminous thatch like crumpled broad-brimmed hats. As we cross the Dorset border the thatch continues, but the walls rise from the limestone which, beginning at Portland, divides into a north-easterly swathe through the Cotswolds and Northamptonshire in gentle shadings of different hues and textures until it reaches the Lincolnshire Wolds, and another running parallel with the coast as the South Downs. The most truly homely inns, like the mellowest homesteads, are fashioned from their own earth without need of alien, imported ingredients.

Too many of the coastal villages, for centuries the home of hardy fishermen and the descendants of explorers and privateer crews, are overrun in summer, their streets too narrow for modern traffic and modern crowds, but congested with them just the same. The best time to get the true flavour is to go in winter, and prove yourself as hardy as the inhabitants. Port Isaac is a little slate-hung village of only a thousand or so people, but its population swells when the sun shines on the pebbly strand. The Golden Lion looks much more comfortably itself when the gales are beating in across the Atlantic and the locals are huddled into the bar for warmth and local gossip. At Clovelly the Lion immediately above the pebbles, with boats drawn right up under its windows, is a Red Lion; and the New Inn, far from new and all the better for that,

provides a welcome staging post for those puffing up the steep, cobbled street from which motor traffic is wisely banned.

At Bideford we are in the world of the great Elizabethan captains and adventurers. It was from here that Sir Richard Grenville set out on his last voyage, and in the Old Ship here that the Brotherhood of the Rose was founded, as recorded by Charles Kingsley. Kingsley's *Westward Ho!* was such a success that a new seaside resort further up the coast took its name as a tourist lure. A great many inns in this region boast of having been patronized by Drake, Hawkins, Grenville and even Grenville's cousin, Sir Walter Raleigh; and they may well have been hearty drinkers in addition to being hearty fighters.

There was once a Ship in Dunster, a village abandoned by the sea but still providing a landmark for shipping with its Conygar Hill tower. In the Middle Ages the abbots of Cleeve, three miles away, had a town residence in Dunster but lost it, along with many other possessions, at the Dissolution. After extensive reconstruction it became an inn, though its impressive projecting porch looks more like a church entrance, even to the chamber over the doorway with its latticed windows; and a high window over the courtyard adds to the impression. Inside there are seventeenth-century additions, including some fine plasterwork, to original Tudor features. In 1779 its name of The Ship was changed to The Luttrell Arms in deference to the manorial family. Just across the street is the yarn market or yarn cross restored by the Luttrells in 1647, serving as a meeting-place for yarn merchants and the local craftsmen and craftswomen—just as the bars of the inns doubtless did, also.

Starting out along the south coast, our first port of call has to be Penzance. Here at the sign of the Dolphin in 1588 Sir John Hawkins set out recruiting seamen to defend England against the threatening Spanish Armada. Here, too, many a vessel from the Americas found its haven and disembarked its men, booty and goods. Tobacco may have been smoked in the Dolphin for the first time in England, and the first imported potatoes were sampled here. The dining-room was used as a makeshift court-room by Judge Jeffreys, prisoners being temporarily housed in the cellars. Quite obviously such a place, which has seen and heard so many things, must also have a ghost. The Dolphin's is, appropriately enough, a grizzled old seafarer who years ago was frequently seen pacing about the place with a three-cornered hat on his head. More recently he has grown shy of showing himself, but from time to time can still be heard walking from the front to the back of the building right above the bar, without ever being known to retrace his steps.

The Old Jolly Sailor at Looe claims to date from the fifteenth century, but nothing without or within seems earlier than the sixteenth. Its differently pitched sections of slated roof present a most attractive appearance at the front, slanting out over first-floor windows or dipping in sharper cat-slides between them, as if separating three gable ends or as if three narrow cottages with passages between had been brought under one many-angled roof.

At Salcombe the Ferry Inn was once the western end of a ferry service plying between here and East Portlemouth on the other side of Kingsbridge estuary. At Stoke Gabriel, near Brixham, the building called Church House is in fact no longer church property but an inn, retaining an outside flight of steps up to a first-floor room where parish meetings were held. Behind the premises a cobbled path leads to the church itself, but there may once have been another, more secretive, means of access: one of Stoke Gabriel's vicars was rumoured to be leader of a smuggling gang, and a tunnel leading from the 600-year-old cellars could have led to the church or the creek, or both.

The Ship at Exeter can turn up its nose at lesser establishments with their dubious assertions of great men's patronage. It is mentioned by name, and most favourably mentioned, in one of Drake's letters; and among its regulars were known to be Grenville, Hawkins, Sir Humphrey Gilbert and Sir Walter Raleigh. Quite a family booze-up, for the Raleighs, Grenvilles and Gilberts were all related.

Buckler's Hard in Hampshire, where the Beaulieu river begins widening towards the Solent, was a centre for constructing the wooden walls of England.

New Forest oak went into many a great ship, including Nelson's favourite *Agamemnon*, whose builder was Henry Adams. Adams lived in what has become the Master Builder's House Hotel, overlooking the wide street where timber was stacked and weathered. In 1963 Earl Mountbatten opened a small but

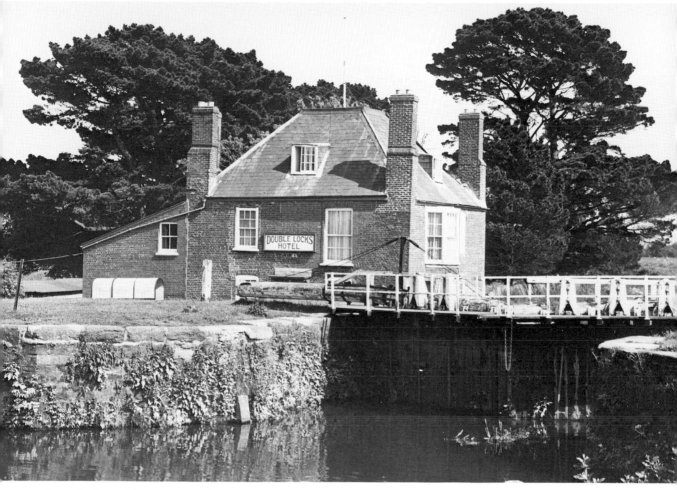

well-stocked maritime museum here.

In this coastline of ragged inlets and moorings are many picturesque and sometimes over-picturesque inns. The sailing fraternity take their pick from dozens around Chichester Harbour and along the Solent; and in the Bosham and Chichester region I have happy memories of the inn at Dell Quay and its lavish fish dishes at the bar.

Although it was the railways which did most to bring holidaymakers to the Channel coast and so build tourist resorts out of fishing villages and hamlets, one or two places had earlier attracted traffic from London. George III's daughter Charlotte was presuaded to favour Bognor with her presence. His son George, Prince of Wales, discovered Brighton and, by his own building schemes and by his influence on others, transformed the little community. By the early nineteenth century there were some 30 daily coach services between London and Brighton. An advertisement from an August 1806 issue of the *Sussex Weekly Advertiser* gives details of one of the regular conveyances:

Sets out from the Nelson Hotel, Worthing, and the Star and Garter, Brighton, Monday, Wednesday and Friday mornings at seven o'clock, arrives at the Swan and Crown Inns, Horsham at ten; at the White Bear, Piccadilly, and the White Horse in the Borough at five in the afternoon. Returns from London, Tuesday, Thursday and Saturday mornings at seven o'clock, and arrives at Horsham at half past one o'clock, and at Worthing and Brighton at five o'clock in the afternoon; calls at the Elephant and Castle and Red Lion, Westminster Bridge.

65 The Double Locks on the Exeter canal in Devon, along which ships of up to 400 tons could reach Exeter from Turf in the Exe estuary

66 The York Hotel overlooking Lyme Bay at Sidmouth, south Devon, in the early nineteenth century

Inside passengers from Worthing to London	£1. 0.0
Outside passengers from Worthing to London	11.0
Inside from Horsham to London	12.0
Outside from Horsham to London	7.0

Some distance inland as it may be, Horsham once had an Anchor Hotel, whose emblem carved in stone with the date 1899A.D. remains above what is now Lloyds Bank. A few yards across the road and round the old town hall is the Bear, one of the most engaging of the houses in the neighbourhood tied to Horsham's own King and Barnes brewery and offering, as they all do, a tasty real beer. And on another corner is the Olde King's Head, established in 1401, a euphoria of old woodwork: ceiling beams, palisades of timber between bar and restaurant, a minstrels' gallery, overhanging and balustraded landings which seem forever trying to find a new direction into some half-remembered past. One of its bedrooms has a four-poster bed; its cellar wine bar is low-ceilinged, warm and jolly, with wattle and daub exposed beside the precipitous stairs and a heavy cellar door with huge lock and handle. My wife and I have spent several days there and enjoyed every minute—though neither of us expected ever to give our custom, if that's the word, to a building which so blatantly proclaims itself in raised relief capitals an INLAND REVENUE OFFICE.

Alarming as this may appear, it refers not to our present tax men but to the Preventive officers who hunted down evaders of duties inland, in conjunction with their coastal Revenue colleagues. In the early nineteenth century it was also, for a spell, the Post Office.

Smugglers operated, in fact, not just along the Sussex and Kent coasts but far inland; and many of the most skilled and ruthless gangs were based in towns far from the sea. Many of them, too, met their just fate at one of Horsham's 'Hang Fairs', when local publicans gleefully profited from the thousands of onlookers arriving for the hanging of a highwayman, burglar or smuggler.

144

Two highwaymen who had held up the Brighton Mail at Forest Row in 1801 were tracked down to an inn in Liverpool and brought to Horsham for trial and execution. In 1803 a known murderer and smuggler whose misdeeds had been winked at by the excisemen because he was one of their paid informers was arrested for murder, let off, and continued a life of crime until recognized and denounced by the landlord of the White Hart in Ditchling; after which he was arrested again, escaped from gaol, but was at last executed in Horsham before a crowd of 3,000.

Smugglers might be regarded with disfavour by tax collectors, but a large part of the population enjoyed their exploits and, where possible, took such hand-outs as were offered.

The free traders

Our first thought when smugglers are mentioned is of men toiling up in darkness from a lonely beach with kegs of brandy on their backs or the backs of their ponies. In fact for a long time the more profitable aspect of smuggling was the illegal export trade in commodities such as wool and, of all things, the sort of black-lead we use in pencils. All through the eighteenth century a brisk trade was carried on through Ravenglass in Cumbria, not the place one normally associates with the owlers, 'gentlemen', or free traders.

Plumbago or graphite, known locally as wadd, had been used by Lake District farmers as a reliable way of marking their sheep before its value as a more sophisticated writing medium was realized, and the local lead pencil industry grew up. It was also a desirable contribution to the manufacture of shot and cannon-balls. Although a 1752 Act of Parliament made it a felony to steal from the wadd 'pipes' in the fells, gangs were soon organized to remove large quantities and sell them off. One of the main exchanges centres was the George in Keswick, where dishonest miners made deals with visiting merchants from abroad. Once the terms had been agreed, consignments were carried by mule to the sea at Ravenglass; and in return, contraband liquor and other foreign delicacies were shipped in from the Isle of Man.

One of the Sussex key points in a similar two-way traffic was the village of Rottingdean, just outside Brighton. As well as exporting large quantities of wool to the Continent, it was

... also noted along the coast for bringing things on shore without paying the revenue duties, for which innocent and beneficial practice (sad to relate) Captain Dunk the Butcher paid £500 and ten of his worthy friends were lodged in Horsham Jaol or in their elegant language were sent off for a few months to colledge to improve their manners.

Captain Dunk lived just behind the Plough, one of several Rottingdean inns which played a part in the 'free trade'. Indeed, it is hard to see how any local hostelry could have survived if it had not played along with the law-breakers.

Smugglers met frequently and brazenly in the Black Horse, founded in 1513 and once apparently called the Black Hole: the fact that its lounge was at one time a blacksmith's forge may account for the compression of names. There is also a White Horse, of sixteenth-century origin, whose cellars were noted for the quality and quantity of old French brandy always available in spite of the Revenue men's vigilance. It was the scene of other diversions, as announced by one of its landlords:

This is to acquaint the public that, on Friday next, 26th May, 1758, at the House of Thomas Clare at Rottingdean, will be Bull-baiting. To begin at Nine o'clock in the morning. Likewise who-sever pleases to bring any Cocks to fight may depend upon having them matched for Five Shillings a Battle. A good Twelve-penny Ordinary at One O'clock.

67 After the 1848 revolution in France, the Bridge at Newhaven, Sussex, was the first refuge of Louis Philippe and his queen

When fashionable coaches and an increase in mail descended on Brighton, the White Horse offered stabling for 40 horses, and was one of the posting houses along the Union Line route from Brighton to Margate. It was also the major auction house for the district, and on its premises in 1813 was sold Rottingdean windmill, which for so long had been used by smugglers to signal danger or a go-ahead to incoming cargoes by the set of its sails. Among the look-out men was numbered Dr Hooker, vicar of the parish from 1792 to 1838, whose bust now watches only the congregation in the church from a position behind the pulpit. Later in the nineteenth century the proprietor of the White Horse ran a horse-bus carrying the mail and a small number of passengers, known because of its restricted space and discomfort as 'the coffin on wheels'. In 1934, to the pleasure of no regular customer and surely to that of no discriminating visitor, the old building was pulled down and replaced by something for which I am tempted to invent a new architectural definition: Housing Estate Hostelry.

Romney Marsh, as every reader of Russell Thorndike's *Dr Syn* novels knows, was the happy hunting ground of the most skilful owlers and duty-free tub transporters. Organizers of the trade might have their headquarters in rural seclusion many miles from the sea, as did the murderous ruffians of the Hawkhurst gang; but the Marsh was their theatre of operations. Churches,

68 *Facing* The Mermaid, Rye, where in 1737 the High Bailiff of Sussex was seized by smugglers and narrowly escaped being exported to France

69 The Union in East Street, Rye—forever the favourite remembered inn of the Rye-born author of this book

barns and inn cellars were used for storage, and even rectories. Sometimes these facilities were paid for in kind, as when brandy was left for the parson, baccy for the clerk. In other cases there might have to be a financial adjustment if the parson himself was a good customer: one clerk taking over the administration of a Kent parish found among debts outstanding from the previous year a sum owed to a well-known smuggler for 'two gallons of gin to drunk at the vestry'.

The Hawkhurst gang were so powerful and so greatly feared that, although they took pains to hide their smuggled goods, they did little to hide their vocation. William Holloway, Rye historian, wrote of a local resident who had seen several of them celebrating the successful running of a large cargo, seated arrogantly in a window of the Mermaid, bragging and smoking their pipes, with loaded pistols on the table before them and 'no magistrate daring to interfere with them'.

The Mermaid is the most celebrated of Rye's surviving inns, but has suffered several interruptions in its career as licensed premises. In the seventeenth and early eighteenth centuries it shared many local functions with the George, from whose balcony it was until recent years the custom to throw hot pennies down to children on Mayoring Day; but around 1750 the Mermaid seems to have fallen out of favour with the Corporation. In 1760 there is a record of 'several Dunghills and two Hog Pounds in the Workhouse Yard late the Maremaid Yard'. Presumably these were removed when the place reopened as an inn, taking in several neighbouring houses. Well on into Edwardian times it had a brick and tile-hung frontage with bay windows, but today is half-timbered and has latticed windows flush with the main surface.

When, years ago, I lived in Rye, my own favourite haunt was the Union, converted over a hundred years ago from a house in East Street and still fitting snugly into the sloping terrace of houses. There indeed did fishermen, trades-people, writers, painters, visitors and 'foreign residents' (i.e. those who had not been born in the town) indulge in 'wit enough to justify the town' and set the whole world to rights—a benefaction of which the whole world, alas, does not yet appear to have taken advantage.

Perched beside steep and perilous steps is the weather-boarded Ypres Castle, under the shadow of the medieval keep which gives it its name, looking out over Walland and Romney Marshes and surely in an ideal position, if any landlord had been so minded, for the reception of contraband from the river below.

Like Rye, the Woolpack Inn, the villages of Brookland and Old Romney, and the town of New Romney were once nearer the sea, and played their part along with Dymchurch in the smuggling trade. The Woolpack, isolated below a sharp turn of the main road to Folkestone, served both the legitimate wool-staplers and the illegal exporters. Its sign derives from the woolsack emblem of the Worshipful Company of Woolmen, the original of which was destroyed in the Great Fire of London. The ingle-nook fireplace and many original beams have lasted many centuries, as have sections of wattle-and-daub wall. When the lounge was converted in 1973, part of the original structure was salvaged to provide an interesting display in a glass case within the porch, including handmade bricks, fragments of wattle and daub, and a twelfth-century ship's timber which had supported the walls for untold years. Entering the main bar—with its familiar warning to tall birdbrains, 'Duck or Grouse'—one finds a long table marked out for shove-penny, played with the 'cartwheel' pennies of the Georgian era. And as lasting evidence of the inn's use by smugglers there is a 'spinning jenny' set in the bar ceiling: a circle of numerals and a clock finger revolving, used for dividing up contraband brought ashore nearby.

In the New Inn at New Romney I am always reminded of the heroine of Sheila Kaye-Smith's unjustly neglected novel, *Joanna Godden*, and the shock displayed by the local farmers when they realized a mere girl intended to run her late father's farm in her own way but follow his example when it suited her, as in taking a meal in the male-filled dining-room of the inn where he had 'put up' every market day for 20 years. I am aware that in the book this first act of defiance took place at the Crown in Lydd, but the two little towns have so much in common that if suddenly set down in one it would take me a minute or two to decide which it was. Taverns in market towns on market days show more similarities than differences, and the atmosphere has changed little from one century to another, as Richard Jefferies' description confirms:

. . . it is not easy to enter, for half a dozen stalwart farmers and farmers' sons are coming out; while two young fellows stand just inside, close to the sliding bar-window, blocking up the passage to exchange occasional nods and smiles with the barmaid. However, by degrees you shuffle along the sanded passage, and past the door of the bar, which is full of farmers as thick as they can stand, or sit. The rattle of glasses, the chink of spoons, the hum of voices, the stamping of feet, the calls and orders, and sounds of laughter, mingle in confusion. Cigar smoke and the steam from the glasses fill the room—all too small—with a thick white mist, through which rubicund faces dimly shine like the red sun through a fog.

In spite of its modern fitments, the bar of the New Inn has an old red plushy look and feel about it, and matt black painted panelling which, with the red padded benches and red striped wallpaper, creates a fine ambience of fading glories. There is a pool table, but it is tucked discreetly away at one end, with steps up to its floor level; and steps at the other end of the bar lead to a pleasant dining area. The juke-box cannot, I grieve to say, be regarded as discreet or unobtrusive.

Heading across Romney Marsh towards the low foothills, the leisurely wanderer can find a dozen agreeable pubs. Some of them would be almost the only building in sight were it not for a neighbouring church, and some of the bars, like the churches, are too large for an apparently non-existent community. But each one has its devotees, who may travel miles to reach it. In my time I have been fond of those at Ivychurch, Newchurch, St Mary in the Marsh . . . in fact, there are few that I have *not* been fond of.

The Walnut Tree at Aldington, above the Marsh, recalls the many meetings

of Dr Syn and his accomplices at Aldington Knoll. On the signboard is shown a
smuggler with his cask and, just coming into the frame, a hand holding a
lantern: a Preventive Officer, or the landlord of the pub waiting for a delivery
by night? The Ransley gang were active in the district around 1823, and had
their look-out stationed in a small window of the inn commanding a view far
over the levels, waiting for a successful delivery to be signalled. Today the
Walnut Tree is proud of its reputation for good food, served in a dining-room
some features of which must be 600 years old, including a noble old fireplace.
Beside this can be seen the entrance, up a step-ladder, to a cupboard bedroom.
The public bar is filled with local notices: activities of the local cricket club, a
county cricketer's benefit match, ex-servicemen's news, and all the sociable
goings-on of a closely-knit community. When I was last there, a less cheerful
notice was displayed:

WHAT'S BIGGER THAN CANTERBURY CATHEDRAL?
Say NO to the Convertor Station.

This was part of a campaign to stop the building of a second nuclear reactor at
Dungeness. With what result? It is too early to say; but not too early to make a
gloomy guess.

And further on, across Kent until we are almost on its north coast, is
Smugglers Corner at Herne. St Martin was buried here in the second oldest
church in the country, and to keep him unsuitable company is also the body of
a Bow Street Runner shot by smugglers. Hidden behind a cellar wall of the
Smugglers inn were found two dozen bottles of claret and burgundy; and a
later deepening of the cellar floor revealed a number of full rum casks.

Facing the east wind

The creeks and inlets of Essex shelter many a smuggling pub, sailing pub and
fishing pub; though the fortunes of the latter have, like the Tollesbury oyster
beds, never quite recuperated from the 1953 floods. If we seek something which
has lasted long in spite of all vicissitudes, we should turn towards the Blue Boar
in Maldon. Here on the hill where Viking invaders defeated the heroic
Byrhtnoth, ealdorman of Essex, is an inn with traces of fourteenth-century
workmanship, named after those earls of Oxford whose Essex seat was at

72 Sailing barges laid up below the windows of the Butt and Oyster at Pin Mill on the river Orwell, Suffolk

Castle Hedingham and whose emblem was the blue boar, which we have encountered in earlier chapters and different localities. The courtyard tells a long history from primitive timber and plaster through more confident half-timbering to the days when this became an important coaching inn and a supplier of horses to the individual rider, with a mounting block to help him into the saddle. On the first floor is a room which once served as ante-chamber to an assembly room, now carved up into bedrooms.

Great sailing barges are laid up at Maldon, as at the barge museum by Sittingbourne in Kent; and there are others up the river Orwell at Pin Mill, lying on the mud under the windows of the Butt and Oyster. The smuggling fraternity flourished here, also, and the true story of Margaret Catchpole which the Reverend Richard Cobbold (whose family name appears in the brewery name of Tolly Cobbold on the inn) related in a colourful novel has led to this whole region being known as 'Margaret Catchpole country'. It was from the far bank of the river that her smuggler lover set out to abduct Margaret and, in spite of his failure, so obsessed her that in the end she sided with him and was sentenced to transportation to Australia. The name of Pin Mill itself has caused endless speculation, from the idea that it may have been a mill standing beside a pin or pound to the romantic story of a local landowner who gave his daughter pin-money from the profits of windmills on his estate. By the water's edge, with high tides lapping alarmingly close under the bar windows, the Butt and Oyster poses similar problems. Long ago there were oyster beds along the Orwell, and doubtless the oysters were packed in butts or tubs. But then, it is known that a patch of ground near the inn once served as archery butts. And, to add to the confusion, the local dialect name for a flounder is a butt. . . .

Anyway, records show that admiralty courts were held from the early sixteenth century on the premises of what was even then known as the Butt and

Oyster, and it has featured in official documents and romantic fiction ever since: one of Arthur Ransome's stories starts only a few doors away. I can think of few inn windows commanding quite such a ravishing view as that from the bar here when the sun is on the river, the passing freighters, and the furled red sails of the resting barges.

As well as smugglers and press gangs, local poachers and rowdies gave hostelers a great deal of trouble. On the way into Ipswich from Pin Mill, the Ostrich at Wherstead suffered from the arrogance of large poaching gangs who needed not just the local constable but a whole detachment of dragoons to quell them. Built in 1612, the Ostrich was thought by some to have taken its name from the aforementioned oyster beds; but it seems more likely that it derived from the ostrich emblem of the Coke family, lords of the manor at the time of its construction. In 1750 its then proprietor inserted a mouth-watering advertisement in the local newspaper:

THOMAS TUNMER

At the OSTRICH and BONE-BRIDGE, nr Ipswich Begs leave to acquaint those Gentlemen, Ladies and others, that are so good to favour him with their Company, that he intends at all Times to have some or all of the following Entertainments, in their proper Seasons, viz Pidgeon Pies, Cold Tongues, Potted Beef, Asparagus, Green Pease, Artichokes, Tarts, Cheese Cakes, Plumb Tarts, etc. etc.

NB My Cherry Ground will be in Perfection this Season.

More inviting, surely, than scampi and chips in the basket?

Just as Kent and Sussex were dominated at one period in their history by the Hawkhurst gang, so the Suffolk smuggling trade reached its professional pinnacle with the activities of the Hadleigh gang. Again, like Hawkhurst, this is a town some considerable distance from the sea; though the river Stour provided a useful connection, and by going into partnership with gangs from Norwich and Yarmouth the Hadleigh smugglers could control a great stretch of East Anglian coast and river banks.

One of the most attractive features of Hadleigh's long main street is the pargeting on house and inn frontages. Although there is plenty of timbering to be found here and in neighbouring villages, the characteristic Suffolk inn has a frontage plastered in pink or some other pastel hue, with relief moulding of flower and animal shapes, or even some purely geometrical designs.

On the Felixstowe side of the river Orwell is an inn with a long smuggling association, the Dooley at Walton. Until recent years it looked across the marshes to the river, but since the expansion of Felixstowe docks it has been hemmed in by factories, warehouses and feeder roads. Its odd name is not the one officially bestowed on it. Serving as an inn to cater both for travellers on the ferry between the Essex and Suffolk banks of the estuary, and for maintenance men on the ferry and the building itself, it was known first as the Ferry House and then the Ferry Boat Inn. Yet everybody calls it the Dooley. One story has it that towards the end of the last century the crew of a steamer returning from India made their visit to the bar as soon as they had been paid off and jokingly called it the Doali Tap, an Indian expression thought to refer to a home for the mentally disturbed. But Allan Jobson, who has written many books on local lore, believes that a likelier descent is from the word 'dole', a boundary mark, pronounced hereabouts as 'doole'.

There is a remarkable number of inner doors in the Dooley, and some of them at remarkable angles. It would not be difficult to stage a Whitehall farce in this setting. But the most practical use was made of these openings and passages by smugglers, who also regularly used two small windows for signalling out on to the estuary: one in a gable end, and one right up in the roof. During several wars and rumours of war the inn has also been a venue for

73 The Sole Bay Inn, backed by Southwold lighthouse, is the 'brewery tap' for Adnams' nearby local brewery, and recalls the 1672 battle between English and Dutch fleets off the Suffolk coast

the garrison from Landguard Fort, only about a mile away. The sheds, warehouses and lorry terminals provide a rather different clientèle nowadays.

On the river Deben, Margaret Catchpole's lover and others operated near Waldringfield and, on the other bank, around the lonely inn at Ramsholt, now much modernized but offering a fine view up and down the Deben.

A few miles up the coast is Orford. The King's Head was for some years the equivalent of one of those Felixstowe bonded warehouses—only nobody worried about the bonding of the goods brought in from Hollesley Bay, which were distributed as rapidly and efficiently as possible. The inn served a more respectable rôle as a coaching house, to be challenged in due course by the Crown and Castle. This building has been so much done up that it is hard to detect anywhere in it the original form of a tavern which there is reason to believe was already here in the time of Elizabeth I. A few years before the Second World War, when Robert Watson-Watt and his colleagues were carrying out secret radar research on Orford Ness, they stayed here and most evenings turned the lounge into a conference room. In his autobiography Sir Robert wonders whether the beer at the Jolly Sailor down the road could really have been as delectable as his memory suggests. Coming as it did from Adnams', the Southwold brewery which to this day remains proudly independent, it must indeed have been all he thought of it.

The Jolly Sailor had a none too jolly origin. In Tudor times it was largely built from the timbers of wrecks. At that time it would have stood closer to the water than now, for the quays of the then thriving port ran right past it up Quay Street. There are many little doors, nooks and crannies associated with smugglers; and the front entrance might have been devised to defeat pursuers, since the steps down into the bar are so precipitous that anyone unfamiliar with them could well pitch head-first to the fine old stone-flagged floor. In the bar hangs an evocative painting of old one-time regulars seated at the huge, heavy table. On another wall is a glass case containing the three Little Dogs of Orford, none of them much larger than a hamster. Nobody knows who presented them to the inn, but it is thought they were Chinese 'muff dogs' brought back by some local sailor. Presumably they were expertly stuffed in China before departure, as one cannot imagine them being very popular nipping about the ship on the long homeward voyage.

A brass marker in the bar shows the level to which the January 1953 floods rose. Many an inn along this coast has a similar souvenir. And many an inn was swept away in earlier inundations. Slaughden, a southern limb of Aldeburgh, was often attacked by the sea, as George Crabbe vividly relates, until early in our own century it almost entirely disappeared, taking with it the Three Mariners inn. Once, as the Anchor, it had been an important place, operating the ferry across the Alde and, according to local gossip, providing more help to smugglers than any other inn of the region.

The Harbour Inn at Blackshore, Southwold, has a sign on the front of the building showing the 1953 flood level, and has suffered several times since. There is also an alarming marker by the quayside at Blakeney in Norfolk.

As for Dunwich, we know that several churches and monastic foundations of what was once the most important anchorage on the east coast have been swallowed by the North Sea; and there must have been several inns taken down with them. All that remains in the diminutive village is the Ship, a rambling sixteenth-century inn which changed its name to the Barne Arms in the nineteenth century in deference to the family owning a large part of what was left of Dunwich. The estate was sold off after the Second World War, and in 1967 the name reverted to that of the Ship. Among other alterations the then

landlord opened up a generous old fireplace which had been hidden for years behind a poky Victorian grate.

There were other enemies to attack the coast. In Southwold, not merely the town sign but the sign of the Sole Bay inn recall the bloody naval engagement off the town in 1672 when the Dutch attacked an English fleet under the command of James, Duke of York. One relic of this encounter is a ferocious figurehead, washed up further along the coast after the battle, which now adorns the frontage of the Red Lion at Martlesham on the A12. And quite recently, in Southwold itself, a cannonball was unearthed near the cliff's edge when a trench was being dug across a yard beside the Lord Nelson. This same inn has an interesting little dormer with a side window, high enough above its neighbours to look straight out to sea. It was probably used by smugglers; and in the First World War led to a landlord with an unusual name being accused of signalling to the Germans.

Great Yarmouth sprawls over the border between Suffolk and Norfolk. As a fishing port, holiday town and business centre it has a variety of inns, hotels and public houses which I have always found livelier than those in its drab rival to the south, Lowestoft. The Star, set in a short way back from the harbour bridge and quays, is one of the oldest and most dignified of its establishments. Along South Quay some impressive merchants' houses survived Second World War bombing, and the Star itself was once such a house, built in 1606 by the town bailiff as a home and business premises. He ran his business from the ground floor, and did pretty well for himself in his living quarters above. Above the fireplace in what is now the coffee room are carved the arms of the Merchant Adventurers of England. In 1780 the house became an inn, still well cared for inside and with attractive use of local materials and style outside: a frontage of knapped flint.

To bring us right up to date on the maritime scene, an inn further across the harbour changed its name not so long ago from the Station Stores to the Rising Flame. Its sign shows a North Sea oil drilling platform with gas being flared off.

And then, as we go round the Norfolk coast past too many pubs in the hands of one major brewery chain, and through some places where that chain has callously closed down the last remaining pub, we come to the Burnhams and a name which deserves to dominate the beginning of a fresh chapter.

10
Heroes and Hauntings

Give me an old crone of a fellow
Who loves to drink ale in a horn,
And sing racey songs when he's mellow
Which topers sang ere he was born . . .

John Clare

On 29 September 1758 a sixth child was born to the rector of Burnham Thorpe and his wife Catherine. An earlier son, Horatio, had died in infancy; but in spite of this they christened the newcomer Horatio Nelson.

It is hardly surprising that the village inn should be the Lord Nelson, and the post office the Trafalgar Stores. Thirsty travellers may rejoice also in the fact that this simple, unfussy old ale-house should be supplied by Greene King, the admirable brewers from Bury St Edmunds. In one of its rooms Nelson treated the villagers to a celebratory supper the night before he left to take command of the *Agamemnon* in 1793.

In that same year a boy from Ingoldsthorpe went to sea aboard the same warship, fought beside his idol in the battle of the Nile, and won rapid promotion. The name of Sir William Hoste may have been overshadowed by that of the great admiral, but is remembered in the name of the Hoste Arms at Burnham Market, a more impressive building than the modern Lord Nelson at the other end of the village.

At Burnham Overy Staithe the local hero appears as just that: the Hero. In Mundesley a hotel called the Royal claims to be 'the Home of Nelson' on the grounds that when at school in North Walsham he often stayed here. So there have to be a Nelson room, a Trafalgar room, and a Hamilton room. Similar attributions are given to rooms in the modern Hotel Nelson above the river in Norwich, and there is a carved figurehead in the foyer, not to mention model naval cannon in the Cannon bar.

In Southwold an inn once known as the Raven switched, as did so many establishments in the early nineteenth century, to the Lord Nelson. And a late landlord of the Red Lion in the same town was, in this last couple of decades, so fervent an admirer that when he realized the dimensions of an upper back room were precisely those of Nelson's cabin on the *Victory* he engaged local craftsmen to fit it out as authentically as possible, complete with slanting transom lights.

Overlooking the river in Chatham, Nelson's Command House belongs to Lloyd's but is leased to Charrington's, who ripped out the guts and rebuilt it following a fire soon after the Second World War, reconstructing the exterior as closely as possible to the original.

There is a Battle of Trafalgar at Portslade in Sussex, a Trafalgar at Greenwich; and at Harwich, Essex, a Trafalgar displaying a representation of the signal flags in Nelson's famous message, 'England expects that every man will do his duty.'

A one-time coaching inn at the end of the regular run from the Bell, Norwich, to Great Yarmouth, shows no immediate reverence for the Norfolk hero, though at one time it tried to follow the fashion. More than two years after the battle of the Nile at Aboukir Bay, having been created a Baron and then been made Duke of Bronte by the King of Naples, Nelson returned to his own country in 1800, and on 6 November landed at Yarmouth. He was accompanied by Sir William Hamilton and Lady Hamilton, about whom there was already a fine flurry of scandal. Newspapers and television did not exist to communicate such gossip to the public, however, and local folk rushed to unharness the horses of the carriage waiting for Nelson and draw it to what was then the most important of Yarmouth inns, the Wrestlers. Here he was greeted by Mrs Suckling, the widowed landlady whose late husband had often boasted in the bar of his relationship with the family of Nelson's mother, Catherine Suckling.

All the Corporation dignitaries rolled up to offer the great man the freedom of the borough. But when the town clerk observed that Nelson had put his left hand on the Bible as the oath was being administered, he politely protested: 'Your right hand, my lord.' 'That, sir', said Nelson, 'I left at Teneriffe.'

Before he left, Mrs Suckling begged his approval for the inn's renaming as the Nelson Arms. 'That would be absurd, as I have but one.' But he accepted the compromise of the Nelson Hotel; which later, inexplicably, chose to revert to the Wrestlers. During the Second World War it was badly damaged by bombing and now remembers its early glories only in a painted frieze of sea battles and ships of the line, culminating in Nelson's arrival at the Yarmouth jetty; and there is a fading *London Chronicle* entry recording that arrival.

In the year before this visit, a local boy had been seized on the premises by the press gang, and later joined the *Victory*. He was one of those who carried Nelson down to the cockpit after the admiral had received his mortal wound... and spent his later years as first keeper of the monument, with stairs inside to a viewing platform, erected in Nelson's memory long before the Trafalgar Square column came into being. Near that monument is now an inn called— but what else?—the Nelson.

And in the great seaman's own county, we might stop a moment to pay our respects to another courageous man. The bar of the Ship in Cromer, much used by local lifeboat men, has a mural featuring that most decorated of all such men, Henry Blogg of Cromer, and the snack bar is the Coxswain's Grill. Perhaps we should allow ourselves an extra emphasis on this spot: *The* Coxswain's Grill.

Royalty, rebels and writers

Although the name of the Royal Oak at Eccleshall in Staffordshire suggests a tribute to Charles II, the inn goes back long before Restoration times. Margaret of Anjou, the powerful wife of the feeble-minded Henry VI, stayed here with her son Edward, Prince of Wales, the night before joining battle at Blore Heath in one of the innumerable tussles between Lancastrians and Yorkists during the Wars of the Roses.

Many an English inn has its proud or shameful associations with rulers and rebels. The Green Man at the top of Putney Hill was built on the site of a smithy where Thomas Cromwell was born. In its bar during the closing years of the last century and the beginning of this, the poet Swinburne was allowed by the watchful Watts-Dunton to have his meagre ration of drink daily.

The Golden Cross in Cornmarket, Oxford, was a monastic inn which, after being sold off to a wine merchant, continued its associations with the Church. Two bishops were born on the premises: one in the twelfth century who became bishop of Worcester, and in 1526 John Underhill, later bishop of Oxford. The inn also lodged Ridley, Latimer and later Cranmer, burnt at the stake at the junction of Cornmarket and the Broad on the orders of Bloody Mary. Their bedroom is still called the Martyrs' Room.

Mary's sister and successor travelled so widely that hostelries competed with each other in claiming 'Queen Elizabeth slept here'. One whose claim seems so circumstantial that it must be true is to be found at Modbury in Devon's South Hams, whose village inn is referred to in certain publications as being Elizabeth's resting place on her way to Plymouth to knight Sir Francis Drake. One room bears the name of the Minstrel Bar in memory of a concert given by 80 of Sir Richard Champerdowne's musicians. Perhaps the queen did lodge there on some occasion, but hardly on that one: for Sir Francis Drake received his accolade aboard ship at Deptford after a sumptuous banquet.

75 The old sign preserved in the yard of the Haycock at Wansford, Cambridgeshire, where Mary, Queen of Scots, spent her last night before being imprisoned in Fotheringhay Castle

A great worry to Elizabeth was her wayward rival, Mary, Queen of Scots, who in the end was taken into protective custody and shipped from one comfortable prison to another. While in Tutbury castle in Staffordshire she was supplied with beer from 'Burton three myles off'. (The present visitor to Tutbury should we well content with the amenities of the attractively half-timbered Dog and Partridge.) One of her last easy-going outings was to Buxton, where she stayed under guard at Old Hall, now the Old Hall Hotel. With some foreboding she scratched a Latin couplet on her bedroom window, which translates as:

Buxton whose fame the milk-warm waters tell,
Whom I perhaps shall see no more, farewell.

Celia Fiennes, the well-connected lady who daringly travelled about the country on horseback in the seventeenth century, with only a couple of attendants, was less royally treated in Buxton Hall, which

... is where the warme Bath is and Well, its the largest house in the place tho' not very good . . . the beer they allow at the meales is so bad that very little can be dranke . . . and the Lodgings so bad, 2 beds in a room some 3 beds and some 4 in one roome, so that if you have not Company enough of your own to fill a room they will be ready to put others into the same chamber, and sometymes they are so crowded that three must lye in a bed . . . no peace and quiet with one Company and another going into the Bath or coming out; that makes so many strive to be in this house because the Bath is in it.

When the doomed Mary Queen of Scots was sent for her final imprisonment at Fotheringhay, she stayed a night at the Haycock in Wansford. After her execution, Fotheringhay castle did not long survive, and in 1626 large quantities of stone from its ruins were used to rebuild the Talbot inn, Oundle. This building derives from a seventh-century monastic hostel, attached to a monastery on the site of what are now Oundle Schoolhouse studies. It was at first called the Tabret, a variation of Tabard, whose complexities we have already met in Southwark; and a cosy bar opening off the courtyard still bears that name. In 1638 the staircase down which the Queen of Scots walked to her death was also incorporated in the inn, complete with windows which today, oddly clipped at an angle by the ascent of the stairs, look down on the court-yard. Panelling in the residents' lounge is also thought to have come from Fotheringhay.

A farmhouse at Fotheringhay is said once to have been the hostel where Mary's executioner lodged; but the Talbot claims that in fact he stayed at the inn and 'partook of pigeon pie, drank a quart of best ale and made a merry discourse with the serving girl till an early hour of the morning'.

Charles I has many inns associated with him. He is known to have stayed three times at the George in Stamford. He paid a fleeting visit to the Ship at Bishop Sutton in Somerset, but found the local Parliamentary Committee were holding a meeting on the premises, so had to go off through the rain to find safer accommodation.

A great curiosity is the Radway Tower on Edgehill, built between 1747 and 1750 by an enthusiastic creator of follies within the grounds of his home, Radway Grange. Now part of the Castle inn, it stands on the spot where Charles I raised his standard in October 1642 before the battle of Edgehill. The tower bar has old weapons, cuirasses and a model cannon, in somewhat odd contrast to the electronic scorer for the dartboard. The gents' lavatory is in a detached mock barbican. After the battle, Charles stayed in a house at Southam and ordered local noblemen to bring their silver valuables so that they could be melted down into coinage for his troops. The fourteenth-century building in which these tokens were minted has become a rambling, mellow inn known as the Old Mint, with beamed ceilings and half-timbered walls within the stony exterior. A collection of swords and guns is displayed in the Armoury bar.

Before the battle of Naseby the king lodged a few nights at the Wheatsheaf in Daventry. In the middle of one night he met in dreams the ghost of Strafford, whose death warrant Charles had reluctantly signed in 1641. Forgiving him, Strafford warned against meeting the Parliamentarians in open combat at this stage. Charles dismissed the dream warning and gave battle, with dire results.

76 Radway Tower in Warwickshire, now a part of the Castle Inn, marks the spot where Charles I raised his standard before the battle of Edgehill

The Saracen's Head at Southwell accommodated Charles before his final failure. Having slept and taken his breakfast, he rode to Newark to order the Royalist garrison to surrender, and surrendered his own royal personage to the Scots in the hope of wheedling them into supporting him against Parliament. Instead, they handed him over to his enemies. In spite of this gloomy echo, the Saracen's Head is an estimable building, with timber and plaster above a ground floor of brick, whitewashed over in the stable-yard but scraped down to its original pink hue at the front. A fine medley of doorways of all shapes and sizes run up one side of the yard towards the stables. Above the archway, facing down a shallow slope beside the minster, a lozenge of the lion and unicorn gives the date 1693. The Crown opposite, with its pattern of

black shuttering, does not disgrace the setting.

After Charles had been taken to London for trial, rumour and speculation simmered in every home and tavern. Anxious for the latest news, a Cavalier named Captain Fanshaw rode from Windsor with Charles's servant, John Dowcett, to intercept a messenger from London. It was all arranged in such a hurry that they knew nothing of the messenger's identity, and had no password. At the Ostrich in Colnbrook they were accosted by a man who said he had 'helpful information' for them; but when the three of them went into the yard, an armed gang set on Fanshaw and Dowcett, tied them up, and shut them away in separate rooms. Fortunately Lord Richmond arrived with a dozen men, gave battle, and killed five of the attackers. Fanshaw and Dowcett were

77 The Old Mint at Southam, Warwickshire, where Charles I produced coinage to pay his troops

soon located and set free.

Further north, the Old Man and Scythe in Bolton has a sign depicting a jester wielding a scythe. This recalls a local gentleman farmer who, when pounced on by a Parliamentary platoon, went on threshing corn in his barn and babbling away incomprehensibly. The soldiers left him to it, not realizing that he had hidden all his valuables beneath the threshing floor. Lord Derby spent his last night in the inn before being executed by the Parliamentarians in October 1651 at the market cross outside. One would like to think that his captors reassured him as amiably as did one of the gaolers in Shakespeare's *Cymbeline*, about to escort Posthumus to his hanging:

But the comfort is, you shall be called to no more payments, fear no more tavern-bills; which are often the sadness of parting, as the procuring of mirth: you come in faint for want of meat, depart reeling with too much drink; sorry that you have paid too much, and sorry that you are paid too much; purse and brain both empty, the brain the heavier for being too light, the purse too light, being drawn of heaviness: of this contradiction you shall now be quit.

Oliver Cromwell is supposed to have spent the night before the battle of Worcester at the Lygon Arms, Broadway, in the room now named after him, with its moulded plaster ceiling and a massive fireplace almost reaching to it.

79 The George, Huntingdon, once owned by Oliver Cromwell's grandfather

During the six weeks after Worcester, Charles II wove a complicated escape route across England with a price of £1,000 on his head. In disguise—rather difficult in view of his height—he stayed at the George in Charmouth, Dorset; possibly at the Kingsbridge in Totnes; and certainly, late on in his flight, at the King's Arms in Salisbury. At Hambledon he was afforded the comforts of a loyal supporter's private house, and not those of the inns later to be associated with the beginnings of cricket. From Hambledon an escort was arranged to deliver him to Brighton and a vessel which would carry him to France. Approaching the river Arun, the party came face to face with the governor of Arundel castle, who fortunately failed to recognize the prize within his grasp. They stopped for refreshment in the George and Dragon at Houghton, an inn still in superb condition today with its unusual buttressed walls on the road between Amberley and the crossroads above Arundel Park.

On through Steyning and Bramber, they resisted the temptations of the numerous inns which have long graced these twin towns. In 1461 four 'common brewers' were recorded in Steyning, sternly enjoined to 'brew not their Ale or Beer of any Musty Malt, or eaten with Wivels'. Two years after Charles had surreptitiously passed this way, John Taylor versified:

August the 18 twelve long miles to Steyning
I rode, and nothing worth the kenning
But that mine Host there was a jovial wight,
My Hostess fat and fair: a goodly sight.
The Sign the Chequers eighteen pence to pay
My Mare ate mortal meat, good Oats and Hay.

The king, crowned in Scone but repudiated in England, reached Brighton and lodged at the George, where the landlord nearly spoiled everything by recognizing him and effusively kissing his hand. At last he was safely despatched on the lugger of a Brighton skipper, Captain Tattersall. When Charles II returned to the throne, Tattersall changed the name of his vessel from the *Surprise* to the *Royal Escape*. Granted various royal favours, he behaved so irresponsibly that in 1663 he was granted a pension in the hope that this would keep him out of mischief. With some of the money he set himself up in what is now the Old Ship, Brighton's oldest inn.

Moving closer to modern times, the George at Ilminster in Somerset has a plaque recording that on Christmas Night 1819 the infant Victoria, later to become queen, stayed here—'the hotel being the first at which she ever stayed'.

And so to writers other than Dickens; for not only could one write a book about Dickensian inns—it has already been done, and more than once. Shakespeare, then? Like Elizabeth I, he is fawned on by so many. But we do know that in 1582 he stayed at the Old Bull in Inkberrow on his way from Stratford to Worcester to collect his marriage certificate. In modern dramatic context it is known as the model for the Bull at Ambridge in the radio serial, *The Archers*.

This chapter was prefaced by a few lines from the Northamptonshire peasant poet, John Clare, brought up in a labourer's cottage next door to the Blue Bell inn, Helpston. Neglected in his lifetime and driven ultimately into the county asylum for the last 23 years of his existence, he was 'discovered' when it was far too late to do him any good. But at least the Blue Bell, where Clare as a youngster worked as a servant, has been preserved in his memory—and the remarkable size of its car park is explained by its dual function, accommodating also visitors to the cottage museum in his birthplace.

Visiting writers, too. Nathaniel Hawthorne, who served as American consul in Liverpool from 1853 to 1857, found the celebrated Rows at Chester 'cramped, ancient and disagreeable'. He also found that the most aged houses seemed mainly to be taverns, among them

. . . the Black Bear, the Green Dragon, and such names. We thought of getting our dinner at one of them; but, on inspection, they looked rather too dingy, and close, and of questionable neatness. So we went to the Royal Hotel, where we probably fared just as badly, at much more expense, and where there was a particularly gruff and crabbed old waiter, who, I suppose, thought himself free to display his English surliness, because we arrived at the hotel on foot.

The Saracen's Head in Lincoln, 'Gray, time-gnawn, ponderous, shabby', received Hawthorne 'hospitably enough, though there is an evil smell of gas, or some other abomination, about our parlor'. His supper sounds appetising enough, goodness knows: cold boiled crab, cold trout, and cold roast beef.

Jeffrey Farnol's swashbuckling novel *The Broad Highwayman* features the Old Cock at Hildenborough in Kent, built in 1502 and still retaining its original ingle-nook fireplace. Its older name was the Cock Horse, meaning the lead horse added to a normal coach team when faced with a particularly steep hill, such as that at River Hill, the next stage between Hildenborough and Sevenoaks: a sort of predecessor of Stephenson's stationary steam engines outside Euston and Lime Street, Liverpool, to help his locomotives up steep gradients.

80 *Facing* In Broadway, Worcestershire, the Lygon Arms has a room named after Charles I and one after Cromwell, who is thought to have stayed here the night before the battle of Worcester

And where would writers in England have been without the work of Tenterden's most celebrated son, commemorated in the signboard of the William Caxton?

Spirits on the premises

Beside the Talbot at Oundle, which we have already visited, a right of way was established in the sixteenth century through Dobb's Yard. Later this changed its name to Drumming Well Lane after a series of disturbing noises. From a well in the yard came the sinister drumming of a march . . . always before some great catastrophe. It presaged the death of Charles I and of Cromwell, and the Fire of London; and the return of Charles II to the throne (obviously reported by a disapprover of the Stuarts!). The sceptical Daniel Defoe recorded that he 'could meet with no person of sufficient credit that would seriously say they had heard it', so he came away dissatisfied. Anyway, after the well had been filled in the premonitory drumming ceased.

Other hostelries keep their ghosts indoors. In a dark corner of the bar of the Bull at Henley-on-Thames there is sometimes an inexplicable smell of snuffed candles. In one bedroom of the Bear at Woodstock the guests' luggage and other belongings are pushed about, and there is the creaking of footsteps across the floor. Lights have gone on unexpectedly, and several occupants have complained to the manager at one time and another of there being somebody

A number of phantom coaches are said still to operate in and out of Farnham. One frequently arrives in the middle of the night at the Hop Bag: nobody ever sees it, but the clatter of hoofs and wheels resounds through the yard. It may have some connection with the coach which long ago brought the news to a girl at the inn that her lover, whom she had been awaiting, had been killed by highwaymen and would now never appear. Another girl waits forever in the yard of the Lion and Lamb at Farnham for the lover who had not died but had simply stood her up.

At the Angel in Guildford a ghostly soldier appeared to a guest in his bedroom for long enough to allow a sketch to be made. His uniform was from the early nineteenth century, and although he has hitherto not reappeared and there is no record of his possible identity, a bullet of the period was found in one of the beams during renovations in 1948.

In Chester the George and Dragon, standing on the site of a Roman cemetery, is said to echo to the tread of a legionary eternally on sentry duty. The Ferry Boat near Holywell in Cambridgeshire has in its floor the gravestone of a forsaken girl who hanged herself by the river: dogs shun the stone, and local women are chary of visiting the pub on the day when legend says the girl did away with herself. At the Chequers in Holbeach, Lincolnshire, there is talk of a card game which still goes on in the church across the road. Four seventeenth-century addicts used to meet in the bar nightly, and when one of them died his maudlin friends decided to play a last hand in the church itself, using the corpse as dummy. The devil appeared and, with uncharacteristic courtesy, warned them to stop. They persisted; and were carried off by the devil. But he allows them to continue their game as ghosts, for ever and ever.

Let us end this chapter where it began, with Lord Nelson. This time the scene is the Lord Nelson in Southwold, Suffolk, for the good reason that the author can vouch for having been present, with a number of reliable witnesses, at a psychic manifestation.

On a busy Saturday lunchtime the then landlord, Eric Woods, was more than usually overworked because his new barmaid, taken on a couple of weeks

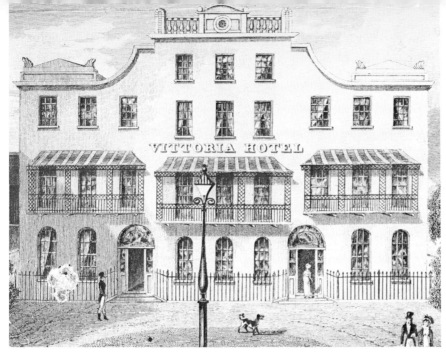

81 A fashionable Cheltenham hotel named after the 1813 battle during the Peninsular War when Wellington inflicted a major defeat on the French

before, had been abruptly called away on family business. Friends of mine with a holiday house in the town had just arrived, and while the husband queued up to buy me a drink his wife commented to me: 'I don't think much of Eric's new barmaid.'

I was rather surprised. 'We all think she's very good indeed.'

When Peter, the husband, returned, he gave me the drink and said: 'Can't say I'm impressed with that new girl of Eric's.'

This time something struck me. 'But you weren't here last week.'

'I'm not talking about last week. I'm talking about the girl who's just served me.'

I pointed out that Eric was on his own behind the bar, and assured them that there had been no girl with him the entire morning. My friends were convinced I was pulling their leg, and when Eric confirmed what I had said they assumed he was in on the joke, and it wasn't a very funny one. Both Peter and his wife, Audrey, gave detailed descriptions which tallied exactly—of a woman with slightly frizzy dark hair, fairly tall, wearing glasses and with a rather large nose. The next day, though realizing that the landlord and I were sincere, they still swore that Peter had been served with drinks by this woman.

Weeks later, after several of the people present had made enquiries locally, an older inhabitant recalled just such a woman as licensee many years earlier: but she and her sister had gone off to Australia. Had she just died there, and come back for a last look at her old inn? Apparently not: the sister had returned, alive, was living some miles away, and there was no report of the woman's death in Australia.

Even later, I was in the bar one winter evening with only Eric Woods and two strangers for company. The couple in the corner had a small, well-behaved dog half asleep between them. Suddenly the door beside me, opening from behind the bar, thumped and I felt a woman brush past me, crossing the room to the outer door. She went out. The dog began all at once to wail and tremble.

'Did anyone come out of that door and walk past me?' I asked Eric.

'No.'

But she did. I knew it, and the dog knew it. And that is *all* I know, for she has never been back.

11

Branch Lines

How fine it is to enter some old town, walled and
turreted, just at approach of nightfall, or to come to
some straggling village, with the lights streaming
through the surrounding gloom; and then, after
inquiring for the best entertainment that the place
affords, to 'take one's ease at one's inn!'

William Hazlitt

This chapter is one for which every reader ought to be able to supply his or her
own version. We all have our own favoured regions, personal routes, pet pubs,
and inns with such happy and maybe intimate memories that we do not wish
anyone to share them. And there are the others which we're willing to recommend to chosen friends: 'the most gorgeous little place, right off the beaten
track', or 'superb food, absolutely superb', or 'if I were you I wouldn't take
the main road, I'd branch off across the moor there and turn left when you
get to . . .'

Too many people in England base all their calculations on and from
London. But even in coaching days the network of posting routes and passenger
services was as complex, and with as many regional branches, as the later
railways. In *Tom Brown's Schooldays* it was the Birmingham Tally-ho which
took Tom to school; and other grandiloquent local names included the
Liverpool Royal Umpire, the Shrewsbury Greyhound, and the Manchester
Telegraph.

Probably most of us have been taken on conducted tours of neighbourhoods
unknown to us, and learned from our accompanying friends of a dozen places
to add to our store of agreeable recollections. And in our turn we can take them
round our own favourite haunts: few of them in stereotyped city streets, and
few on a main highway.

Once while attending a wedding in Leamington Spa I had the chance of
exploring a region with which I was unfamiliar. In Leamington itself the
Regent was awe-inspiring, with its stained glass window on the double
staircase commemorating the Prince Regent, and Regency décor and framed
prints everywhere. This being June 1979, I found a little card on the bar table
recommending a First Lady Cocktail 'in honour of our first lady Prime
Minister'. I asked various wedding guests what they supposed the ingredients
to be, and without actually trying the concoction awarded the palm to the
man who suggested it must be a sweet sparkling wine topped by three inches
of candy floss, with a deep aftertaste of vinegar. What would Mr Pickwick have
made of a woman Prime Minister? Or, heaven help us, Prinny himself?

I stayed in the comfortable Lord Leycester in Warwick, which had only two
minor disadvantages. Every hour on the hour throughout the day four choruses
of 'The Minstrel Boy' rang out from the carillon of the neighbouring church,
until the day I was leaving, when the tune became 'There's no place like
Home'; and in the dining-room, although the taped background music was
quiet and genuinely in the background, it consisted of a limited number of

tapes, so that if one spent any time there eating, the same tunes came round and round again. There are two or three popular songs which I shall never be able to listen to again without expecting another specific one to follow immediately.

And then I was driven at leisurely pace about the countryside. The Saracen's Head at Balsall Common was a nicely timbered, welcoming place for a Sunday lunchtime, with a snug little porch, sprightly latticed windows peeping into the restaurant and odd corners, a deep fireplace, and bars in different styles— one with thick, yellowing plaster, another smoothly papered. And there was more good timber and plaster at the Bull's Head in Wootton Wawen, on the old road from Stratford to Birmingham: a thirteenth-century building much modernized, but not too appallingly. Another old coaching inn was the Boot at Honiley; and again one has to add 'much modernized'.

Within such easy reach of Coventry, local inns are bound to cater for businessmen bringing clients out to lunch and, at weekends, for the suburbanites of both Coventry and Birmingham. It is to their credit that so many of them do it without sacrificing all their original quality.

In 1764 Charles Dibdin, prolific composer of such nautical ditties as 'Tom Bowling', was on tour with a theatrical company and had recommendatory letters to 'many respectable connections' in the neighbourhood of Birmingham. He made a number of trips in convivial company, one of which threatened to incapacitate him for the evening's performance:

On one of these occasions, a party of us went to dine at the Bull, at Meriden. There had been nothing like hard drinking, and every man was completely sober; but, it was agreed, before we got on our horses, to see the cellars, which are of an immense extent. The age of the ale, and all its different qualities, was, as usual, the theme of the landlord; and we tasted till I, in particular, began to be severely cut, as it is called. I felt myself extremely affronted, and left the company very abruptly. When I came into the air, I was dreadfully intoxicated; but, the only sensation I felt, was anger at my companions, who, I was convinced, had gone to the cellar for no other purpose than to make me in that pickle. I got to the stable, made the ostler saddle my horse, and off I set towards Birmingham. I had got on, I dare say, nearly half way, when I saw something before me, which appeared to be a great deal of gravel on the road. I found the horse unwilling to go on, but I whipped and spurred, and presently I had fallen from his back, and found myself surrounded with cows, which, no doubt, with their red hides, I had mistaken for the gravel. I was presently on the ground, and was determined to lie still . . . At length they all passed me, and I felt no injury. I got up, and looked about, but found no horse. The poor devil had enough of it, and was gone back to his stable, so that I had to walk, or rather stagger, to Birmingham in the best manner I could.

The Fleur de Lys at Lowsonford opens up a new vista. Its secluded dining-room, in what must have been a timbered barn, is reached by steps up to a half landing, while its bars on different levels seem to belong to an amalgamation of other buildings. Fleur de Lys meat pies, known throughout the Midlands, originated here, but are now produced in a factory above the Grand Union canal where it cuts between Warwick and Leamington Spa. Another canal, the Stratford and Avon, runs right past the inn, and there is a serving hatch in the wall for the benefit of canal users and visitors sprawling on the grassy bank.

Broads, Fens and waterways

We get a whole new group of names along the rivers and canals of the country: the Ferry, the Bridge, the Three Pickerels, and of course our old oceanic friend, the Anchor. At Acle on the Broads, what was once a guest-house for Weybridge Priory became first the Angel and then the Bridge, its rather unimaginative post-war reconstruction garnished by a thatched rotunda. Like many an inn by these waterways, it relies mainly on passing cruisers for its trade, and offers fishing facilities and the use of a well-stocked shop. Moorings and accommodation are available at various places on the water's edge, such as the Anchor at Coltishall with its pleasant garden.

82 The Cutter on the river Ouse at Ely, Cambridgeshire, with the old maltings in the background

Canals have their own characteristic inns, many of them called the Boat or the Navigation. But a large number of these came into being not just to serve the barges and, nowadays, the holidaymakers: they slaked the thirst of the navigators, or navvies, digging the canals. The Load of Hay on Haverstock Hill in London may not have a particularly nautical ring to it, but during the construction of the Grand Union canal it was a regular Saturday night meeting-place of navvies whose foremen had kept them as disciplined and sober as possible during the week. Now was the time for settling pent-up quarrels: and if there was nothing to fight about, then enough drink would provide an excuse for a fight anyway, until the pavement outside was a pillow for bloodied heads.

Men working on the cut of the Ouse between Adelaide and Littleport in the Fens made use of a hostelry in Ely opened for their benefit in 1830, on the site of old maltings. The Cutter was in fact fashioned around a group of maltsters' cottages. As well as drinking, the navvies and the bargees who followed when the cut was open played skittles in the large skittle alley which has now disappeared under a modern car park.

On comparatively short stretches of the Great Ouse, the Old Bedford and the New Bedford, are quite a few cottages which once catered for men erecting and maintaining the banks. As licensed premises they offered food, drink and accommodation; and were much valued as emergency shelters during times of flood, when workers were out trying to locate and repair damage. Built by the drainage contractors, such makeshift inns were put up for auction annually, along with toll gates and bridges. Many surviving houses, among them a few which are still pubs, can show sheds in their yards where horses were stabled and fed. Near Welches Dam were the Three Fishes and the Princess Victoria; and about a mile away at Manea were the Anchor, the Ship and the Chequers, of which only the Ship is still trading, mainly as a holiday centre for anglers. At Welney, of four busy hostelries only the Three Tuns survives.

Where the Staffordshire and Worcestershire canal joined the river Severn there grew up the town of Stourport. By one of its locks and toll houses was established the Tontine Hotel, whose name gives away the means of its foundation: a tontine is a method by which subscribers receive an annuity from the profits during their own lifetime, each share increasing as other holders die off, until one survivor inherits the lot.

Other backwaters flourished. Bedford on the river Ouse was adjudged by Defoe a handsome and well-built place:

> . . . and though the town is not upon any of the great roads in England, yet it is full of very good inns, and many of them; and in particular we found very good entertainment here.

On the embankment stands the Swan, built in 1794 by the sixth duke of Bedford—whose family crest was the swan—to replace an earlier building in one of whose rooms John Bunyan's wife begged his judges to set him free. A little way up the hill, on the corner of Silver Street, a plaque in the pavement marks the site of the prison in which he was in fact incarcerated. There is another Bunyan connection in the hotel itself: as part of Henry Holland's design, looking both outside and inside like fashionable Georgian assembly rooms or a superior London club, the stairway was one dismantled and brought here from Houghton House, the 'House Beautiful' of *Pilgrim's Progress*. A modern extension at the rear has been done with rare good taste, its bricks matching without mimicking the hue of the original old stonework across the courtyard, believed to have been part of fifteenth-century Bedford castle.

Seeking out hidden beauties along the by-ways, the German traveller Carl Philipp Moritz found in 1782 that in England

> A traveller on foot . . . seems to be considered as a sort of wild man, or an out-of-the-way being, who is stared at, pitied, suspected and shunned by every body that meets him.

At Nuneham in Oxfordshire an innkeeper refused to feed or shelter him; at Eton he was told they had no intention of lodging anyone such as himself; and although he was grudgingly given a room in Windsor he had to share it with a drunkard 'who came crashing to bed with his boots on'. But at the Mitre in Oxford, though arriving late, he had a 'very decent bed-chamber' and 'prince-like attendance' after assuring the waiter that he must not think, because Moritiz had arrived on foot, 'that therefore I should give him less than others gave'.

I wonder if he found time next day to seek out the Turf, tucked away down its alley as if to defy all save the thirstiest and most persistent to find it; or to proceed on foot to Godstow and the delectable Trout above its eternally singing weir?

Peaks and valleys

Not all the most desirable inns snuggle down into picturesque rural corners. Some of the bleakest may well be the most welcome sight of all to wayfarers on windswept, rocky heights. What more appealing on a dark night or in a

83 The Trout at Godstow, Oxfordshire, near the nunnery where Henry II's mistress, the fair Rosamond Clifford, was buried

howling gale than the lights of the Tan Hill inn, over 1700 feet up on Stonesdale Moor, right on the boundary between Cumbria and North Yorkshire? There is no village within miles; not even the tiniest hamlet. The inn came into being, on what had once been a drove road over the moors, to serve miners from the open-cast coal pits in the valley below; and must also have been visited frequently by the grateful keeper of a toll-house a short distance away on the windswept thoroughfare. The innkeeper lived rent free and had half of his licence paid in return for his looking after the pits when there was nobody working there. In due course they ceased to be worked altogether, and with the coming of the railways the toll road lost most of its custom, so that the inn's licence was allowed to lapse until renewed in 1903. Those three-foot-thick walls still keep the cold out; and the whole place comes to turbulent life when, every May, a major sheep sale is held beside the inn.

Only 40 feet closer to sea level is the Cat and Fiddle on the borders of Cheshire and Derbyshire. And at 1476 feet between Windermere and Patterdale is the Kirkstone Pass inn, once appropriately called the Traveller's Rest. There is another Traveller's Rest in what claims to be the highest village in England, Flash, once a centre for illegal prize-fighting and cock-fighting, and giving its name to 'flash' or counterfeit coins in which its inhabitants specialized.

Writing in 1906, Charles Harper observed that a visit to Buxton without a trip to the Cat and Fiddle would be as foolish as a visit to Egypt without seeing the Pyramids. He disapproved of the hundreds of trippers in their waggonettes and brakes; and would probably find their successors these seventy-odd years later little more to his fancy. But I have many times been glad of the existence of that inn on the bleak road between Macclesfield and Buxton.

Beyond Buxton lies Bakewell, where in the middle of the nineteenth century two large inns were run by one landlady. The White Horse no longer exists, but the Rutland Arms is still there. This landlady's brother-in-law, Joseph Paxton, created the glasshouses at Chatsworth and the greater Crystal Palace in London, while Mrs Greaves herself created the Bakewell pudding, or Bakewell tart as it is now more commonly known. It all came about through a misunderstanding with one of her hotel staff. The cook was instructed to pour a mixture into a pastry case and then add jam on top, but she put the jam in first, so that during cooking the top acquired a dark golden hue, and the whole mixture had a distinctive new flavour.

In the vales and on the hillsides of Derbyshire the inns, like houses and whole villages of the region, seem to grow out of the mountain limestone and millstone grit: some almost black, some with a brighter sandstone, many with heavy stone-slabbed roofs, and basaltic chunks known as toadstones. They may look outside, but they are warm inside. You can take your pick: Castleton, Tidesmill, Wirksworth . . . and a whole string of them along the favourite assembly area for dedicated walkers, the Hope valley.

I have pleasant recollections of another of those conducted tours which only an unfriendly puritan would describe as a pub-crawl. This one started from Malvern and led first to the Wellington, perched on a slope outside the town, with bars on different levels to adjust to that slope. One bar manages to have three windows on three sides, each commanding a far view of hills and tilting fields. Then there was the Plough and Harrow near the show-ground, at its busiest during the annual Three Counties Show. In the compact little village of Hanley Castle, with pretty timbered and whitewashed cottages, is the fifteenth-century Three Kings with its colourful sign of the three wise men. Brick and slate have been added to good effect over the original structure, and within is just the right sort of bar parlour: faded and cheerful, offering simple snacks and real ale. And just down the road, Upton on Severn has more inns in proportion to population than any other little town I can remember being in. The Lion, associated with Fielding's *Tom Jones*, and the Old Anchor with its

84 Reputedly the highest hostelry in England—the Tan Hill Inn, Yorkshire

85 The George in the Derbyshire village of Tideswell, known for the exuberance of its Wakes Week and for the annual well-dressing ceremony

86 Originally the dower house of Haddon Hall in Derbyshire, the Peacock at Rowsley was often visited by Izaak Walton when fishing the Wye and the Derwent

adjoining shop frontages have both been used for film and television programmes, and are likely to be used often again. There is brisk and profitable river and riverside traffic round the corner, next to the Star.

In Malvern itself is a hotel which grew out of quite a different sort of establishment. In 1843 Dr James Manby Gully and his partner came to what was then a small hillside town of about 2,000 people, and brought fame to the place and profit to themselves with their Malvern water cure. Before the numbers coming for hydropathic treatment led to an increase in hotels and boarding-houses, and the population swelled to 8000, Dr Gully lodged most of his patients and carried on his practice in two houses, to one of which he added his personal crest in stone tablets along the façade. These adjoining buildings were linked by a bridge with coloured glass panels. Since male and female patients were strictly segregated, the men in one side and the women in the other, this glassy corridor became ruefully known as the Bridge of Sighs. Today both parts belong to the Tudor Hotel. Very little damage has been done to the basic layout, and the bridge is still in place; though the present proprietors make no attempt to divide the sexes. Perched high on the hill, the hotel's bar and many of its bedrooms command a wide prospect of the plain towards Bredon, and on a clear day it is easy to pick out Worcester cathedral and parts of the Cotswolds and the Severn valley.

It was a pity that, after he had done so much good, Dr Gully's career should end in disgrace. Falling in love with one of his patients in Malvern, a young widow, he retired early and followed her to London; quarrelled with her, but was reconciled after her second marriage; and then was implicated in the murder of this second husband, Charles Bravo, though the trial jury finally ruled that there was 'not sufficient evidence to fix the guilt upon any person or persons'.

87 The Plough and Harrow, Drakes Broughton, Worcestershire

For unhurried exploration, what more rewarding than Ashdown Forest? Signboards of the Oak or the Sussex Oak recall the days when this really was a forest, and its timbers were needed for ships and for the Wealden iron furnaces. Particularly agreeable is the little weatherboarded Oak at Ardingly, with its sloping ceilings and odd angles indoors, beamed low ceiling and ingle-nook. And on the other side of Wakehurst Place from Ardingly, there's the fourteenth-century White Hart. On the crossroads peak of steep Turner's Hill, the Crown was announcing last time I called in there an annual pilgrimage by coach to the Merrydown Wine Company at Horam, leaving at three in the afternoon and returning at one in the morning, after a tour of the winery and an evening of dancing and drinking in Eastbourne. 'You are advised', said the notice concerning the trip, 'to take the following day off.'

Beyond East Grinstead, the Castle in the National Trust village of Chiddingstone has a solid and delightful saloon bar with attractive alcoves, festoons of dried Kentish hops, and a fireplace stacked with logs. And if we want to wander under the Downs, maybe to. . . .

But no. Stop following *me* around. Make your own discoveries; choose your own favourites; and cherish them.

12

The Case is Altered?

When you have lost your Inns drown your empty selves,
for you will have lost the last of England.

Hilaire Belloc

Two men running a Warwickshire inn as partners fell out with each other and took the question of ownership to court. Judgment was given that they should divide the premises between them, one running one end, his rival the other. This wrangle thus ended with a change of the original agreement via a court case: The Case is Altered.

Such an explanation is offered for an inn's unusual name. But elsewhere there are other explanations. It has been asserted that in one village an Irish priest called Casey, driven from his church by Protestant reformers, continued to celebrate Mass secretly in the local inn, which came to be known as Casey's Altar, and then The Case is Altered. Contesting this there is an Ipswich inn built especially to cater for troops stationed in local barracks during the conflict with Napoleon, which prospered until the troops were demobbed and the barracks pulled down. Watching his customers disperse, the landlord could only lament: 'The Case is Altered.'

How much are our inns, taverns, pubs, hostelries, hotels, ale-houses and tap-rooms altering, before our very eyes, with or without our consent?

In 1784 the young François de la Rochefoucauld, visiting England to learn the language and customs of the country, marvelled:

I could not help being astonished that men who have received a good education and might well be engaged upon something else should find pleasure—a pleasure renewed day after day—in meeting with other men in order to eat and drink.

Prolonged bouts of tippling and talking in 'fine inns' continued to amaze him. But would he not have found that assiduous exchange of conversation preferable to the few snatches of sentences which today can, only at intervals, penetrate the boom and screech of juke-boxes, over-amplified radios and tape recorders which dominate all our bars and restaurants today? In the *Sunday Times* of 31 August 1980 I nodded helpless agreement to a Valerie Tallis of Bradwell-on-Sea who asked plaintively whether anyone had thought of compiling a guide to pubs without juke-boxes, in which civilized conversation was accompanied only by the clink of glasses and the sound of the beer pumps on the bar. Even when it is obvious that most of the occupants of a bar don't want such a noise, it will still go on. Unlike Ms Tallis, however, I am not in favour of the negative approach. Advertising premises 'without' something has a defeatist ring to it. Let's be positive. Beneath the familiar 'Pub Food' or 'Bar Snacks' stuck to the posts of signboards or in a window, let us have a nice plain statement: 'Tavern Talk'.

89 Rowlandson's view of the White Lion at Ponder's End, Middlesex. Obviously in need of a car park and petrol pumps!

Regrettably we have some powerful Philistines lined up against us. The owner or tenant of an inn may have some say in what goes on under his roof. When it comes to managed inns and pubs, which means the majority of licensed houses in the land, the company's District Sales Manager decides what machines should be installed. Architects and designers have to blend these in with the general décor, unless they are added later on the DSM's advice, in which case they are all too often dumped in what seems the most convenient corner, whether this ruins the layout or not. Every managed pub should theoretically have two AWP machines. AWP is a term which may not trip easily off the tongue of the regular coming in for his sociable pint: it means Amusement With Profit. When I first came across this concept, including all the electronic gadgetry and the pool tables and such other such distracting wasters of space, I protested that it must detract from the consumption of beer, which was surely the prime purpose of opening the pub doors morning and evening. I was soon disillusioned. Profit on machines often exceeds the profit on liquor. Pool tables gross incredible sums. 'Nowadays', I was told, 'you can't afford *not* to put one in.' The space taken up, driving steady drinkers away, can be justified by the huge rake-off. And music in relation to food and drink is carefully calculated in relation to the probable clientèle. Some 'music houses' drive people away because their promoter has not understood the district or general atmosphere; in which case they are often closed down for a few months to let the reputation fade, then reopened with new decorations and a big local advertising splash.

Let us be as fair as possible in these distressing circumstances. It is not new for an inn to be a place supplying not merely food, drink and rest, but entertainment. There were always songs, social functions, and the appearances of strolling players. From 1772 onwards the Greyhound at Dulwich was a meeting-place for the Dulwich Club, attended by Dickens, Thackeray and Mark Lemon; and when it was sold off for building development in 1897 its grounds included a pleasure garden and a couple of cricket pitches. Behind the Wheatsheaf in Watford, the young Henry Irving swaggered on in 1856 as a member of Holloway's Portable Theatre. Both respectable inns and sleazy pubs sponsored a variety of undesirable entertainments. After public 'mains', that is to say cock-fighting contests, were made illegal in 1849, patrons with a taste for blood turned to ratting, wherein dogs were matched in pub rat-pits to kill the greatest number of rats in the shortest possible time. Less savagely there were bowling greens, skittle alleys, billiard tables and such social amenities as slate clubs and sick clubs. Different regions, different pastimes. At Ranworth on the Norfolk Broads a riotous annual contest has been established in the local inn: after a boozy argument some years back about who could pluck chickens the fastest, there is now a seasonal race, lasting on average 12 minutes, to find the most skilled turkey and bantam plucker of the year.

Not even the most earnest Victorian reformers denounced all diversions on licensed premises. Charles Booth, deploring the evils of drink and its resultant misery, nevertheless praised publicans who strove to make their houses more attractive:

Look more closely at the signs in their windows. There is hardly a window that does not show the necessity felt to cater for other wants besides drink. All sell tobacco, not a few sell tea. 'Bovril' (a

90 'The interior of a country ale-house' by George Morland. Where shall we put the fruit machine and the juke-box when we modernize this out-of-date place?

well-advertised novelty) is to be had everywhere. Hot luncheons are offered, or a mid-day joint; or 'sausages and mashed' are suggested to the hungry passer-by; at all events there will be sandwiches, biscuits, and bread and cheese. Early coffee is frequently provided, and temperance drinks too have now a recognized place. . . . No doubt in all these things there is an eye to the ultimate sale of drink, but every accessory attraction or departure from the simple glare of the gin palace is an improvement. In order to succeed, each public-house now finds itself impelled to become more of a music hall, more of a restaurant, or more of a club, or it must ally itself with thrift. The publican must consider other desires besides that for strong drink. Those that do not, will be beaten in the race.

Those foregoing paragraphs might, in essence, well have been written today. Yet somewhere between then and now there was a strange hiatus. For several decades of the twentieth century few pubs troubled to offer even sandwiches, let alone a hot luncheon or 'sausages and mashed'; a request for coffee would have been met with incredulously raised eyebrows; and the old music hall tradition had apparently died away forever. Yet now—due, we are told, to the number of folk who take Continental holidays and return dissatisfied with English pubs and English grub, or lack of it—every hostelry is suffused with the

91 & **92** Transformation and tribute: the Jolly Farmer (*right*), William Cobbett's birthplace in Farnham, Hampshire, now renamed in his honour (*facing*)

smell of frying chips, of scampi and chicken and steak, and sizzling with music . . . if that is the word. Pubs advertise disco evenings; experimental plays are performed in a back bar; and country inns offer bargain breaks complete with string quartet or piano recitals.

'We're only here for the beer'—only a minority of us, it would seem.

And what, then of the trappings of these part-time snack bars, concert halls, recital rooms and amusement arcades?

An owner may shape and reshape his premises to his own taste, if he can afford it. A tenant may strike a deal with the brewery and hope to come out of it without too big a hole in his pocket; though, as we have seen, any improvements he may make will certainly push his rent up. A manager will do as he is told: the architect's department of the company will handle all the design, the materials, and the problems of planning permission where relevant.

I talked to one such architect, more enlightened than some of his fellows, who assured me that the chain for which he works has learned from past mistakes. At one time there was an ill-conceived campaign against such Victorian pubs as had survived in London, and the breweries ripped out as much Victoriana as possible, replacing it with vinyl, formica and chrome. In the 1970s it was realized that this had been a misguided policy, and the trend was reversed, with results almost as silly: Victorian gimmickry was done to death. Now the tendency is to get back as closely as possible to the original period décor without forcing things too much. Each building has its own basic feeling and, commented my informant, 'The interior has to match the promise of the exterior.'

The Railway near Putney station was a nice Victorian pub which it was decided in 1965 to turn into a 'music house' with a disco, visiting groups on certain evenings, and so on. Bars were made garishly modern, and survivals of the old days torn out. Instead of putting the premises on their feet, this got them a bad reputation in the locality, until it was decided to close the premises for several months, maybe a year, and try to undo the damage. Plans were drawn up for a basement wine bar and a carvery restaurant. An embossed Victorian ceiling which someone had painted black all over had to be carefully restored, and old and new materials more satisfactorily blended than before. The total cost worked out at about £200,000.

As in any business, the balance between construction or renovation costs and the estimated return is a tricky one. A new inn on a virgin site, such as on a new housing estate where of course there has never been a pub before, has to be planned with the greatest care. With no idea what trade to expect, the architects are usually given a fairly low budget to start with, which makes it hard to design anything more ambitious than a straightforward, somewhat spartan drinking-house. Occasionally chances are taken; but the department can be in trouble from its bosses if those guesses don't work out.

New shopping precincts can pose a similar challenge. Among the sites allocated for various kinds of shop, one or more units may be offered to brewers for tender. In a big company, the sales chiefs and designers work out what they can get out of the shell thus offered, cost the whole project, and decide how much they are prepared to pay the developers for that unit. The brewery which can do the job cheapest and still sell the economically sound quantity of beer, wines and spirits is, obviously, going to be able to put in a better tender. Developers nearly always accept the highest offer. Occasionally they may query the design, but this is a formality. In any case, the design shown to them may bear little relation to the finished job. In the early stages the architects will have worked out a quick feasibility scheme, priced for tender purposes. Often a company will have only a week or so in which to gather information, visit the developer, and submit details. Obviously this is nowhere near long enough. As a general rule, once a tender has been accepted, the architect's department will start from scratch again and re-design the premises to suit themselves.

When a company takes over some dilapidated old building, perhaps bought from retiring tenants, the job of converting it has to be very carefully priced, and a detailed scheme submitted to the company's internal planning committee. As an example, an old tavern in Peckham which had been neglected by its ageing tenant and so had lost business to smarter establishments in the neighbourhood, was costed out at around £60,000, split between capital and revenue. 'Revenue' covers basic items of maintenance and repairs which would have to be done anyway to make a building habitable. 'Capital' refers to major building extension and alteration. The capital investment should be recuperated, plus 25 per cent, within two years. If the project cannot guarantee that, it will be abandoned, or severly modified: it is rare to let property go, and if all else fails a reasonably cheap job will be done on simple decoration of the bars instead of extensive modifications. If the pub gets going and the position improves, later extensions can be considered.

District Sales Managers have to budget for what beer and other drinks they can expect to sell, and this figure is compared with what the design and building folk want in order to do their part of the job to the best of their ability.

Things can go wrong—or go unexpectedly right—during the actual conversion. 'On site,' Peter Davies of Charrington's has told me, 'any number of features can change. You may have designed something in exact detail, but then when you're ripping walls out you find some marvellous stuff underneath that's been forgotten for years. Once I found a whole stained glass window under a wall lining. And then you've got to be ready to modify a plan on the spot, to make the best of what's shown up. Too much brutish ripping out was done in the fifties. Now we do our level best to recondition.'

Historical associations can provide the basis for a 'theme pub'. Not far from the Archway Tavern on Highgate Hill in north London is the stone by which Dick Whittington is said to have been persuaded by the sound of Bow bells to turn back and become thrice Lord Mayor of London. A case in the bar of the pub holds a mummified object which is said to be Whittington's cat. And the Whittington Stone has been fitted out with a number of gimmicks, far from authentic—since historical evidence and verifiable relics of Dick Whittington are, to put it mildly, rare—but, let's be fair, pleasant gimmicks. At Bembridge on the Isle of Wight, the Pilot Boat inn has been built in the shape of an inn; and the nautical flavour of the Burgh Island Hotel off Bigbury on the Devon coast is enhanced by the stern of HMS *Ganges* built right into one wall. I find it rather agreeable, too, that the Duke of Bristol, a centre for local jazz sessions, should in recent times have acquired a signboard featuring the late Duke Ellington.

Designers and builders encounter some awkward moments which are none of their fault. Some years ago, work on a pub site in Watling Street, London, was held up for two years because Roman remains had been unearthed and the whole site had to be investigated by experts. Unfortunately less scrupulous developers who had heard about this made a swift decision, when they dug their way into mounds of bones in a hitherto unknown Plague burial site, not to report it: they filled in with concrete before the archaeologists got to know about it. And I have heard of a listed building in a development area which was blocking a brewery's plans; and which just happened to burn down one night, clearing the way for them to proceed.

So the work goes on. Hotels, motels, and pubs, with their 'Amusement With Profit' machines and their ceaseless thudding of over-amplified bass from speakers tilted from the ceiling or set on window ledges right by your left ear. Sometimes it is more pleasant in the wine bars which have been springing up in recent times, run by young people who still like to talk and listen to their friends. Even there, one has to be suspicious: it is much easier to get a wine licence than a full licence, because of the smaller scale of the operation, so this can often be just a foot in the door, with plans for applying for a full 'on' licence later. And then the takeovers threaten, the machines rattle and bellow, and the conversation is drowned.

But if that is what the public wants, or can be persuaded to want, are some of us just being crotchety and old-fashioned in complaining? The inn, as we have established, has always been a place of entertainment; and if one generation's entertainment is different from that of its predecessors, who has the right to condemn? Old pub games such as cribbage are played less; but darts still fly dangerously across many a public bar. Fewer establishments have bowling greens, but enough of them survive to ensure that the sport will not die out. Steel quoits teams are coming back into fashion in some country areas; and I think that many such pastimes, after a spell in the doldrums, will gather new strength and live on long after the bleeping electronic diversions have run out of current.

Above all, let there still be talk: the good jokes and the bad jokes, the sudden spontaneous flare of inspired argument, and the weird remarks which float across a bar in an unexpected lull. 'I don't care how badly a man does it as long as he does it'—the demure girl who uttered these words in my hearing could not see why her innocent remark about interior decorating should arouse such laughter. And I recall a friend's wife coming back smiling from the ladies' lavatory after overhearing the complaint from an older lady there: 'I've only just noticed, sitting here—I've got odd shoes on.'

Oh, the bad jokes in pokerwork or glossily printed cards behind the bar! 'If you think our barmaid's beautiful, don't drive home.' 'We've agreed with the bank not to cash cheques, and they've agreed not to serve beer.' And the arch names over the lavatory doors: His and Hers, Damsels and Cavaliers . . .

The catch phrases are contagious. In a basement wine bar in Copenhagen I deciphered the following from a plaque on one of the benches, and puzzled over it for a while:

Man skal ikke vaere tosset for at vaere her, men det hjaelper.

It dawned on me. It was nothing but our old friend, 'You don't have to be crazy to work here, but it helps.'

Let's not despair. The good places are still there for the finding. There is still, somewhere, that unspoilt country inn off the beaten track, sustained by local hospitality and local conversation. Not the droning of imitation rustics or the squealing of the Jag-and-gin set, but the knowledgeable talk of a living community, accompanied by beer from a local independent brewery. Or it may be a hotel right in the middle of an industrial town, telling you things you have never heard before and could hear nowhere else. The coach that rumbles past is not drawn by horses but by resonant horse-power, and the coaching yard is a car park; but this is still an English inn.

I remember good talk, and I expect to hear more. I remember George Carruthers and the Union in Rye, and Petter Leggett and the Red Lion in Southwold; and the Yorke Arms in Ramsgill, the Drayton Arms in South Kensington, the Lygon Arms in Chipping Campden, and so many more . . . all different, yet each a vital ingredient in an invigorating diet.

Each reader will complain about the innumerable omissions from this book. I plead guilty. There are too many places to be visited in one lifetime, and each and every one of us can do no more than make a brief, affectionate selection. In itself that is a cheering thought. With so many treasures left to be discovered, who would ever want to give up the quest? I for one propose to persevere and to take philosophically, with tankard in hand and a log fire suffusing the ingle-nook with its glow, the warning epitaph in Yoxford churchyard, Suffolk:

Life like an inn where Travellers stay
Some only breakfast and then go away
Others to dinner stay and are full fed
The oldest only sup and go to bed
Long is his bill who lingers out the day
Who goes the soonest has the least to pay.

No, I am in no great hurry to be gone. Nor, in spite of ever-rising prices, can I see myself ever begrudging the investment when the rewards are so great. Tell the landlord not to be too impatient. We must still have a few minutes' grace, a few more minutes for drinking up, before those awesome words put an end to it all:

Time, gentlemen, please!

93 *Facing* Paille-maille, the ancient French croquet-style game which gave Pall Mall in London its name, is still played on a special court behind the Freemason's Arms, Hampstead Heath

94 The Frogmill at Andoversford, much expanded and modernized—but in good local materials

BIBLIOGRAPHY

In my opening pages I said how well the history of a typical inn through the ages might be told in the form of a novel. Before I had finished typing this final version I came across just such a novel—*A Wayside Tavern* by Norah Lofts (Hodder & Stoughton, 1980)—and find that the author has done a splendid job.

Anyone researching the subject of inns and contrasting past with present must always be indebted to the 'Road' books of C. G. Harper published in the early years of this century; and, for an assessment very shortly after the Second World War, there are the booklets on English Inns by my old colleague, W. G. Luscombe. Among specific titles which I would especially recommend as being not only invaluable for checking references but, which is just as important, eminently readable in themselves, are:

Askwith, Lord, *British Taverns* (Routledge, 1928)

Borer, Mary Cathcart, *The British Hotel Through the Ages* (Lutterworth Press, 1972)

Cooper, William, *Smuggling in Sussex* (Frank Graham, 1966)

Drackett, Phil, *Inns and Harbours of North Norfolk* (RAC, 1980)

Dunn, Michael, *Penguin Guide to Real Draught Beer* (Penguin, 1979)

Hackwood, Frederick W., *Inns, Ales, and Drinking Customs of Old England* (1909)

Harper, C. G., *The Old Inns of Old England* (Chapman & Hall, 1906)

Harper, C. G., *Historic and Picturesque Inns of Old England* (E. J. Burrow, 1926)

Johnson, W. Branch, *Hertfordshire Inns* (Hertfordshire Countryside, 1962)

Jusserand, J. J., *English Wayfaring Life in the Middle Ages* (Methuen, 1961)

Long, George, *English Inns and Road-Houses* (Werner Laurie, 1937)

Matz, B. W., *The George Inn, Southwark* (Chapman & Hall, 1918)

Matz, B. W., *The Inns and Taverns of Pickwick* (Cecil Palmer, 1921)

Monckton, H. A., *A History of English Ale and Beer* (Bodley Head, 1966)

Rainbird, G. M., *Inns of Kent* (Naldrett Press, 1949)

Richardson, A. E., *The Old Inns of England* (Batsford, 1934)

Spiller, Brian, *Victorian Public Houses* (David & Charles, 1972)

Stanley, Louis T., *The Old Inns of London* (Batsford, 1957)

Thompson, Leonard P., *Smugglers of the Suffolk Coast* (Brett Valley Publications, 1968)

Thompson, Leonard P., *Inns of the Suffolk Coast* (Brett Valley Publications, 1969)

Watney, John, *Beer is Best* (Peter Owen, 1974)

INDEX

Numbers of illustrations are given in *italics*.